Religion, Law, and Freedom

A Global Perspective

Edited by Joel Thierstein
and Yahya R. Kamalipour

Foreword by Cees J. Hamelink

Westport, Connecticut
London

Library of Congress Cataloging-in-Publication Data

Religion, law, and freedom : a global perspective / edited by Joel Thierstein and Yahya
  R. Kamalipour ; foreword by Cees J. Hamelink.
       p.   cm.
    Includes bibliographical references (p.   ) and index.
    ISBN 0–275–96452–3 (alk. paper)
    1. Religion and law.   2. Freedom of information.   I. Thierstein, Joel, 1961–   II.
  Kamalipour, Yahya R.
  BL65.L33R446   2000
  291.1'772—dc21   99–088506

British Library Cataloguing in Publication Data is available.

Library of Congress Catalog Card Number: 99–088506
ISBN: 0–275–96452–3

First published in 2000

Praeger Publishers, 88 Post Road West, Westport, CT 06881
An imprint of Greenwood Publishing Group, Inc.
www.praeger.com

Printed in the United States of America

10 9 8 7 6 5 4 3 2 1

For Sally and Emily

J. T.

For Mah, Daria, Shirin, and Niki

Y.R.K.

Contents

Tables and Figures

FIGURE

Foreword

Cees J. Hamelink

Religion continues to be a factor of great significance in the world today. The majority of the world's people identify themselves as belonging to one of the main religions. Moreover, even if people do not acknowledge formal links with religious institutions, many are likely to state that they are religious. Around the world, one observes a considerable and even growing interest in movements and programs that address the core issues of human spirituality. This is not always recognized in the world's mainstream mass media, which show a tendency to either totally neglect religious issues (apart from papal visits to countries such as Cuba, or clerical scandals) or to represent religious peoples in stereotypical ways, such as equating religion with fundamentalism. Much of the coverage of the Rushdie case in Western news media brought to the surface a stunning lack of knowledge about the Islamic world.

It is important for an understanding of the complexities of the contemporary world that this book focuses on the intriguing linkage between religion, law, and freedom. This book comes at a time when people around the world are struggling with the conflict between independently defined religious and moral identities and the demand for globally shared values.

The fiftieth anniversary of the Universal Declaration of Human Rights (December 10, 1998) reminded the world that the international community has adopted a universal catalogue of moral standards that apply across borders and cultures. This universalism is not ignorant about the real existence of greatly varying cultural practices and preferences across the globe. It is actually implicit in the international human rights norms that these differences must be respected. However, this respect should not undermine those values that people universally share.

Among these values is the moral standard of human freedom as an inherent dimension of the sacredness of human nature. The notion of freedom is critical to an understanding of the delicate and often troubled relationship between religions and human rights law. Although there are different interpretations through time and locality, one finds that the main religious ethical systems perceive freedom and responsibility as inseparable elements of an essential interactive process: the human being cannot be free without responsibility and cannot act responsibly without being free.

In the major religious movements around the world, strong support exists for the implementation of the international human rights regime. Many of the world religions (Christianity, Judaism, Islam, Hinduism, and Buddhism) recognize that they share the core of the regime (i.e., its respect for human dignity and its basic principles such as tolerance, integrity, and equality).

The religious support for human rights, however, is not universally shared. It remains in many quarters a contested issue. In fact, in countries with a strong religious presence there often is a great disparity between the theory and practice of human rights.

There is also a long history of gross human rights violations by religious movements. Moreover, there are traditional religious movements (fundamentalists of various origins) and all kinds of new religious sects that perpetrate human rights violations as part of their sacred mission and limit the freedom of conscience of their followers. In the history of religions, an essential human rights principle such as ''freedom of thought, conscience, and expression'' has always been a contested issue, since it fundamentally challenges the institutional hierarchy in religions. Even if religious movements recognize the universality of the human rights principles, their local interpretation may be influenced by religious idiosyncrasies that are difficult to harmonize with these principles. These conflicting interpretations are often defended with references to the Western and imperialist nature of the human rights regime. This is corroborated by the fact that many countries are indeed experiencing a process of cultural colonization (sometimes referred to as McDonaldization) of which the introduction of human rights is perceived as an important part. This is reinforced by the fact that Western nations (in particular, the United States) have so often practiced ''human rights imperialism'' in the pursuit of their foreign policies.

Against these observations, the supporters of human rights in religious movements will propose that conflicting interpretations of human rights principles can be resolved by rethinking religious doctrines. However, this may not be so easy, since there are real differences between religious and secular conceptions about the very notion of ''rights.'' The disparity between the secular conception that rights are derived from inherent human dignity is not so easily reconciled with the theocentric position that rights are the gift of God. In the latter view, rights are obtained on the basis of the fulfillment of obligations toward the Divine Will. Here it should also be recognized that in most world religions the dominant discourse is about duties, not about rights.

In the religious world of Islam, another complex question is whether Islamic conformity with human rights principles also implies that Shari'a should be in conformity with human rights standards. Shari'a comprises "the laws derived from the Qu'ran, the Sunnah—the Hadith and decisions of Muhammed, Ijma'— the consensus of opinion of the Ulama (Judges) and Ijtihad—the counsel of judges on a particular case" (Traer, 1991, p. 115). If conformity with Shari'a is demanded, as certainly the fundamentalist theologians would say, then there is an insurmountable problem. Whereas the Qur'an may contain paragraphs that support religious liberty, this is not the case in Shari'a and has often not been the political practice in Muslim countries where the state has the responsibility to enforce the Shari'a.

Shari'a fundamentally rejects basic human rights principles such as non-discrimination and equality. "It is impossible for Shari'a to acknowledge any set of rights to which all human beings are entitled by virtue of their humanity, without distinction on grounds of religion or gender" (An-Na'im, 1995, p. 238).

The theme of this book brings together two essential moral institutions: religion and the law. There is an important commonality between the two. It is interesting to note that in some secular societies the law is often referred to as the last religion.

Essential to the major religious traditions are texts that, through parables, prophetic visions, and poetic expressions, provide us with moral insights for how we should conduct our lives. The laws around the world also contain standards and prescriptions for our conduct. They frequently take their inspiration from prevailing moral standards and tell us what we should or should not do.

Sometimes religion and law reinforce each other; sometimes they conflict with each other. The laws of the land may protect religious freedom, and religious institutions may encourage their members to obey the law. Both religion and law relate in important ways to communication freedom. They may either protect and reinforce communication freedom, or they may hamper communication freedom.

What unites them is that neither can exist without communication. Religion cannot live without vehicles that distribute its stories, spread its mission, and facilitate its propaganda. In most religious traditions, communication is not only a right; it also constitutes a duty. In the Islamic tradition, the Prophet has been quoted as saying, "He who remains silent about truth is a dumb evil."

An item of considerable contestation has always been (and remains) the question of the freedom to propagate one's religious doctrines. This raises the complex phenomenon of the claim to exclusivity in truth and faith that many religions make. If there is no other truth than the Jewish, Christian, or Islamic faith, then the tolerance of deviating opinions becomes almost impossible. Moreover, the recognition that other religions (and religious sects) deserve respect for their rights has not always been an easy matter. Most religions have great difficulties with the basic human rights notion of inclusivity (i.e., the standard of inclusion or exclusion). Even when religions speak out against social exclusion and discrimination, they may at the same time make theological arguments that their religious truth and tradition are exclusive and superior to other beliefs.

Legal systems need communication, since many of them adopt the essential rule that everyone within their jurisdiction should know the law and that lack of knowledge of the law (*ignorantia iuris non excusat*) provides no excuse for unlawful conduct. But to do justice requires enormous efforts to teach the members of any society about the legal standards they are supposed to obey. In many countries around the world, widespread ignorance about legislation and judge-made law exists. Yet people are supposed to know the law. The principle that ignorance of the law is no excuse is based upon the equation of common law with common sense. This is particularly troublesome in countries where imported legal systems may not reflect indigenous moral standards.

Regrettably, the importance of this book is underlined by the fact that almost everywhere in the world communication freedom is under serious threat. The space for media freedom is, in many countries, under pressure from a variety of interferences. These may come from public authorities, private interest groups, or individuals. Pressures are exerted upon the media by governments that fire prominent journalists who ask awkward questions, advertisers who seek to influence the direction of broadcast programming, or criminals who decide to execute investigative journalists. Religious institutions may also contribute to the pressures on communication freedom by practicing various forms of censorship.

The most problematic feature of the relationship between religion and law and communication freedom is that both subject the extent of the freedom standard to an even higher norm. The European Convention for the Protection of Human Rights and Fundamental Freedoms (1950), for example, recognizes, in art. 10 the freedom of expression but subjects the exercise of this right to restrictions prescribed by law and necessary in a democratic society; restrictions in the interests of national security, territorial integrity, or public safety; and restrictions for the prevention of disorder or crime, the protection of health or morals, and the protection of the reputation or rights of others, preventing the disclosure of information received in confidence or maintaining the authority and impartiality of the judiciary.

However reasonable this may sound, these provisions imply that limits to communication freedom are established that are not unequivocal or uncontested. Several of the restrictive categories (such as national security and the protection of morals) can be politically interpreted by states in very different and arbitrary ways.

In the Cairo Declaration on Human Rights in Islam, adopted by the Organization of the Islamic Conference (August 1990), art. 22 (a) provides, ''Everyone shall have the right to express his opinion freely in such manner as would not be contrary to the principles of the Shari'a.'' In this case, communication freedom is restricted by reference to certain moral principles. Opinions that undermine the morality of Shari'a are not permitted. A critical problem with this ground for restriction is that there is no single Shari'a that is valid for the whole Islamic world. What Shari'a requires in Somalia may be prohibited in Iran. An additional problem is that in several Islamic countries, the exercise of Shari'a is coupled with the dominant political regime, and its interpretation is not guided by an independent judiciary but by the arbitrariness of political powers.

There may be good and valid reasons for legal and religious limits to communication freedom. But then censors always have good reasons! The core problem is that if we take the formulations in the cited documents, the limits are usually elastic in their interpretation. It may be true that only in a world of angels can moral principles be absolute. Since the world has to operate with a somewhat less benign species, limits are needed to protect against the harm that people inflict upon each other when they are not restricted. However, even though no type of freedom will ever be absolute, it should still be considered that whenever limitations are permitted the basic principle is in danger of erosion. This requires serious and critical reflection on how to define the "limit to limits." If qualifiers are very general and open to different interpretations, then there is a serious risk that the very core of the provision is under threat. Sweeping and malleable exceptions leave a large degree of discretion for government officials and courts of law to judge between permissible and non-permissible expressions. Since restrictions threaten to undermine fundamental moral principles, it is crucial to avoid arbitrariness, particularly in a world that is characterized by highly unequal power relationships. The recognition of human dignity and the insight that its realization requires the greatest possible degree of freedom to express oneself should be at the core of the argument about law, religion, and freedom. Whenever law or religion proposes to restrict communications freedom, the extent of elasticity should be minimized.

It is a great relief that a foreword does not need to conclude with solutions, recommendations, or even suggestions for more research. Still, I propose one specific recommendation.

One of the most urgent tasks for the twenty-first century is the promotion of a culture of human rights. As the international community in 1998 celebrated the fiftieth anniversary of the Universal Declaration of Human Rights, the great challenge now is the worldwide realization of respect for the moral standards proclaimed by the Declaration. Realization requires a more effective machinery for enforcement, monitoring, publicity and, more than anything else, the establishment of a cultural environment in which respecting human rights becomes the norm of ordinary, decent behavior of individuals and collectives. In the creation of a human rights culture, the contribution of religion is vital. Early in the new century, I would like to see UNESCO convene an international meeting on religion and human rights. This book should be on the required reading list for that conference.

REFERENCES

An-Na'im, A. A. (1995). Toward an Islamic hermeneutics for human rights. In A. A. An-Na'im, J. D. Gort, H. Jansen, & H. M. Vroom (Eds.), *Human rights and religious values: An uneasy relationship?* (pp. 229–242). Grand Rapids, MI: William B. Eerdmans.

Cairo Declaration on Human Rights in Islam, Art. 22 (a) (1990).

European Convention for the Protection of Human Rights and Fundamental Freedoms, Art. 10 (1950).

Traer, R. (1991). *Faith in human rights: Support in religious traditions for a global struggle.* Washington, DC: Georgetown University Press.

Acknowledgments

This collaborative project has been accomplished through the efforts of many individuals and institutions around the world. We wish to express our sincere gratitude to the contributing authors of this volume. Without their support and cooperation, this project could not have become a reality. We would also like to thank the contributors' academic institutions for providing financial, administrative, and/or secretarial support during the course of this project.

We would like to acknowledge the support of our respective institutions, Purdue University Calumet and Baylor University, for their tangible and intangible support for this project. We would also like to acknowledge Dr. Saul Lerner, Dean of the School of Liberal Arts and Social Sciences at Purdue University Calumet; Dr. William L. Robinson, Head of the Department of Communication and Creative Arts at Purdue University Calumet; Dr. Lee Polk, Chair of the Department of Communication Studies at Baylor University; and Dr. Michael Korpi, Chair of the Telecommunication Division of the Department of Communication Studies at Baylor University.

We would like to thank Sally Thierstein for reviewing the submitted chapters and for offering her editorial assistance during the course of this project. We are grateful to Elisabetta Linton, acquisition editor at Greenwood Press, and to the entire marketing and production team for their valuable support.

Finally, we would like to express our appreciation to our friends, family members, children, and colleagues for their support and understanding throughout this project. We would like to extend special thanks to Dr. William Loges and Dr. Eldred Thierstein for their editorial assistance.

Introduction

We have just enough religion to make us hate, but not enough to make us love one another.

—Jonathan Swift, 1706

People crushed by law have no hopes but from power. If laws are their enemies, they will be enemies to laws; and those, who have much to hope and nothing to lose, will always be dangerous, more or less.

—Edmund Burke, 1777

Many politicians of our time are in the habit of laying it down as a self-evident proposition, that no people ought to be free till they are fit to use their freedom. The maxim is worthy of the fool in the old story, who resolved not to go into the water till he had learnt to swim. If men are to wait for liberty till they become wise and good in slavery, they may indeed wait for ever.

—Lord Macaulay, 1827

The global community is growing; most individual cultures are being diluted. Many nations are taking steps to prevent the dilution of their cultures by foreign media contents and to counter moral influences.

Protecting domestic moral values and beliefs, often built on religious foundations, affects a country's legal limitations on the flow of information and communication. Conversely, the structure of a nation's communications system affects the nation's legal structure as well as its religious ideology. The relationships among law, religion, and the mass media manifest themselves in many different areas, including culture, politics, and international and intercultural communication.

In general, the values and strength of a country's dominant religion often determine the type of government or legal structure a country has. Even in nations where there is a separation of church and state, the dominant religion of the society impacts on the system of governance. For example, the United States, which espouses the separation of church and state, based its Constitution and republican system of government on the organizational structure of the Presbyterian Church. There were more Presbyterians in the Continental Congress than men of any other religion.

Furthermore, the evangelical nature of the dominant religion of a particular country affects the exportation of cultural values, beliefs, or icons of that culture to other nations through the global media. Many countries have begun to recognize this influence and have attempted to construct legal barriers to restrict the importation of foreign media. Religious mores are major factors in nation-states' sensitivity toward the importation of foreign media, such as music, videos, TV programs, movies, and the Internet.

A country's religious dogma, legal structure, and media systems are seldom static. Historically, as these three societal elements have changed, so have the dynamics of their relationships. Even in today's global information age, religion, law, and the media systems of nations are still very much intertwined. The various global perspectives presented in this book illustrate the relationship among religion, law, and communication freedom.

THE IMPETUS FOR THIS BOOK

Religion, Law, and Freedom: A Global Perspective is the result of a three-year collaborative project. This book grew from a conversation between the editors about law and ethics (the source of which are a community's religious mores) three years prior to its publication. The discussion centered on whether law and ethics should be viewed separately, whether one impacts the other, and whether one could be studied or taught without the other. The result of the discussion was that a relationship did exist. From that result came the hypothesis for this book. A relationship exists between the religious mores of a country, the legal system of a country, and the communications freedom in that country, and throughout human history, these three forces have influenced, shaped, and reshaped societies. The chapters that follow are evidence gathered on the subject of the hypothesis.

THE GOAL OF THIS BOOK

The goal of *Religion, Law, and Freedom: A Global Perspective* is to provide a framework for analyzing the perceptions and misperceptions of the relationship between the religious ideology, legal system, and communication freedoms of several selected nations of the world. This book also is intended to present a multifaceted analysis of the relationship between a country's religious ideology, legal system, and communications freedoms.

THE STRUCTURE OF THIS BOOK

This book consists of 15 chapters, authored or co-authored by 17 international scholars specifically for this book, representing many regions (Africa, America, Europe, Asia, the Middle East) and nations of the world, including China, Germany, Iran, Israel, Japan, Latvia, Nigeria, Singapore, the United Kingdom, and the United States. The chapters are organized based on the contributors' emphases on religion, law, and freedom into the following sections:

Part I: Perspectives on Eastern and Western Religions. Chapters in this section examine Eastern and Western perspectives and principal issues and views concerning the definition of religion and freedom, including the First Amendment of the Constitution of the United States; the legal protection of religion and freedom of expression in the European Union; and the multiple meanings of political, legislative, and religious powers constructed and pursued by Buddhist clerics and government officials in Medieval China.

Part II: Press Freedom in Religious and Secular Societies. Chapters in this section explore freedom of expression, freedom of the press, religious censorship, state-religion relationships, and problems associated with religion, politics, and freedom. The nature of freedom and communication systems in religious and non-religious countries, including China, Iran, Israel, Latvia, and Nigeria, and the impact of new telecommunications technologies on law, communication, and freedom are also examined.

Part III: Journalism, Advertising, and Ethical Issues. The focus of the chapters in this section is on the relationship between communication and ethical issues throughout the world. The chapters examine communication and ethical issues in Islamic societies, ethical concerns about advertising, the commodification of females in Singapore, and the ethics of intercultural exploitation. Furthermore, the possibility of forming a World Organization of Muslim Journalists, including the boundaries and frontiers of communication from an Islamic perspective, is considered.

Part IV: Religion, Politics, Media, and Human Rights. Chapters in this section examine the impact of mass media on religion, human rights, freedom, and intercultural communication. Issues such as media coverage of religious groups, media coverage of Salman Rushdie's case in Germany and selected Islamic countries, media coverage of the Japanese royal family and religion, media development within the Communist framework in China, and the utility of human rights in the engagement of religion in world politics are explored.

It should be noted that the ideas and opinions presented in this book do not necessarily reflect those of the editors or the publisher. The chapters were selected to provide the reader with a variety of perspectives on religion, law, and freedom throughout the world.

THE RELEVANCE OF THIS BOOK

This book will be of particular interest to students, teachers and researchers in mass communications, international communications, intercultural communications, political science, sociology, religion, journalism, and comparative studies. In addition, it will appeal to the general readers and researchers outside of the academic community who are interested in the subjects of religion, law, and culture.

Religion, Law, and Freedom: A Global Perspective presents readers with some of the important values of different cultures around the world. In some cases, several perspectives are provided on one particular culture. Through the study of the religious mores that a culture has valued enough to apply as laws and the ways in which those laws affect communications freedom, a greater understanding of a culture can be achieved.

World harmony can come without conflict through understanding the values of other cultures. However, it is not the position of the contributors to this book that the only or best way to achieve world harmony is without conflict or even through understanding. Rather, it presents readers with a variety of perspectives on the relationship among religion, law, and freedom. From the chapters that follow, readers can draw their own conclusions about the best way to resolve cultural conflict brought about by the growing global community.

Part I

Perspectives on Eastern
and Western Religions

Chapter 1

Historical Perspectives on Contemporary Freedom in America

Ron Manuto

One of the extraordinary contributions of the European Enlightenment was its emphasis on individual reason and experience rather than on authority or tradition. In order to achieve the quality of mind necessary for self-government, people would be left to their own resources rather than to the dogma of the church or the controlling devices of the state. The spirit of the age wiped away given "truths," leaving human beings only with questions and more questions. The relief from personal anguish—that modern sense of inner chaos—often found in the religious experience would be replaced with the conditions of uncertainty. Nothing is given, yet anything is possible. Though problematic, the very existence of uncertainty is what makes the democratic experiment possible. The answers to social, scientific, or political complexities cannot be found in the metaphysics of being but only in each other, in common discourse, in common places of discussion and debate. The elimination of rank, that social distance between the rich and powerful on the one hand, and the average person who historically had been denied the right to participate on the other hand, could now be eliminated.[1]

For some—those of privilege who still hold to social Darwinist fantasies—the elimination of class distinctions based on rank threatens the natural order of things. It is a prescription for social disaster, if not open revolt. Yet Thomas Jefferson and James Madison gambled the nation's destiny on the elimination of class distinctions based on rank. The fact that they attempted to diminish the authority and political influence of religion is not to suggest that either man was anti-religious or atheistic, merely that self-rule was the one overriding principle to which all others would have to concede. Within the framework of constitutional liberty, religious practice and self-government were simply separate spheres of human action. As the principal architects of the First Amendment,

Madison and Jefferson were two of the nation's most formidable students of history, particularly the empiricism and pragmatism that were essential features of the European Enlightenment. They understood as few others the need for a separation between civil and religious affairs if the country was to avoid conflict. However, the effort of the founding fathers in ensuring the separation of church and state was not what it first appeared to be, nor was it unique to American political experience (Levy, 1986; Stokes & Pfeffer, 1964).

JOHN LOCKE

While the origins of the separation thesis run as far back as Greece in the fourth century B.C. and continue throughout the great periods of development in the history of Western civilization, it was John Locke who had the most profound effect upon the political theories of Madison and Jefferson (Richards, 1986; Sheldon, 1991). In "A Letter Concerning Toleration" (Locke, 1689), Locke makes a compelling case for the separation of church and state. Their differences make them irreconcilable. Religious organizations are private entities with private interests. They are rarely if ever democratic. Members must accept and adjust to the hierarchy of authority as it is composed. A democratic state founded on a social contract also demands obedience, but the power shifts may be more mediated by historical circumstance and people's interpretation of the events in their lives. If the institutions of government fail to secure the rights that they were created to guarantee, the contract itself may be altered or abolished.

Locke argues that if a separation between church and state cannot be achieved, one will eventually be in conflict with the other.

If this be not done, there can be no end put to the controversies that will be always arising between those that have, or at least pretend to have, on the one side, a concernment for the interest of men's souls, and on the other side, a care of the commonwealth. The commonwealth seems to me to be a society of men constituted only for the procuring, preserving, and advancing their own civil interests. Civil interests I call life, liberty, health, and indolence of body; and the possession of outward things, such as money, lands, houses, furniture and the like . . . now that the whole jurisdiction of the magistrate reaches only to these civil concernments, and that all civil power, right and dominion, is bounded and confined to the only care of promoting these things; and that neither can nor ought in any manner to be extended to the salvation of souls, these following considerations seem unto me abundantly to demonstrate. (Locke, 1689, p. 3)

Locke gave three reasons for separating the two spheres of activity. First, he claimed that civil authority had no right to force a particular religious belief on a citizen, because nowhere had God granted such a right; in addition, public consent could not grant such power, because no individual could reasonably abandon the care of her or his salvation to another. Religious choice was an inward experience; only the individual human mind could choose and believe. Second, civil authority could only deal with "outward force"; true religion was an internal, private act of persuasion and judgment. Locke suggested that no amount of coercion or torment could effectively change the manner in which a person frames her or his spiritual life. Last, Locke granted the possibility that the law, with its force of penalty, could change one's thinking. After all, it is the primary method of social conditioning and adjustment to the world as it exists. But to the truly religious, coercion cannot help with the issue of personal salvation. Force only extinguishes the light of individual reason; it propels one further down the road to resignation, ignorance, ambition, or the general super-stitions of culture. Religious choice, Locke insists, is a "free and voluntary" act. Any other view violates not only the integrity of the person but the notion of a deity as well.

Locke cites his own existence as proof, when he states:

I have a weak body, sunk under a languishing disease, for which (I suppose) there is one only remedy, but that unknown. Does it therefore belong unto the magistrate to prescribe me a remedy, because there is but one, and because it is unknown? Because there is but one way for me to escape death, will it therefore be safe for me to do whatsoever the magistrate ordains? Those things that everyman ought to sincerely inquire into himself, and by meditation, study, search, and his own endeavors, attain the knowl-edge of, cannot be looked upon as the peculiar possession of any sort of men. Princes, indeed, are born superior unto other men in power, but in nature equal. Neither the right nor the art of ruling does necessarily carry along with it the certain knowledge of other things, and least of all true religion. (Locke, 1689, p. 9)

Locke's eloquent statement on the absolute need to separate religious and civil matters stems from his deep spiritual values. It is precisely from these values that he builds the case that the state should be barred from corrupting the religious experience. Spiritual questions are deeply private; civil ones are public. It is Locke's idea that the protection of one's mental life is all important, which gives his argument weight and thus captured the imaginations of Madison and Jefferson.[2] As with the Sophists in Ancient Greece, political theorists and artists in the Renaissance, and writers such as Locke during the European En-lightenment, a new faith in humanity took root in America in the last third of the eighteenth century. It is precisely this faith in things and ideas human that led to the establishment of religious freedom. Stokes and Pfeffer (1964), two of the most respected scholars of America's religious history, claim:

The idea of progress, which had become so dominant toward the close of the eighteenth century, should be added to the factors contributing to the development of complete religious freedom in the United States. This idea . . . assumed not only the worth and potentiality of man but his right to do his own thinking; it held out a glorious future for humanity. . . . In fact, as has often been pointed out, the Enlightenment really constituted a new religious faith, with human progress as its goal. A movement for the enfranchisement of the human spirit and the attainment of great new social ends for the world was in the air. (Stokes & Pfeffer, 1964, p. 38)

JAMES MADISON

It was in the context of the "idea of progress" that the shape of church and state relations in the newly forming government came to be so carefully considered. Madison was instrumental in attempting to preserve the dictates of conscience and in resisting the attempt to establish any one religion as part of the national government. When a bill was introduced to the Virginia legislature to impose a tax for the support of Christian teachers, Madison wrote "A Memorial and Remonstrance Against Religious Assessments" (1785), which is considered one of the classic, most influential statements for religious freedoms in American history (Stokes & Pfeffer, 1964). Madison provides the sitting legislators with 15 individually numbered arguments in his assessment. A careful reading reveals a close connection with the work of Locke. For example, in argument one, he states:

Because we hold it for a fundamental and undeniable truth, "that Religion or the duty which we owe to our Creator and the conviction, not by force or violence." The Religion then of every man must be left to the conviction and conscience of every man; and it is the right of every man to exercise it as these may dictate. This right is in its nature an unalienable right. It is unalienable; because the opinions of men, depending only on the evidence contemplated by their own minds, cannot follow the dictates of other men: It is unalienable also; because what is here a right towards men, is a duty towards the Creator. It is the duty of every man to render to the Creator such homage, and such only, as he believes to be acceptable to him. This duty is precedent both in order of time and degree of obligation, to the claims of Civil Society. . . . We maintain therefore that in matters of Religion, no man's right is abridged by the institution of Civil Society, and that Religion is wholly exempt from its cognizance. True it is, that no other rule exists, by which any question which may divide a Society, can be ultimately determined, but the will of the majority; but it is also true, that the majority may trespass on the rights of the minority. (Madison, 1953, pp. 299–300)

And again, in argument two:

Because if religion be exempt from the authority of the Society at large, still less can it be subject to that of the Legislative Body. The latter are but creatures and viceregents of the former. Their jurisdiction is both derivative and limited: it is limited with regard to the coordinate departments, more necessarily it is limited with regard to constituents. The preservation of a free government requires not merely, that the metes and bounds which separate each department of power may be invariably maintained; but more especially, that neither of them be suffered to overleap the great Barrier which defends the rights of the people. The Rulers who are guilty of such an encroachment, exceed the commission from which they derive their authority. . . . The people who submit to it are governed by laws made neither by themselves, nor by an authority derived from them. (1953, p. 302)

Madison's stirring attack against any relationship continues with an examination of the resulting civil strife when the two domains are mixed. He also contends that neither needs the other for its existence; on the contrary, any overlap would destroy moderation and harmony. And, as did Locke, Madison claimed that an establishment of religion was a contradiction of Christianity; every page of the Bible disavowed a dependence of the powers of this world to affect or control religious thought.

THOMAS JEFFERSON

Thomas Jefferson was probably this nation's most gifted advocate and architect of liberty. His work covered a remarkable 60-year period of the inquiry, study, and practice of civil affairs. To a man who could not live without books, it is not surprising to find in him the single greatest expression of religious freedom and equality in our early history, most notably in "Notes on Religion" (1776) and "A Bill for Establishing Religious Freedom" (1779) (Jefferson, 1943). Though empirical and pragmatic in nature, Jefferson understood the importance of religion in everyday life. It was a critical part of the makeup of human beings. Further, he felt that no one had the right to prejudice another in civil life because one was of another faith. No one had the authority, least of all the state, to make judgments about another's soul. It belonged solely to the person. If the people neglected or abused the life of the soul, it was not the business of the state to remedy the situation. In addition, Jefferson saw civil authority much in the same fashion as Locke, whose language he freely adopts. The magistrate has only that power which people give; the people cannot grant to the magistrate, even through democratic means, power over another's soul. According to Jefferson, they could not because no man can abandon the care of his soul to another, even if desirable: "The life and essence of religion consists in the internal persuasion or belief of the mind" (1943, p. 944).

"A Bill for Establishing Religious Freedom" was Jefferson's greatest achievement. It became the foundation for the new Republic on questions of religious freedom and the model for the other states as they began the difficult task of rewriting their constitutions after the Revolutionary War. So strongly did Jefferson feel about the work that he asked that the title and his name as author be engraved on his tombstone. Jefferson's bill was introduced into the Virginia legislature in 1779, but because of the controversy it aroused, it was not approved until 1786. Section I of the bill provides a rationale for the proscriptions in Sections II and III. Jefferson's argument was consistent with themes developed by Locke and Madison. Any attempt, he argued, to influence religious thought by temporal punishments led only to meanness and hypocrisy; reason, not coercion, was the method to salvation. He observes that:

Our civil rights have no dependence on our religious opinions, any more than our opinions in physics or geometry; and therefore proscribing any citizen as unworthy the public confidence by laying upon him an incapacity of being called to offices of trust or emolument, unless he profess or renounce this or that religion opinion, is depriving him unjudiciously of those privileges and advantages to which, in common with his fellow citizens, he has a natural right . . . the opinions of men are not the object of civil government, nor under its jurisdiction; that to suffer the civil magistrate to intrude his powers into the field of opinion and to restrain the profession and propagation of principles on supposition of their ill tendency is a dangerous fallacy, which at once destroys religious liberty, because he being of course judge of that tendency will make his opinions the rule of judgment, and approve or condemn the sentiments of others only as they shall square with or suffer from his own . . . that truth is great and will prevail if left to herself; that she is the proper and sufficient antagonist to error, and has nothing to fear from the conflict unless by human interposition disarmed of her natural weapons, free argument and debate; errors ceasing to be dangerous when it is permitted freely to contradict them. (Jefferson, 1943, p. 947)

In Sections II and III, the requirements of the law are specific. No man was to be required to support any religious establishment, nor should any religious opinion damage his civil rights. Religious freedom is a natural right, and any future attempt to abrogate such a right would constitute an infringement.

The battle over this bill was a significant one. It pitted the Episcopal Church, long established in Virginia, against the Baptists, Presbyterians, and Lutherans, who were seeking more equitable treatment. Stokes and Pfeffer (1964) believe that the bill's final passage not only guaranteed religious freedom for Virginia but for the entire nation. It became the model for other states as well as for the early drafts of the Constitution.

The long road to religious liberty and the level of religious diversity we share today was not an easy one. Unfortunately, not even the eventual passage of the Bill of Rights resolved the issue of church-state relations. While on its face the First Amendment appeared to clearly deal with questions of religious liberty, it is important to remember that even after its passage in 1791 many of the states had religious establishments. The Constitution did not prohibit the states from establishing a religion; only the federal government was so prohibited. Indeed, Robert Cord (1982) argues:

The First Amendment was intended to accomplish three purposes. First, it was intended to prevent the establishment of a national church or religion, or the giving of any religious sect or denomination a preferred status. Second, it was designed to safeguard the right of freedom of conscience in religious beliefs against invasion solely by the national Government. Third, it was so constructed in order to allow the States, unimpeded, to deal with religious establishments and aid to religious institutions as they saw fit. Nor does there appear to be any historical evidence that the First Amendment was intended to provide an absolute separation or independence of religion and the national state. The actions of the early Congresses and Presidents, in fact, suggest quite the opposite. (Cord, 1982, p. 15)

There was a serious conflict over the precise powers of state governments, as opposed to the federal government, to regulate religion. No one could anticipate the kind of tough religious cases that would later find their way to the Supreme Court, nor could anyone anticipate the complex problems thrown to the federal judiciary when interpreting the language of the First Amendment. Clearly everyone seeks the fullest measure of religious liberty. But did the admonition "no law" mean literally no law? And if so, did this prohibition apply to the states? The evidence seems to suggest that while Congress was barred from passing laws on establishment and free exercise questions, the states were under no such restriction.

THE SUPREME COURT

The narrow interpretation of the First Amendment argues not for the complete separation of church and state, but for equity between the two. Neither the states nor the national government can establish a church, nor can they levy taxes for religious purposes. There is no absolute or inherent "wall of separation." According to Levy (1986), there was political pressure but not legal pressure to disestablish, and pro-establishment parties were forced to make concessions to the growing sentiment against any establishment.

Even the passage of the Bill of Rights left the states free to do many things, including imprisoning religious heretics or political radicals. The Bill of Rights was simply not intended to apply to the states, even though some states such as Virginia had comparable laws. However, in 1868, the Fourteenth Amendment was ratified. Whether or not the framers of the Fourteenth Amendment, which was specifically aimed at preventing states from violating the due process rights of blacks, intended to apply the protections of the Bill of Rights to the states is still unclear.[3] The Supreme Court resisted the application of key provisions of the Bill of Rights to the states for 57 years. The change in judicial thinking came almost unnoticed in a 1925 free speech case, *Gitlow v. New York* (1925). The controversy involved the constitutionality of a state sedition statute. Though the Court ruled the statute valid, it tentatively incorporated the Fourteenth Amendment into its justification. The incorporation theory went from dictum to holding in *Fiske v. Kansas* (1927), and it eventually went from just the free speech clause to nearly the entire Bill of Rights. In *Fiske*, the defendant was accused of violating a state sedition law. This time the Court ruled that his First Amendment rights had been violated as incorporated by the Fourteenth Amendment. This far-reaching doctrine of applying the Bill of Rights to the states under the Fourteenth Amendment began in *Gitlow* and was to have a revolutionary impact on all aspects of the civil rights of Americans, including their religious rights.

The Establishment Clause and Free Exercise Clause

The proper measure of the exact relationship between church and state is ultimately left to the Supreme Court. Thomas Paine, in *The Rights of Man* (1791), wrote that the earth belongs to the living; government from the grave was dangerous because it could not take into consideration new complexities, new realities; hence, there were times when the terms of the original social contract should and must be violated. Jefferson by and large agreed and argued that no society could make a perpetual Constitution or even a perpetual law. He believed that political or legal action should be governed by reason, not precedent. Precedent should only act as a guide (Parrington, 1927). Beginning in the late 1940s, this was essentially the position that the Supreme Court took in regard to establishment cases.

While the Court, previous to 1947, had ruled on issues of establishment, the cases were few in number and minor in consequence. *Everson v. Board of Education* (1947), however, was probably the single most important case in the area of establishment clause law. For the first time since the ratification of the Constitution, the Court attempted to develop a comprehensive interpretation. The decision was important in two ways: (1) It applied the First Amendment to the states through the Fourteenth Amendment to make prohibitions of the First Amendment applicable to action by the states abridging religious freedom; and (2) The Court characterized what was meant by the establishment of religion. Writing for the majority, Justice Hugo Black defines the establishment clause in the following manner:

The "establishment of religion" clause of the First Amendment means at least this: Neither a state nor Federal Government can set up a church. Neither can pass laws which aid one religion, aid all religions, or prefer one religion over another. Neither can force nor influence a person to go to or to remain away from church against his will or force him to profess a belief or disbelief in any religion. No person can be punished for entertaining or professing religious beliefs or disbeliefs, for church attendance or non-attendance. No tax in any amount, large or small, can be levied to support any religious activities or institutions, whatever they may be called, or whatever form they may adopt to teach or practice religion. Neither a state nor the Federal Government can, openly or secretly, participate in the affairs of any religious organizations or groups and vice versa. In the words of Jefferson, the clause against establishment of religion by law was intended to erect a "wall of separation between Church and State." (*Everson v. Board of Education*, 1947, pp. 15–16)

Citing Jefferson's words of a "wall of separation" is a bit of a distortion. It defeats rather than supports Black's position, because Jefferson was never against the separation of church and state in education.[4] It appeared as though

Black could have simply focused on the Fourteenth Amendment without reference to the First Amendment. Even so, *Everson* still ranks as the key establishment clause case, the one from which all others flow.

As with the establishment clause, the one principle that emerged most clearly as the theoretical rationale for the free exercise of religion was the protection of religious liberty. The desire for religious autonomy and the concern with the potential for state intervention led the framers to include the free exercise clause in the Constitution. Hence, its purpose was to secure religious liberty against the government's infringement. Yet, free exercise clause cases were virtually nonexistent in the Supreme Court until *Reynolds v. United States* (1878).

George Reynolds was a Mormon. At that time, a primary tenet of the religion was the practice of polygamy. Reynolds reported that in refusing to practice polygamy when circumstances permitted, he would be punished with eternal damnation. Surprisingly, Reynolds was not a polygamist "by nature." He established that he committed the act of polygamy as a testament of faith in accordance with church authorities. In delivering the opinion for the Court, Chief Justice Morrison Waite observed that "religion" was not defined in the Constitution; this would be a serious issue in later cases. He also recognized that Congress was prohibited from passing legislation restricting the free exercise of religion. However, in determining the scope of that prohibition, Waite's reasoning suggests that:

Congress was deprived of all legislative power over mere opinion, but was left free to reach actions which were in violation of social duties or subversive of good order . . . we think it may be safely said there never has been a time in any State of the Union when polygamy has not been an offense against society, cognizable by the civil courts and punishable with more or less severity . . . it is impossible to believe that the constitutional guaranty of religious freedom was intended to prohibit legislation in respect to this most important feature of social life. Marriage, while from its very nature a sacred obligation, is nevertheless, in most civilized nations, a civil contract, and usually regulated by law. (*Reynolds v. United States*, 1878, p. 250)

This case represents the Court's first statement of the belief-action distinction. While the freedom to believe was absolute, the freedom to act was not. To this day, there are serious questions surrounding the doctrine. First, the state is supposed to remain neutral in religious matters. However, in *Reynolds*, the Court appears to be reacting to no more than a religious action that conflicts with traditional values. The question of the substantive harm of polygamy never arose but is merely assumed. The violation of a "sacred" tradition was sufficient to warrant the suppression of Reynolds' religious practices. The Court continues to emphasize the belief-action dichotomy as a rationale for state intervention and/or regulation in nearly all of its subsequent free exercise, as well as free speech, cases.[5]

The Court appears to view religious belief and conduct as more essential or critical than other categories of expression, what some scholars have called a "preferred position."[6] If so, then the application of such a preference would seem to demand that the Court clearly define what it means by religion. What constitutes religion, and why is it deserving of a level of protection beyond that afforded to free speech? There are dangers in an explicit definition. By defining religion, the Court could inadvertently limit the view of what religion is, or it could foster too orthodox a description. However, to avoid the task or to remain neutral could seriously erode the meaning of the rights within the establishment and free exercise clauses. When refusing to define religion, how then could the Court seriously or defensibly invalidate a law prohibiting the free exercise thereof? Yet in the absence of a workable definition of religion, the purpose and meaning of the freedom of religion clauses are called into question. One cannot reasonably carve out a class or a category of special rights unless a definition of the class is forthcoming. Religious diversification presents new challenges to the Court. In this context, tradition does not offer reasonable guidelines.

The Inability to Define Religion

The Court's first attempt to cope with a definition of religion came in *United States v. Ballard* (1944). Guy and Edna Ballard, founders of the "I Am" movement in 1930, were charged with using the mails to defraud by means of "false and fraudulent representation." The Ballards claimed to have had supernatural powers to heal incurable diseases. The state argued that the Ballards knowingly had no such powers and intended to cheat unsuspecting people of their money and property. Writing for the majority, Justice William Douglas said that the freedom to believe embraces the right to hold theories of life and death that others may find heretical and that people may believe what they cannot prove. He states:

Many take their gospel from the New Testament. But it would hardly be supposed that they could be tried before a jury charged with the duty of determining whether those teachings contained false representations. The miracles of the New Testament, the Divinity of Christ, life after death, the power of prayer are deep in the religious convictions of many. If one could be sent to jail because a jury in a hostile environment found those teachings false, little indeed would be left of religious freedom. . . . The religious views espoused by the respondents might seem incredible, if not preposterous to most people. But if those doctrines are subject to trial before a jury charged with finding their truth or falsity, then the same can be done with the religious beliefs of any sect. When the triers of fact undertake that task, they enter a forbidden domain. The First Amendment does not select any one group or any one type of religion for preferred treatment. It puts them all in that position. (*United States v. Ballard*, 1944, p. 495)

The Court implicitly altered the traditional view of religion to include what others might find incredible or even preposterous. To limit religion only to a Judeo-Christian ethic would strike not only at the diversity of faiths but at the shield of protection for all faiths. In 1961, in *Torcaso v. Watkins*, the Court appeared to take the first step in enlarging its view of religious status. In this case, the Court struck down a Maryland test for public office requiring a belief in God. It identified several religions that did not reflect a belief in God yet were nonetheless religious faiths deserving protection—Taoism, Ethical Culture, Secular Humanism, and others. Though it was following a somewhat ambiguous course by defining religion on a case-by-case basis, the Court continued to sever its tie to a theistic model of religion.

In *United States v. Seeger* (1965), the Court demonstrated that *Torcaso* was not an aberration. Seeger sought exemption to the Universal Military Training Act as a conscientious objector. However, he did not belong to an orthodox or a traditional religious organization. The Court held that religious belief could be no more than a "sincere and meaningful belief which occupies in the life of its possessor a place parallel" to that filled by the more traditional views of God.[7] Seeger did not claim a belief in a Supreme Being but a belief in "goodness" and "devotion to goodness" in a religious sense. Applying this expanded view, the Court allowed Seeger an exemption to the Universal Military Training Act.

Several years later, in a strikingly similar case, *Welsh v. United States* (1970), the Court extended its range of religious protection even further to people with deeply held moral or ethical beliefs that function as an equivalent of religion. What constitutes a religion entitled to constitutional protection is now any belief that is "sincerely" held. If the Seeger/Welsh definition is fully applied, anyone can legitimately seek a religious exemption, a situation, some commentators have argued, that has led to judicial indiscretion and First Amendment chaos. According to Ingber (1986), the legal contours of religion are seriously problematic. He argues:

Analysis of the Court's interpretive response to the religion clauses discloses more than residual ambiguity; it reveals extreme judicial schizophrenia. While explicitly acknowledging the need to distinguish religion from other belief systems in order to retain the semblance of a system of law, the Court remains unwilling to commence the task. Conscious of our nation's religious diversity and concerned with the dangers of exclusion inherent in any effort at definition, the Court consistently has circumvented establishing criteria for classification. . . . On the rare occasions when definition of some sort was unavoidable, the Court rejected its earlier theistic understanding and embraced a concept broad enough to encompass virtually all sincere positions of moral or ethical conscience. (Ingber, 1986, p. 264)

The view that there is something deeply wrong with the Court's treatment of religion is not restricted merely to scholars such as Ingber. Justice Antonin Scalia (1987), comments about the confusion:

We have said essentially the following: Government may not act with the purpose of advancing religion, except when forced to by the Free Exercise Clause (which is now and then); or when eliminating existing government hostility to religion (which exists sometimes); or even when merely accommodating governmentally uninhibited religious practices, except that at some point (it is unclear where) intentional accommodation results in fostering of religion, which is of course unconstitutional. (*Edwards v. Aguillard*, 1987, p. 2605)

The uncertainty over the definition makes its application under the establishment and free exercise clauses dysfunctional. Scholarly definitions of religion as having to do with questions of "ultimate" meaning have not been granted legal recognition because they are in such dramatic contrast to the assumptions of the principal framers, which essentially had to do with matters of conscience tied to theism.

However, if the Court gives wide latitude to a definition of religion, another set of problems arises. Should the level of protection granted to religion exceed the level of protection already guaranteed by the free speech clause? If the process of the development of religious thought is no different than the development of thought in art, medicine, politics, or culture, are two distinct levels of protection justified?

The courts have upheld the distinct operation of religion and state. It is not that one does not influence the other, they do. However, the operations of each remain distinct and separate.

NOTES

1. The idea that all people must have equal standing finds its fullest expression in the due process and equal protection clauses of the Fourteenth Amendment. And even here, it took the Supreme Court decades to extend the Bill of Rights to the power of the states. See *Brown v. Board of Education* (1954); *Gitlow v. New York* (1925); *Reynolds v. Sims* (1964); and *Shelly v. Kramer* (1948). Under Chief Justice Earl Warren's tenure, the Court accelerated the incorporation of the Bill of Rights as a limitation on state power.

2. It is important to remember that Jefferson and Madison are not alone on the issue of the separation of church and state. Benjamin Franklin, John Witherspoon, George Mason, George Washington, Patrick Henry, Thomas Paine, and Charles Pickney, to name a few, all made significant contributions, though perhaps not as complete or forceful as those of Jefferson and Madison.

3. See Graham (1968), Fairman (1949), Morrison (1949), and Frankfurter (1965). Though a detailed evaluation is beyond the scope of this book, the Fairman/Morrison discussion of incorporation was one of the most vivid and far-reaching in legal and academic circles. Both men agreed that there was no evidence that Congress intended to impose federal standards (in the first eight amendments to the Constitution) on the states. In other words, on the basis of the principle of fairness and equity, it might be desirable, but there was no evidence to suggest that it was ever the intent of the legislature to do so. The issue is absolutely critical and is still one of deep concern to those holding different philosophies about law, democracy, and the just powers of the Supreme Court. The incorporation of the Fourteenth Amendment has radically altered American social and political life. It became the basis of renewed political divisiveness, particularly where

traditional state laws and practices regarding race and religion were subsequently held unconstitutional. Neither *Brown v. Board of Education* (1954) or the separation of church and state would have occurred at the state level without the application of the Bill of Rights to the states.

4. Jefferson advocated and expected students at the University of Virginia to attend religious worship. He always argued that religious ideas were as important as any other body of thought. He felt that religious sects on campus were not only useful but necessary to the educational process.

5. The Court has always assumed that the state was free to regulate religious action. However, in *Sherbert v. Verner* (1963), it placed a heavy burden on the state to justify its interest in doing so. In a following case, *Employment Division, Department of Human Resources v. Smith* (1990), the Court held that *Sherbert* did not apply to generally applicable criminal statutes but only to the unemployment compensation field, thus severely diminishing free exercise rights set forth in its opinion in *Smith*.

6. In extending a high level of protection to religious free exercise, some have argued that the Court is less sensitive to the due process rights of nonreligious groups (Marshall, 1983).

7. In *United States v. Seeger* (1965), the majority relied heavily on progressive theologians such as Paul Tillich. Tillich believed that the center of religion could be found in the term *ultimate concern*, which could only be found in a person's experience, not objective reality. It is an expansive view of religion as a unique experience that gives meaning and purpose to a person's life. It is not any doctrine or idea per se, but the experience as motive that constitutes religion (''Towards a constitutional definition of religion,'' 1978).

REFERENCES

Brown v. Board of Education, 347 U.S. 483 (1954).

Cord, R. L. (1982). *Separation of church and state: Historical fact and current fiction.* New York: Lambeth Press.

Edwards v. Aguillard, 107 S. Ct. 2573, 2605 (1987).

Employment Division, Department of Human Resources v. Smith, 110 S. Ct. 1595 (1990).

Everson v. Board of Education, 330 U.S. 1 (1947).

Fairman, C. (1949). Does the Fourteenth Amendment incorporate the Bill of Rights? *Stanford Law Review, 2*: 5–139.

Fiske v. Kansas, 274 U.S. 315 (1927).

Frankfurter, F. (1965). Memorandum on ''incorporation'' of the Bill of Rights into the Fourteenth Amendment. *Harvard Law Review, 78*: 746–767.

Gitlow v. New York, 268 U.S. 652 (1925).

Graham, H. J. (1968). *Everyman's constitution.* Madison, WI: State Historical Society of Wisconsin.

Ingber, S. (1986). Religion or ideology: A needed clarification of the religion clauses. *Stanford Law Review, 41*: 233–333.

Jefferson, T. (1943). *The complete Jefferson* (S. K. Padover, Ed.). New York: Duell, Sloan & Pierce.

Levy, L. W. (1986). *The establishment clause: Religion and the First Amendment.* New York: Macmillan.

Locke, J. (1689). A letter concerning toleration. In R. M. Hutchins (Ed.), *Great books of the Western world* (pp. 3–17). Chicago: Encyclopedia Britannica.

Madison, J. (1953). *The complete Madison* (S. K. Padover, Ed.). New York: Harper.

Marshall, W. P. (1983). Solving the free exercise dilemma: Free exercise as expression. *Minnesota Law Review, 67*: 545–594.

Morrison, S. (1949). Does the Fourteenth Amendment incorporate the Bill of Rights? *Stanford Law Review, 2*: 142–175.

Towards a constitutional definition of religion. (1978). *Harvard Law Review, 91*: 1056–1089.

Paine, T. (1791). *The rights of man.*

Parrington, V. L. (1927). *Main currents in American thought* (Vols. 1–2). New York: Harcourt, Brace.

Reynolds v. Sims, 377 U.S. 533 (1964).

Reynolds v. United States, 98 U.S. 145 (1878).

Richards, D.A.J. (1986). *Toleration and the Constitution.* New York: Oxford University Press.

Sheldon, G. W. (1991). *The political philosophy of Thomas Jefferson.* Baltimore: Johns Hopkins University Press.

Shelly v. Kramer, 334 U.S. 1 (1948).

Sherbert v. Verner, 374 U.S. 398 (1963).

Stokes, A. P. & Pfeffer, L. (1964). *Church and state in the United States.* New York: Harper & Row.

Torcaso v. Watkins, 367 U.S. 488 (1961).

United States v. Ballard, 322 U.S. 78 (1944).

United States v. Seeger, 380 U.S. 163 (1965).

Welsh v. United States, 398 U.S. 333 (1970).

Chapter 2

Religion, Religious Expression, and the Law in the European Union

Manny Paraschos

INTRODUCTION

Whenever the legal systems of human rights protection in the United States and the European Union (E.U.) are compared, the results usually show more similarities than differences: Both systems offer clear and strong support for the rights of citizens vis-à-vis the State. Two of these rights, freedom of expression and freedom of worship, have always been at the heart of what defines the character of the open, capitalist, and pluralistic democracies traditionally known as the West.

Freedom of expression and its corollary, freedom of the press, have evolved in similar paths in the United States and in the E.U. countries. In fact, with the exception of national security protection and limits on broadcast violence, the European and American legal systems currently view defamation, privacy, obscenity, state secrecy, journalistic source protection, and media ownership concentration with considerable similarity.

However, where freedom of worship is concerned, the European concept differs significantly from what the First Amendment allows in the United States. The European notion, although tolerant and even accommodating of non-majority faiths, often allows State interference on expression deemed offensive by the State's dominant religion. While progress has been made and some E.U. nations have moved away from the historic ''State church'' concept, considerable support still exists for the idea that expression on religious issues is more restrainable than other types of expression. Such support has found validation even in the E.U.'s highest court, the European Court of Human Rights.

At the threshold of the twenty-first century, this is especially painful for the E.U. countries, because despite their unequivocal commitment to religious pluralism as well as freedom of expression, they have to find legal ways through which to appease the "offended" religious sensibilities of the majority of their faithful constituents. This is accomplished mainly through the offense of "blasphemy," which criminalizes offensive religious expression.

The problem is exacerbated by the increasing diversity of the E.U. countries, which must abide by the E.U. founding principle of the "free movement of goods, services, capital, and people." It is the "free movement" of all these entities, in fact, that has forced the E.U. countries to confront with greater frequency the challenges presented to their respective religious establishments by the ever-increasing numbers of immigrants and communication technologies.

The concepts of freedom of expression and religious expression, even with limits, are naturally interwoven and must be viewed together in order to better assess the intricacies of the balancing act that recently has preoccupied the legal energies of many of these nations.

Two factors seem to explain this contentious legal environment: (1) the majority of these E.U. countries are religiously homogeneous or, in other words, are dominated by one religion; and (2) these countries harbor a deeply rooted respect for minority viewpoints. The strain in the relationship between these two competing viewpoints has taken its toll, and recently there have been considerable signs of intolerance toward minorities in several E.U. countries. Although these outbursts may reflect a public attitude shift that is economically driven but temporary, they should be viewed with alarm.

THE LEGAL CONTEXT

The issues of religion and expression are addressed mainly by the Council of Europe (COE), which is to cultural and human rights issues what the E.U. is to economic issues. All of the E.U. member countries belong to the Council. The COE constitution is the 1950 European Convention of Human Rights and Fundamental Freedoms (ECHRFF), and its final judicial arbiter is the European Court of Human Rights (ECHR) in Strasbourg, France. It is the Court's function to assess the European compatibility of individual countries' laws and court decisions with the European Convention. The Court's decisions are binding on COE members.

Article 9 of ECHRFF says:

1. Everyone has the right to freedom of thought, conscience and religion; this right includes freedom to change his religion or belief and freedom, either alone or in community with others and in public or in private, to manifest his religion or belief, in worship, teaching, practice, and observance.

2. Freedom to manifest one's religion or belief shall be subject only to such limitations as are prescribed by law and are necessary in a democratic society in the interests of public safety, for the protection of public order, health or morals, or for the protection of the rights and freedoms of others.

Article 10 of ECHRFF says:

1. Everyone has the right to freedom of expression. This right shall include freedom to hold opinions and to receive and impart information and ideas without interference by public authority and regardless of frontiers. This article shall not prevent States from requiring the licensing of broadcasting, television, or cinema enterprises.

2. The exercise of these freedoms, since it carries with it duties and responsibilities, may be subject to such formalities, conditions, restrictions, or penalties as are prescribed by law and are necessary in a democratic society, in the interests of national security, territorial integrity, or public safety, for the prevention of disorder or crime, for the protection of health or morals, for the protection of the reputation or rights of others, for preventing the disclosure of information received in confidence, or maintaining the authority and impartiality of the judiciary.

The above texts serve as benchmarks for national legislation and offer abundant support for free expression and worship, although they also clearly provide a warning that these freedoms are not absolute. Obviously, by U.S. First Amendment standards, some of these warnings are not friendly.

Finally, one other key transnational document that encompasses provisions on expression and religion is the E.U.'s 1989 Directive on Transfrontier Television, which protects free expression but also prohibits programming that might encourage "hatred on the grounds of race, sex, religion, and nationality" (art. 22) and advertising that might offend "religious or political beliefs" (art. 12). It also forbids the interruption of religious services for commercial purposes (art. 11).

National Constitutional Provisions

Expression in Austria is addressed by art. 13 of the 1867 Basic Law, which says that:

Everyone has the right to express his opinion freely, within the limits established by law, in speech, in writing, in print or in pictorial form. The press may neither be subject to censorship nor to the license system. Administrative postal prohibitions cannot be extended to apply to printed matter in the country. (Basic Law of Austria, 1867)

On freedom of worship, art. 14 says:

Everyone is guaranteed complete freedom of conscience and creed. The enjoyment of civic and political rights is independent of political belief. Nevertheless duties incumbent on nationals may not be prejudiced by religious beliefs. No one can be forced to observe a ritual act or to participate in an ecclesiastical ceremony in so far as he is not subordinate to another who is by law invested in such authority. (Basic Law of Austria, 1867)

Article 15 guarantees autonomy, "subject to the general laws of the land," to "every Church and religious society recognized by law" (Basic Law of Austria, 1867). Furthermore, the 1919 constitutional Treaty of Saint-Germain, art. 63, provides that Austrians "shall be entitled to the free exercise, whether public or private, of any creed, religion or belief, whose practices are not inconsistent with public order or public morals."

Belgium's 1831 constitution, art. 19, combines guarantees for both "freedom of worship, public practice of the latter," and "freedom to demonstrate one's opinions on all matters," except "for the repression of offenses committed using this freedom." Article 20 guarantees that no one can be obligated to contribute "in any way whatsoever to the acts and ceremonies of a religion," or "not to observe the days of rest." Article 21 forbids the State from being involved in church affairs.

Denmark is one of the few countries in the E.U. that has an official State religion. Its 1953 constitution's Preamble, ¶ 4, establishes "the Evangelical Lutheran Church" as the national church and provides for its support by the State. Article 67 allows freedom to congregate and worship, "provided that nothing contrary to good morals and public order shall be taught or done." Article 68 outlaws the obligation for any citizen to contribute to "any denomination other than the one to which he adheres," and art. 70 prohibits discrimination based on religious affiliation as well as the avoidance of civic duty on the same grounds. On the issue of expression, art. 77 says, "Any person shall be at liberty to publish his ideas in print, in writing and in speech, subject to his being held responsible in a court of law. Censorship and other preventive measures shall never again be introduced."

The 1919 Finnish constitution, ch. II, § 8, allows a citizen "the right, provided that the law or good custom are not infringed, to practice a religion in public and in private," and also the freedom to "renounce the religious community to which he belongs and to join another religious community." Section 9 says that "the rights and obligations of a Finnish citizen shall not depend on" his/her religious affiliation, if any. Although Finland does not have an official State religion, the Evangelical Lutheran Church is referred to several times in the 1919 constitution. Section 83 concerns the organization and administration of the church, § 87 provides for presidential appointments of bishops and archbishops, and § 90 makes reference to special legislation that governs "appointment procedures" in the Evangelical Lutheran Church and the Greek Orthodox Church. Regarding expression, § 10 guarantees citizens' freedom of speech "without prior restraint . . . as long as they do not infringe on the law or good custom."

In France, art. 10 of the Declaration of the Rights of Man and of the Citizen (1789), says, "No one must suffer for his opinions, even for religious opinions, provided that his advocacy of them does not endanger public order." Article 11 says, "Free communication of thought and opinion is one of the most valuable rights of man; thus every citizen may speak, write and print his views freely, provided only that he accepts the bounds of his freedom established by law.''

The Basic Law of Germany (1953), art. 4, guarantees "freedom of faith, of conscience, and freedom of creed, religious or ideological," "the undisturbed practice of religion," and that "no one may be compelled against his conscience to render war service involving the use of arms." Article 5 guarantees a citizen "the right freely to express and disseminate his opinion by speech, writing and pictures and freely to inform himself from generally accessible sources. Freedom of the press and freedom of reporting by means of broadcasts and films are guaranteed. There shall be no censorship." But § 2 of the same article says, "These rights are limited by the provisions of the general laws, the provisions of law for the protection of youth and by the right to inviolability of personal honor."

Greece is another country that has a State religion. Its 1974 constitution starts with the mention of the Holy Trinity, and art. 3 says, "The dominant religion in Greece is that of the Christian Eastern Orthodox Church. The Greek Orthodox Church, which recognizes as its head Our Lord Jesus Christ, is indissolubly united, doctrinally, with the Great Church of Constantinople."

Also relevant is art. 13:

1. Freedom of conscience in religious matters is inviolable. The enjoyment of personal and political rights shall not depend on an individual's religious beliefs. 2. There shall be freedom to practice any known religion; individuals shall be free to perform their rites of worship without hindrance and under the protection of the law. The performance of rites of worship must not prejudice public order or public morals. Proselytism is prohibited. 3. The ministers of all known religions shall be subject to the same supervision by the State and to the same obligations to it as those of the dominant religion. 4. No one may be exempted from discharging his obligations to the State or refuse to comply with the law by reason of his religious convictions. (Constitution of Greece, 1974)

The 1974 Constitution of Greece, art. 14, § 1, guarantees that "Everyone has the right to express and disseminate orally, in writing or through the press his thoughts respecting the laws of the Nation." Section 2 says, "The press is free. Censorship and any other preventive measure are forbidden." Section 3 says, "The confiscation of newspapers or other publications, either before or after their circulation, is forbidden." Court-ordered, post-circulation confiscation, however, is allowed in cases involving, among others, "offenses against the Christian or any other known religion" and in the case of "an obscene publication patently offensive to public decency."

The 1937 Constitution of Ireland also starts with a strong religious tone:

In the Name of the Most Holy Trinity, from Whom is all authority and to Whom, as our final end, all actions both of men and States must be referred, We, the people of Eire, Humbly Acknowledge all our obligations to our Divine Lord, Jesus Christ, Who sustained our fathers through centuries of trial.

Article 40, 6. i, guarantees, "subject to public order and morality . . . the right of the citizens to express freely their convictions and opinions." It also says:

The education of public opinion being, however, a matter of such grave import to the common good, the State shall endeavor to ensure that organs of public opinion, such as the radio, the press, the cinema, while preserving their rightful liberty of expression, including criticism of government policy, shall not be used to undermine public order or morality or the authority of the state. . . . The publication or utterance of blasphemous, seditious, or indecent matter is an offense which shall be punishable in accordance with law. (Constitution of Ireland, 1937)

In 1984, Italy moved away from its traditional "State religion" concept by renewing the constitution's art. 7 and providing that "State" and "Church" are "independent and sovereign" and by guaranteeing, in art. 19, that citizens "are entitled to freely profess their religious convictions in any form, individually or in associations, to propagate them and to celebrate them in public or in private, save in the case of rites contrary to morality" (Constitution of Italy, 1984).

Furthermore, art. 20 provides that religious organizations will not suffer special legal or financial burdens, and art. 21 guarantees that "All are entitled freely to express their thoughts by word of mouth, in writing, and by all other means of communication. The press shall not be subjected to authorizations or censorship of any kind." Restrictions may be imposed, the article says, "only by order of the judicial authorities for due and motivated cause, and only in those cases expressly authorized by the laws regulating the press." Only in cases of "absolute urgency . . . distraint [*sic*] may be applied." "Printed publications, entertainment and all other public demonstration running contrary to public morality are forbidden," the article concludes (Constitution of Italy, 1984).

Article 24 of the 1868 constitution of Luxembourg says, "Freedom of speech in all matters and freedom of the press shall be guaranteed, subject to the repression of offenses committed in the exercise of these freedoms. No censorship shall ever be introduced." Article 19 guarantees "freedom of religion and of public worship, as well as freedom to express one's religious opinions," as long as they do not violate a law "in the exercise of such freedoms."

The 1815 constitution of the Netherlands, art. 6, says:

1. Everyone shall have the right to manifest freely his religion or belief either individually or in community with others, without prejudice to his responsibility under the law. 2. Rules concerning the exercise of this right other than in buildings and enclosed places may be laid down by Act of Parliament for the protection of health, in the interest of traffic and to combat or prevent disorders.

On expression, art. 7, says:

1. No one shall require prior permission to publish thoughts or opinions through press, without prejudice to the responsibility of every person under the law. 2. Rules concerning

radio and television shall be laid down by Act of Parliament. There shall be no prior supervision of the content of a radio or television broadcast. 3. No one shall be required to submit thoughts or opinions for prior approval in order to disseminate them by means other than those mentioned in the preceding paragraphs, without prejudice to the responsibility of every person under the law. The holding of performances open to persons younger than sixteen years of age may be regulated by Act of Parliament in order to protect good morals. 4. The preceding paragraphs do not apply to commercial advertising.

The Constitution of Portugal (1976), art. 37, provides the citizen with "the right to express and make known his or her thoughts freely by words, images or any other means, and also the right to inform, obtain information and be informed without hindrance or discrimination." Censorship is outlawed.

Religious expression is addressed specifically in art. 41:

1. Freedom of conscience, religion and worship shall be inviolable. 2. No one shall be prosecuted, deprived of rights or exempted from civil obligations or duties because of his convictions or religious practices. 3. No one shall be questioned by any authority about his or her convictions or religious practices, except for the gathering of statistical data that cannot be identified individually, nor shall anyone be prejudiced by his or her refusal to reply. 4. The churches and religious communities shall be separate from the State and shall be free to organize and exercise their own ceremonies and worship. 5. The freedom to teach any religion within its own denomination and the use of its own means or public information for the pursuit of its activities, shall be safeguarded. 6. The right to be a conscientious objector shall be safeguarded in accordance with the law. (Constitution of Portugal, 1976)

The Constitution of Spain (1978), art. 16, declares that "There shall be no state religion," and it instructs public authorities to take into consideration the religious beliefs of Spaniards as they deal with the "Catholic Church and the other confessions." It also guarantees "freedom of ideology, religion and worship of individuals and communities," although restrictions are allowed "to maintain public order protected by law."

Further, art. 20, § 1, guarantees, among other things, the right to "freely express and disseminate thoughts, ideas and opinions by word of mouth, in writing or by any other means of divulgation" [*sic*], the right to "literary, artistic, scientific and technical production and creation," and the right to "freely communicate or receive truthful information by any means of dissemination whatsoever" (Constitution of Spain, 1978). Section 2 outlaws censorship, and § 4 says that these freedoms may be limited "by the right to honor, to privacy, to personal reputation and to the protection of youth and childhood" (Constitution of Spain, 1978).

Sweden's constitutional references to expression are probably the world's most extensive, and they incorporate the provision on freedom of worship. Two of Sweden's four main constitutional documents are the 1949 Freedom of the Press Act (first written in 1766) and the 1992 Fundamental Law on Freedom of

Expression. The third, the 1974 Instrument of Government, says, in ch. 2, art. 1,

All citizens shall be guaranteed the following in their relations with the public administration: 1. freedom of expression: the freedom to communicate information and to express ideas, opinions and emotions, whether orally, in writing, in pictorial representations, or in any other way; 2. freedom of information: the freedom to obtain and receive information and otherwise acquaint oneself with the utterances of others. . . . 6. freedom of worship: the freedom to practice one's own religion either alone or in the company of others.

Article 12 says that these freedoms may be curtailed "only to achieve a purpose acceptable to a democratic society" (Instrument of Government, 1974). Article 13 allows for some restrictions with regard to "the security of the Realm, the national supply, public safety and order, the integrity of the individual, the sanctity of private life or the prevention and prosecution of crime," but it also requires that these restrictions pay particular attention "to the importance of the widest possible freedom of expression and freedom of information in political, religious, professional, scientific and cultural matters" (Instrument of Government, 1974). It is interesting to note that although Sweden does not have a State religion, its constitutional document, the Act of Succession (1810), art. 4, does require that the king "always profess the pure evangelical faith, as adopted and explained in the unaltered Confession of Augsburg. . . . Any members of the Royal Family not professing this faith shall be excluded from all rights of succession."

The United Kingdom has no constitution, Bill of Rights, or other executive, parliamentary, or judicial document that defines a citizen's rights, the implication being that British citizens are free to express whatever they wish, as long as their expression does not violate a law.

National Statutes and ECHR Cases

Blasphemy normally is the crime that most directly addresses the issue of offensive expression about religion. Other statutes that affect religious expression or behavior are those concerning proselytism, while there are cases that invoke various ECHRFF articles to show religious discrimination. Most of these laws and cases emanate from countries with a "dominant religion." The Court's most sensitive task is to decide if the alleged State interference was within the allowable limits mentioned in the various ECHRFF articles and, eventually, if its application was "necessary in a democratic society."

1. Blasphemy. There are two landmark cases that set the tone for blasphemy law in Europe—*Otto-Preminger-Institut v. Austria* (1993) and *Wingrove v. the United Kingdom* (1995). In both cases, the European Court of Human Rights found that national blasphemy statutes had been properly enforced.

The first case was started in May 1985, when the Otto-Preminger-Institut für audiovisuelle Mediengestaltung, a private institute promoting the arts in Innsbruck, Austria, announced the upcoming showing of "The Council in Heaven," a "satirical tragedy" based on the author's 1895 conviction for blasphemy. The film's promotional material explained that:

[The film] starts from the assumption that syphilis was God's punishment for man's fornication and sinfulness at the time of the Renaissance, especially at the court of the Borgia Pope Alexander VI. In Schroeter's film God's representatives on Earth carrying the insignia of worldly power closely resemble the heavenly protagonists. Trivial imagery and absurdities of the Christian creed are targeted in a caricatural mode and the relationship between religious beliefs and worldly mechanisms of oppression is investigated. (*Otto-Preminger-Institut v. Austria,* 1993)

The Innsbruck Roman Catholic Diocese requested that the public prosecutor disallow the film's presentation. After a private showing of the film to local legal authorities, before its public showing, the film was ordered confiscated for violating the blasphemy act, § 188 of the Austrian Penal Code (1992):

Whoever, in circumstances where his behavior is likely to arouse justified indignation, disparages or insults a person who, or an object which, is an object of veneration of a church or religious community established within the country, or a dogma, a lawful custom or a lawful institution of such a church or religious community, shall be liable to a prison sentence of up to six months or a fine of up to 360 daily rates.

A year later, the regional court upheld the confiscation as appropriate, because in the film:

God the Father is presented both in image and in text as a senile, impotent idiot, Christ as a cretin and Mary Mother of God as a wanton lady with a corresponding manner of expression and in which the Eucharist is ridiculed. . . . The conditions of section 188 of the Penal Code are objectively fulfilled by this portrayal of the divine persons—God the Father, Mary Mother of God and Jesus Christ are the central figures in Roman Catholic religious doctrine and practice, being of the most essential importance, also for the religious understanding of the believers—as well as by the above mentioned expressions concerning the Eucharist, which is one of the most important mysteries of the Roman Catholic religion, the more so in view of the general character of the film as an attack on Christian religions. (*Otto-Preminger-Institut v. Austria,* 1993, p. 5)

Articles 13 and 4 of the Basic Law of Austria (1867) (see National Constitutional Provisions section above) were the Institute's defense, and art. 17a of same provided "freedom for artistic creation and of the publication and teaching of art." However, all Austrian courts upheld the confiscation decision, and the case reached the European Court of Human Rights in 1993.

In its decision, the Court, referring to ECHRFF art. 10.2, said that these "rights and freedoms" come with "duties and responsibilities," or

an obligation to avoid as far as possible expressions that are gratuitously offensive to others and thus an infringement on their rights, and which therefore do not contribute to any form of public debate capable of furthering progress in human affairs. This being so, as a matter of principle it may be considered necessary in certain democratic societies to sanction or even prevent improper attacks on objects of religious veneration. (*Otto-Preminger-Institut v. Austria*, 1993, p. 15)

The Court admitted that it was not "possible to discern throughout Europe a uniform conception of the significance of religion in society," and therefore, it was impossible for it to "arrive at a comprehensive definition of what constitutes a permissible interference with the exercise of the right of freedom of expression where such expression is directed against the religious feelings of others" (*Otto-Preminger-Institut v. Austria*, 1993, p. 15). For that reason, the Court felt it had to allow "a certain margin of appreciation" to local authorities "in assessing the existence and extent of the necessity for such interference" (1993, p. 15). The Court also warned that such "margin of appreciation" is not unlimited and "it goes hand in hand with Convention supervision" (*Otto-Preminger-Institut v. Austria*, p. 15).

Finally, the Court, by a 6–3 vote, held that:

The Court cannot disregard the fact that the Roman Catholic religion is the religion of the overwhelming majority of Tyroleans. In seizing the film, the Austrian authorities acted to ensure religious peace in that region and to prevent that some people should feel the object of attacks on their religious beliefs in an unwarranted and offensive manner. It is in the first place for the national authorities, who are better placed than the international judge, to assess the need for such measure in the light of the situation obtaining locally at a given time. In all the circumstances of the present case, the Court does not consider that the Austrian authorities can be regarded as having overstepped their margin of appreciation in this respect. (*Otto-Preminger-Institut v. Austria*, 1993, p. 17)

In dissent, three judges said that such a drastic measure, as the "complete prevention of the exercise of freedom of expression," can be acceptable only if the offending behavior "reaches such a high level of abuse, and comes so close to a denial of the freedom of religion of others, as to forfeit for itself the right to be tolerated by society." Their conclusion was:

We do not deny that the showing of the film might have offended the religious feelings of certain segments of the population of Tyrol. However, taking into account the measures actually taken by the applicant association in order to protect those who might be offended and the protection offered by Austrian legislation to those under 17 years of age, we are, on balance, of the opinion that the seizure and forfeiture of the film in question were not appropriate to the legitimate aim pursued. (*Otto-Preminger-Institut v. Austria*, 1993, p. 21)

The United Kingdom's *Wingrove* (1995) case involved an 18-minute video entitled "Visions of Ecstasy," written and directed by Nigel Wingrove, who submitted it to the British Board of Film Classification so that it might be legally sold, rented, or shown. In September 1989, the board rejected Wingrove's application, relying on the British blasphemy law, which says:

Every publication is said to be blasphemous which contains any contemptuous, reviling, scurrilous or ludicrous matter relating to God, Jesus Christ or the Bible, or the formularies of the Church of England as by law established. It is not blasphemous to speak or publish opinions hostile to the Christian religion, or to deny the existence of God if the publication is couched in decent and temperate language. The test to be applied is as to the manner in which the doctrines are advocated and not to the substance of the doctrines themselves. (*Wingrove v. the United Kingdom*, 1995, p. 3)

The objectionable manner to which the board referred was the depiction of an erotic relationship between Jesus Christ and St. Teresa of Avila, the sixteenth-century Carmelite nun and convent founder. The film depicted St. Teresa in a black habit, stabbing her hand and spreading her blood over her breasts and clothing, spilling communion from a chalice and licking it up from the ground, kissing Christ fastened onto the cross, which is lying on the ground, and finally sitting astride him, "seemingly naked under her habit, all the while moving in a motion reflecting intense erotic arousal and kisses his lips. For a few seconds, it appears that he responds to her kisses" (*Wingrove v. the United Kingdom*, 1995, p. 3).

The board's decision objected not to the integration of "religious ecstasy" and "sexual passion," which "may be of legitimate concern to an artist," but to its actual presentation, which was "bound to give rise to outrage at the unacceptable treatment of a sacred subject." The decision also said:

Because the wounded body of the crucified Christ is presented solely as the focus of, and at certain moments a participant in, the erotic desire of St. Teresa, with no attempt to explore the meaning of the imagery beyond engaging the viewer in an erotic experience, it is the Board's view, and that of its legal advisers, that a reasonable jury properly directed would find that the work infringes the criminal law of blasphemy. . . . If the male figure was not Christ, the problem would not arise. (*Wingrove v. the United Kingdom*, 1995, p. 5)

The *Wingrove* defense rested solely on ECHRFF art. 10, and the Court, much like in *Otto-Preminger-Institut*, took into consideration both paragraphs 1 and 2 of art. 10, thus focusing on limitations "necessary in a democratic society" and on a "not unlimited margin of appreciation" enjoyed by all member States in the interpretation of the balance between rights and responsibilities.

In its decision, the Court observed that although they are becoming obsolete, blasphemy laws are still in effect in several European countries, and minus a "sufficient common ground in the legal and social orders of the Member States," it is difficult to conclude that such restrictions are "unnecessary in a democratic society and thus incompatible with the Convention." Furthermore, the Court conceded that:

A wider margin of appreciation is generally available to the Contracting States when regulating freedom of expression in relation to matters liable to offend intimate personal convictions within the sphere of morals or, especially, religion. Moreover, in the field of morals, and perhaps to an even greater degree, there is no uniform European conception of the requirements of the "protection of the rights of others" in relation to attacks on their religious convictions. *(Wingrove v. the United Kingdom*, 1995, p. 21)

The Court observed that since the U.K. blasphemy law did not prohibit "'matter" but only "'manner" of presentation, "it was not unreasonable for the national authorities, bearing in mind the development of the video industry in the United Kingdom, to consider that the film could have reached a public to whom it would have caused offense" *(Wingrove v. the United Kingdom*, 1995, p. 24). Therefore, by a 7–2 vote, the Court found no violation of art. 10, because "it cannot be said that the authorities overstepped their margin of appreciation" 1995, p. 24.

It should be noted that the Court's emphasis on the "content v. form" differentiation in offensive religious expression seems to be at odds with its view on offensive political expression. In fact, art. 10, the Court had said a few years earlier, "protects not only the substance of the ideas and information expressed, but also the form in which they are conveyed" *(Oberschlick v. Austria*, 1990, p. 25).

The law of blasphemy had been used in England only once since 1922; in 1979, it was used to find blasphemous a poem that attributed homosexual acts to Christ *(Whitehouse v. Lemon/R*, 1979). The law's usefulness, however, has come under attack recently because it has been interpreted to protect only the Christian religion and especially the Anglican Church. When in 1991, for example, British Muslim groups challenged Salman Rushdie's "The Satanic Verses" on the grounds that it was blasphemous, a British Divisional Court ruled that "as the law now stands it does not extend to religions other than Christianity" *(R. v. Bow Street Magistrate's Court ex parte Choudhury*, 1979), p. 318).

Failure to prosecute the *Rushdie* case prompted a letter to influential Muslims from then Minister of State at the Home Department, John Patten. The letter stated that the government had carefully considered the Muslims' argument about amending the law to accommodate other religions, but concluded that it would be unwise to do so for a variety of reasons, not the least of which was "the clear lack of agreement over whether the law should be reformed or repealed. . . . An alteration in the law could lead to a rush of litigation which would damage relations between the faiths'' (*Wingrove v. the United Kingdom*, 1995, p. 15).

Patten concluded his letter with what may be an omen for the future of blasphemy laws everywhere:

I hope you can appreciate how divisive and how damaging such litigation might be, and how inappropriate our legal mechanisms are for dealing with matters of faith and individual belief. Indeed, the Christian faith no longer relies on it, preferring to recognize that the strength of their own belief is the best armour against mockers and blasphemers. (*Wingrove v. the United Kingdom*, 1995, p. 15)

But while the Court has drawn the limits of tolerance on artistic expression of religious themes, it has given the news media considerably more freedom to disseminate information that might be interpreted as offensive. In 1985, for example, Olaf Jersild of the Danish Broadcasting Corporation presented a program that featured representatives of the Greenjackets explaining their racist and xenophobic beliefs in the crudest of terms (''A nigger is not a human being, it's an animal,'' etc.), and he was convicted by Danish courts for violating the country's anti-discrimination law. The Penal Code of Denmark (1985), art. 266b, punishes those who ''publicly or with the intention of disseminating it to a wide circle of people, makes a statement, or other communication, threatening race, color, national or ethnic origin or belief.''

In reversing the Danish courts, the European Court of Human Rights said that the intent of the program was informational, not propagandist, and therefore it fell within the sweep of the freedom of expression protection of art. 10. ''Not only does the press have the task of imparting such information and ideas,'' the Court said of Jersild's topic, ''the public also has a right to receive them'' (*Jersild v. Denmark*, 1993, p. 20). Although *Jersild* did not concern religion, the Danish penal code provision utilized by the Danish prosecutors outlaws religious as well as racial discrimination.

The Court's tolerant attitude toward offensive speech in *Jersild* points to a strain in its decisions that demonstrates a courageous intent on its part to take on ''dominant religion'' countries and even rule against them. For example, it told the Irish government that its ban on the distribution of abortion information by clinics was ''over-broad and disproportionate'' in relation to its proclaimed purpose of protecting public morals. The Court, in short, found that this '' 'perpetual' restraint on provision of information to pregnant women concerning abortion facilities abroad, regardless of age, state of health or their reasons for seeking counseling on the termination of pregnancy'' violated art. 10's freedom of expression guarantee (*Open Door Counselling Ltd. and Dublin Well Woman*, 1992, p. 30).

Finally, the blasphemy provision of the Penal Code of Holland, art. 147, which prohibits insult against "any religion in public, orally or in writing," has not recently been tested in court.

2. Proselytism. The Court continued to use the "content v. form" yardstick in measuring expression offensiveness in other instances involving religion. In cases of proselytism, for example, even in "dominant religion" countries such as Greece, where the practice of proselytism is constitutionally precluded (see National Constitutional Provisions section above), the Court said that:

A distinction has to be made between bearing Christian witness and improper proselytism. The former corresponds to true evangelism, which a report drawn up in 1956 under the auspices of the World Council of Churches describes as an essential mission and a responsibility of every Christian and every Church. The latter represents a corruption or deformation of it. It may, according to the same report, take the form of activities offering material or social advantages with a view of gaining new members for a Church or exerting improper pressure on people in distress or in need; it may even entail the use of violence or brainwashing; more generally, it is not compatible with respect for the freedom of thought, conscience and religion of others. (*Kokkinakis v. Greece*, 1992, p. 17)

It is impossible, the Court said, to punish a Jehovah's Witness conversation with a Greek Orthodox chanter's wife without "flouting fundamental human rights" (*Kokkinakis v. Greece*, 1992, p. 16). The Greek courts' conviction of a Jehovah's Witness for doing just that, the Court said, was an inappropriate punishment for the "legitimate aim pursued" by the State, and therefore, not "necessary in a democratic society . . . for the protection of the rights and freedoms of others" (1992, p. 17). The Court, in a 6–3 vote, decided that the Greek courts had violated art. 9 of the Convention.

In a similar case, this time involving ministers of the Pentecostal Church, Greek courts were reversed again, albeit not on all counts. In this case, the Court reiterated its view that art. 9 encompasses "freedom to manifest one's religion, including the right to try to convince one's neighbor" as well as its objection to "improper proselytism," which might include "offers of material or social advantage or the application of improper pressure." Since the case involved ministers, who also happened to be officers in the Greek army, the Court found that their conviction violated art. 9 in connection with their proselytizing civilians. However, the Court found no violation of art. 9 in the case of their proselytizing their army subordinates, because the latter felt "a certain degree of pressure owing to the applicants' status as officers" (*Larissis and Others v. Greece*, 1998, p. 3). In short, the Court said that the statute limiting proselytism was correctly applied by the Greek courts in the second instance where its application was found to be within the allowable limits of "freedom to manifest one's religion or belief" of ECHRFF art. 9.

3. Discrimination. In other cases from "dominant religion" countries, the Court continued to refine the boundaries of propriety and fairness in the competition between the dominant and minority religions. It found, for example, that it is discriminatory to exempt from military service the ministers of the dominant religion but not the ministers of minority religions, such as those of Jehovah's Witnesses (*Tsirlis and Kouloumbas v. Greece*, 1996, p. 7). The Court, in particular, found that the military authorities had practiced religious discrimination by illegally detaining the defendants, a violation of ECHRFF art. 5, on unlawful deprivation of liberty.

The Court, however, allowed to stand under the "national margin of appreciation" rule the suspension of Jehovah's Witnesses from high school for refusing to participate in independence day parades (*Efstratiou v. Greece*, 1996, p. 3). The decision said that "It is not for the Court to rule on the Greek State's decisions as regards to the setting and planning of the school curriculum." The Court added that it could "discern nothing, either in the purpose of the parade or in the arrangements for it, which could have offended the applicant's pacifist convictions." Furthermore, the Court said,

The obligation on the pupil does not deprive her parents of their right "to enlighten and advise their child, to exercise with regard to their child natural parental functions as educators, or to guide their children on a path in line with the parents' own religious or philosophical convictions." (1996, p. 23)

In short, the Court, in this instance, found no violation of ECHRFF art. 2 of protocol 1, which guarantees children "the right to education" and parents the right to ensure that such an education is in accordance with their own "religious and philosophical convictions."

Finally, the Court decided that it was discriminatory, based on religious grounds, for the Austrian courts to refuse to award custody of two children to their mother who, after her divorce from their father, had become a Jehovah's Witness. The Court said that "there has been a difference in treatment and that that difference was on the ground of religion," and therefore there was a violation of ECHRFF art. 8, the guarantor of "respect for . . . private and family life" (*Hoffman v. Austria*, 1992, p. 15). Furthermore, according to the Court, the Greek government discriminated on religious grounds and thus violated art. 9 when it unnecessarily delayed giving authorization to Jehovah's Witnesses to operate a house of worship despite their timely application, as prescribed by law (*Manoussakis v. Greece*, 1995, p. 20).

CONCLUDING THOUGHTS

The above record of laws and judgments shows that considerable progress has been made among E.U. members in moving away from "State religions" and in creating an environment of religious pluralism and tolerance. The European Court of Human Rights, on the other hand, has provided adequate legal support for these notions and has shown a remarkable willingness to rule against "dominant religion" countries in guaranteeing freedom of speech and freedom of the press on religious issues.

However, the above record also points to some clear differences between the United States and the countries of the European Union on this issue.

First, the U.S. legal commitment to the concept of a meticulous separation of church and state and an almost absolute right of free speech, concepts that have long been both admired and scorned in Europe, is in contrast to European traditions in which religious institutions have historically played a significant role in civic life. It should come as no surprise, therefore, that Europe's social, political, and legal institutions reflect that role. The first two parts of this chapter demonstrate this position by pointing to the official, often murky, church-state relationship in the legal instruments of the various countries.

Second, the commitment of the E.U. nations to freedom of worship—and by extension to the protection of religious diversity and freedom of expression— has sometimes created awkward situations when expression has been deemed offensive to a country's dominant religion. The result often has been the acceptance of a double standard, an acknowledgment that expression about religion can be limited more easily than other types of expression (i.e., political). This comes at a time when there are clear tendencies in European law to match the more liberal U.S. view on defamation and other types of laws.

Third, the incongruity generated by this double standard has necessitated the refinement of free expression law interpretation in order to clarify that the "content" of religious expression is not punishable, but that the "manner" of that expression is. Unfortunately, even the European Court of Human Rights has been unable to guarantee consistency in the interpretation of art. 10 on all cases.

Finally, in grappling with these inconsistencies, lawmakers and judicial bodies in Europe seem to be saying that they are less concerned with protecting religious symbols and more with respecting the religious sensibilities of their constituents.

In other words, the debate should go on as long as it is civilized. But since civility is debatable as well, the issue is bound to continue confounding E.U. nations as long as blasphemy remains a crime.

REFERENCES

Act of Succession, art. 4 (1810).
Austrian Penal Code, § 188 (1992).
Basic Law of Austria, arts. 13–15, 17a (1867).
Basic Law of Germany, arts. 4, 5 (1953).
Constitution of Belgium, arts. 19–21 (1831).
Constitution of Denmark, preamble, ¶ 4, arts. 67, 68, 70, 77 (1953).
Constitution of Finland, §§ 8, 9, 10, 83, 87, 90 (1919).
Constitution of Greece, arts. 3, 13, 14 (1974).
Constitution of Ireland, preamble, art. 40 (1937).

Constitution of Italy, arts. 7, 19–21 (1984).

Constitution of Luxembourg, arts. 19, 24 (1868).

Constitution of the Netherlands, arts. 6, 7 (1815).

Constitution of Portugal, arts. 37, 41 (1976).

Constitution of Spain, arts. 16, 20 (1978).

Declaration of the Rights of Man, arts. 10, 11 (1789).

Directive on Transfrontier Television, arts. 11, 12, 22 (1989).

Efstratiou v. Greece, 77 Eur. Ct. H.R. (ser. A) (1996).

European Convention of Human Rights and Fundamental Freedoms, arts. 2, 3, 9, 10 (1950)

Freedom of the Press Act (1949)

Fundamental Law on Freedom of Expression (1992).

Hoffman v. Austria, 15 Eur. Ct. H.R. (ser. A) (1992).

Instrument of Government, ch. 2, arts. 1, 4, 12, 13 (1974).

Jersild v. Denmark, 298 Eur. Ct. H.R. (ser. A) (1993).

Kokkinakis v. Greece, 3 Eur. Ct. H.R. (ser. A) (1992).

Larissis and Others v. Greece, 140 Eur. Ct. H.R. (ser. A) (1998).

Manoussakis v. Greece, 59 Eur. Ct. H.R. (ser. A) (1995).

Oberschlick v. Austria, 204 Eur. Ct. H.R. (ser. A) (1990).

Open Door Counselling Ltd. and Dublin Well Woman, 375 Eur. Ct. H.R. (ser. A) (1992).

Otto-Preminger-Institut v. Austria, 295A Eur. Ct. H.R. (ser. A) (1993).

Penal Code of Denmark, art. 266b (1985).

Penal Code of Holland, art. 147.

R. v. Bow Street Magistrate's Court ex parte Choudhury, 1 All ER 306 (1979).

Treaty of Saint-Germain, art. 63 (1919).

Tsirlis and Kouloumbas v. Greece, 54 Eur. Ct. H.R. (ser. A) (1996).

Whitehouse v. Lemon/R, [1978] 68 Cr. App. R 381; [1979] AC 617.

Wingrove v. The United Kingdom, 19 Eur. Ct. H.R. (ser. A) (1995).

Chapter 3

Law and Religious Freedom in Medieval China: State Regulation of Buddhist Communities

Tanya Storch

INTRODUCTION

The question of government control and religious freedom in modern Chinese society has been actively debated in academic literature (*Buddhism under Mao*, 1972; Chan, 1953; Harvey, 1990, chap. 12; Sponberg, 1982; Wright, 1971, chap. 6). On the other hand, religious freedom in classical Chinese society has never been a subject of a discussion. This chapter will fill in this gap by presenting information about government regulation of Buddhist communities in the seventh through twelfth centuries of Chinese history. Whereas scholars have analyzed several aspects of the Chinese Buddhist community, or sangha, including the sangha's role in the country's economy (Gernet, 1956), its social functions (Ch'en, 1976), the principles of the monastic discipline to which it adhered, and the exemplary lifestyles created by its members (Kieschnick, 1997), limited analysis has been done regarding the political and legal influence of the sangha.

The most general observation, based on what is known from the dynastic chronicles and Buddhist histories, is that, despite the immense popularity of Buddhist ideology during many Chinese dynasties, the official status of the sangha was very low. All its activities were strictly regulated by the government, and a single decree of an emperor was enough to end its existence (Ch'en, 1973, chap. 7; Tsukamoto, 1948; Zurcher, 1959, chaps. 3–5).

A comparison of the Buddhist community's representation in Chinese government and its representation in the governments of Sri Lanka, Burma, Thailand, Cambodia, Laos, and Tibet (Rahula, 1966; Snellgrove and Richardson, 1968; Spiro, 1970; Suksamran, 1977; Tambiah, 1996; Tucci, 1950) shows that in China Buddhists were totally subjected to the state. Unlike Buddhists in the previously mentioned countries, Chinese Buddhists were not allowed to become members of the government or even to participate in the selection of government members. Nor were Chinese Buddhists allowed to publicly express opinions about government decisions. Similarly, they did not have the right to select the head of their own community, but they were forced to accept the nominee of the government. Also, the Chinese government was the only government in Buddhist history that issued laws under which each person who made a decision to join the sangha was obligated to seek the permission of the government before seeking the approval of the sangha. Monks and nuns who had joined the community without government permission and senior monks and nuns who had received an ordination were subject to legal persecution in the form of beating with sticks and exile (Qingyuan, 1934, fascicle 12, 50–51).

The nature of the relationship between the sangha and the state becomes clearer upon an examination of the original political documents of the country, such as the state laws and regulations found in the Tanglu shuyi (The Tang Dynasty Code with Commentaries and Explanations), compiled in 653; Song xingtong (The Criminal Code of the Song Dynasty), compiled in 963; and Qingyuan tiaofa shilei (The Laws and Regulations of the Qingyuan Era Selected According to Categories), compiled in 1202. In the following sections of this chapter, four aspects of the above-mentioned documents will be presented. First, the laws that regulated the right to join the Buddhist communities will be presented. Second, the punishments for religious sins will be discussed. Third, the freedom to preach and proselytize will be addressed. And finally, the laws governing the right to a Buddhist education will be analyzed.

GOVERNMENT CONTROL OF THE RIGHT TO BECOME A MEMBER OF A BUDDHIST COMMUNITY

Certainly during the Tang dynasty (618–907) but supposedly even at an earlier date, Chinese law would recognize a person as a member of the Buddhist community only if such a person permanently withdrew from society and lived in a monastery. A person who received a full ordination as a Buddhist monk or nun but who refused to live in a monastery was not treated as a member of the community.

Monks and nuns who lived in the monasteries were regarded as a separate category of people distinct from all other citizens of the country. Judging by the nature of the regulations imposed upon the members of the sangha, it appears that the reasons for distinguishing between monastic Buddhists and the rest of the population had little to do with the principles of Buddhism. Rather, the distinction was due to government concerns, most notably the fact that monks and nuns did not pay taxes and were exempt from forced labor.

The legal system created numerous conditions that made it extremely difficult, if not impossible, for most taxpayers to join the sangha. For example, the head of a family could not become a monk unless he had three adult sons who paid taxes.

Other serious legal limitations on joining a Buddhist community were designed to provide support for the family. Thus all males under age 19 and all females under age 14, by which time the marriages were usually arranged, were prohibited from joining the sangha. People whose parents and grandparents were dead and therefore could not approve of their descendants' decision were not allowed to join the sangha. Similarly, males of any age who did not have male progeny could not become monks until they had sons left in their lineage.

Another regulation that prohibited people from entering the community included laws preventing convicted criminals and citizens who had been noticed in some criminal behavior from joining the sangha. Behavior such as bearing a tattoo or participating in a secret religious group constituted criminal behavior under such laws. Also monks and nuns who had been forcefully returned to their secular position by state regulations could never again join the community.

If a person did not run afoul of any of the above prohibitions, he or she was allowed to become a member of the community. Still, one could not be formally ordained without first obtaining a government-issued certificate known as a *gaodie*. The *gaodie* had to be received from the local imperial officials by each person who decided to become a monk or a nun. It gave permission to the abbot and to the senior monks and nuns in the monastery to ordain a new member of the community.

Under the laws, receiving government permission was the only way to join the community. Under any circumstances, joining a Buddhist community without a *gaodie* was considered a serious crime that was prosecuted. During the Tang dynasty (618–907), the punishment for this crime was one year of labor in the camps for those ordained without permission and 100 blows by the thick stick for those who conducted the ordination (Tanglu, 1936, p. 12). During the Song dynasty (960–1276), the punishment was three years of labor in the camps for those ordained and two years of labor in the camps for those who performed the ordination (Qingyuan, 1934, p. 50).

The state controlled the number of people allowed to take the vows of a monk or a nun. It must be noted that in China becoming a monk or a nun was always believed to be the most effective way to achieve ultimate salvation in Buddhism. Based on the actual social and family traditions of the country, becoming a monk or a nun also was the only way to live one's life according to the principles of Buddhism. Failure to join the sangha meant participation in the ancestral cults, where animals were killed, and blood, meat, and wine were abundantly used for sacrificial purposes. Likewise, remaining in the family meant that the person would be forced to break the vow of abstention from sex, because children could not refuse marriages set up by their parents.

From a modern perspective, the interference of the Chinese state with a person's decision to join the Buddhist community is a violation of personal religious freedom. Most Christians and Muslims would look upon the fact that an individual's right to devote one's life to spiritual perfection was controlled by the government as a violation of personal freedom. From a Buddhist perspective, setting up an obstacle to a person's taking the vows of upasaka means creating bad karma for many generations. Nonetheless, laws prohibiting people from joining the Buddhist community always had intellectual defenders.

Historically, Confucian scholars were one such group of defenders. Whenever the ideological influence of Buddhism on individual members of the Chinese government became strong, government members donated land to the Buddhist communities and allowed large numbers of people to join them. In reaction, the Confucian scholars began a critical campaign against such government members (*Cambridge History of China*, 1979, pp. 589–906; Ch'en, 1976, pp. 225–226; Wright, 1951). The scholars accused the members of the sangha of being lazy, of doing no useful work for society, and of tricking uneducated farmers out of all of their money for the sake of a better rebirth. According to the Confucian scholars, the lands given to the monasteries could be better used for recreation and farming. The Confucian scholars also claimed that people who went into monasteries would be much happier if they stayed with their families.

It is interesting that the opinions of West China specialists are similar to the Confucians. The existence of laws against the sangha is most commonly explained by saying that if the government did not protect itself against the sangha by controlling the taxpayers and the land, the country's economy would collapse (Ch'en, 1976; Gernet, 1956; Weinstein, 1987; Zurcher, 1959).

The criminal laws discussed in the following section may or may not be interpreted as the suppression of religious freedom. From a Buddhist perspective, taking someone's life, stealing, or engaging in sexual misconduct are not social crimes but *parajika*, or deadly sins, which will bring about countless rebirths in hell. Yet to exempt someone from criminal prosecution in a case of murder, stealing, or rape on the basis that this person is going to be punished in hell is a form of religious freedom that modern people will not be willing to give to Buddhists or other religious groups.

GOVERNMENT PUNISHMENT OF MONKS AND NUNS FOR RELIGIOUS TRANSGRESSIONS

According to Buddhist teachings, all monks and nuns must observe five basic precepts (*panca-silani*). These precepts are the five abstentions from: (1) harming living beings, (2) taking what is not given, (3) misconduct concerning sense-pleasures, (4) false speech, and (5) unmindful states due to alcoholic drinks or drugs (Oldenberg, 1879; Prebish, 1975).

Buddhist communities accepted regulations, known as *vinaya*, which held that the punishment for transgressions against the *panca-silani* must be carried out by the members of the sangha. In China, a violation of the five precepts by a member of the Buddhist community was believed to be a ''state problem,'' subject to state regulation. Hence transgressions against any of the above-mentioned five precepts were prosecuted as criminal offenses and punished accordingly.

The laws treated the first Buddhist precept of not injuring a living being as applying to homicide, thus excluding offenses against animals and other beings mentioned in the Buddhist *vinaya*. Furthermore, the legal definition of homicide was in accordance with the social views of the time. For example, killing a slave was not considered as reprehensible as killing a free person. This distinction between slaves and free people constitutes another contradiction in the Buddhist religion. Thus if the abbot killed a slave in the monastery, he was punished by 100 blows by a thick stick. If a layperson killed his own slave, he received the same punishment (Tanglu, 1936, p. 3).

The legal system also assumed a somewhat peculiar position in dealing with situations in which members of the community injured or killed each other. In such cases, the offender and the victim were treated as though they were relatives. Therefore, if a younger monk injured or killed a senior monk, it was treated as a crime committed by a nephew against his uncle. If the injury or murder occurred among monks of the same age, it was treated as an offense that happened between two cousins (Tanglu, 1936, p. 6).

The explanation for this peculiar position lies in the fact that Chinese law punished homicide and physical violence between the members of a family several degrees harder than the same crime committed by people who were not related. By treating the members of the Buddhist community as though they were actual relatives, the laws punished them more severely than they would have if they were not Buddhists.

The rationale for the increased harshness of the law against physical violence among the Buddhists rested on the premises of the Buddhist religion, which taught peaceful and quiet behavior. Still, disrespect for Buddhist beliefs and practices can be seen in the fact that family ties were forced back upon those who had publicly renounced them at their ordination.

Punishments for stealing property by one member of the sangha from another, unlike laws relating to violence, were not based on an imposed family relationship. Rather, the law treated the criminal and the victim as non-relatives. If the law treated monks and nuns as family in theft cases, they would be punished two degrees harder for the same crime, because stealing from a relative (just like killing or injuring a relative) was a more severe crime than the same crime against a non-relative.

It is hard to explain why the law viewed the members of the sangha as relatives in the cases of homicide and physical injury and as non-relatives in the case of stealing property. One possible reason is that the government was less tolerant toward physical fights in the communities than it was toward stealing property. Another possibility is related to the capitalist ideology in Chinese society. Capitalist ideology regards a person's property (but not a person's life) as an individual rather than a collective issue. The punishment for stealing seems to support the "capital ideology" explanation very well, for it was based on a money or silk equivalent to the property stolen. For example, if the stolen property cost 10 *pi* (*pi* is a measure of silk), the punishment was 10 blows by a thin stick. If the damage was equal to 100 *pi*, the punishment was 100 blows, and so on (Tanglu, 1936, p. 6).

In cases of sexual misconduct, monks and nuns also were treated as not having a family relationship. Yet the punishments for sexual transgressions were always two degrees harder for members of the sangha than they were for lay-people. The writers of the code specifically explained that the reason for that was that sexual impurity polluted the principles of Buddhism. The punishment for sexual misconduct was a beating with thick sticks and exile to a labor camp. In some cases, the offenders were permanently excluded from the sangha. It is worth noting that in cases of sexual misconduct, nuns were punished one degree harder than monks for the same crime.

Breaking the fourth precept, abstention from false speech, was punished as severely as sexual misconduct. The crime of false speech was interpreted by the authors of the law as preaching false doctrines. For that reason, it will be discussed in the next section, which deals with the freedom to preach and prose-lytize.

If the fifth vow, abstinence from alcohol, was violated, the offender was punished in a relatively minor way on a first or second offense, by 50 to 100 blows by a thin stick. Yet an addiction to liquor was punished quite severely, by exile and even a permanent loss of status in the Buddhist community.

THE GOVERNMENT DECIDED WHEN AND WHAT THE MEMBERS OF THE SANGHA COULD PREACH

According to the laws of the Tang and Song dynasties, monks and nuns were not allowed to preach or otherwise propagate their religion except on occasions sanctioned by the government. If a member of the community was seen preaching Buddhism, regardless of whether or not his or her preaching contained any anti-government statements, he or she was punished with 100 days of detention.

This detention was inside the Buddhist monastery, but it was a government official who imposed it on a monk or a nun convicted of criminal behavior. Understandably, preaching Buddhist sutras that contained anti-government or apocalyptic-messianic messages (Buswell, 1990; Nattier, 1991; Zurcher, 1981) was punished more severely. In such cases, the punishment was two years of exile to a labor camp (Qingyuan, 1934, p. 51; Tanglu, 1936, p. 3).

Monks and nuns could not move outside the monasteries at will. This seems particularly ironic if one remembers that the Buddhist disciplinary code required them to go out daily to beg for food. If monks or nuns had to leave the monastery to participate in an outside ceremony or for other respectful reasons, the law required them to obtain written permission from an abbot of the monastery and from two other senior monks. Failure to comply with this regulation was punished by 100 blows with a thick stick (Qingyuan, 1934, p. 2).

If a monk decided to travel outside of the province whose government issued his *gaodie*, he needed two letters of recommendation, one from the abbot and the other from a local government officer. These letters were supposed to guarantee his good behavior to the government of the province where he traveled.

Members of the sangha who went on a pilgrimage to Buddhist sites located outside China were detained and interrogated by local officials upon their return to China. After the interrogation, they were forced to reside in one of the largest monasteries in the capital of the province to which they returned after their pilgrimage. This was done so state authorities could continue to observe and control the pilgrim's behavior and communications. Additionally, the returned pilgrims were not allowed to travel outside the monastery where they were forced to reside (Qingyuan, 1934, pp. 50–51).

The reasons behind such restrictions are easy to guess. These were laws against espionage, with which the monks were often associated through the Chinese government. The question of whether monks and nuns actually carried out such an activity on any significant scale has not been investigated. The state also had a policy against foreign monks or nuns coming to China as missionaries or pilgrims. According to the Tang and Song codes, each foreign monk or nun who did not carry a Chinese government certificate for travel was persecuted by 80 blows by a thick stick and expatriated.

GOVERNMENT OFFICIALS WERE RESPONSIBLE FOR THE MORAL AND TEXTUAL EDUCATION OF THE MEMBERS OF THE SANGHA

Through the laws, the state also appeared as an ultimate moral authority for the sangha. This is evident from the fact that the government reserved the right not merely to punish nuns and monks according to its laws but actually to measure their moral accomplishments. Periodically, government officials conducted a "cleansing" of Buddhist communities all over the country. The purpose was to evaluate the "purity" of monks and nuns and to keep in the monasteries only those who had lived their lives strictly according to Buddhist principles. People whom the government committee found morally impure were forced to leave the monastery and return to their families. Any person who was returned to secular status could never become a monk or a nun again (Qingyuan, 1934, p. 50).

Government-sponsored persecutions of the Buddhists' moral impurities were designed to deliver a message that the government's role in the life of the sangha was by far greater than that of a secular ruler. Laws regarding Buddhist images and symbols outside and even inside the monasteries were supposed to work to the same end.

One such law says that monks or nuns who destroy a Buddhist image or a symbol must spend four years in a labor camp and then live in permanent exile at least 3,000 miles away from their own monastery. The comment to this law specifies that, for this crime, the Buddhists were punished several degrees harder than all other citizens, because the former must be taught a lesson in how to respect their own religion (Tanglu, 1936, p. 19).

State officials controlled the area of Buddhist textual education as well. They decided which Buddhist texts the monks and nuns of the empire should study. They also conducted examinations for the monks and nuns. These examinations were modeled on the Confucian-type examinations that the officials themselves had to take before working for the government. A member of the community who did not pass the examination was permanently excluded from the community (Qingyuan, 1934, p. 50).

Texts for Buddhist examinations were chosen by the officials and not by the Buddhist scholars. The abbot of the community had no right to petition for a change in the text in which his community was supposed to be examined. Furthermore, the examination was conducted by the officials.

The text most commonly chosen for the examination during the Tang and Song dynasties was *Mahaprajna-paramita-sutra*. The examined person was given four characters, and he or she was expected to relate exactly to which part of the sutra they belonged. Failure to identify the appropriate part of the text on the basis of the four characters made the person flunk and lose his or her position in the community (Qingyuan, 1934, p. 50).

Monks and nuns were encouraged to study Chinese classical texts such as *Analects (Lunyu)* by Confucius or *Classics of Poetry (Shijing)*, but they were forbidden from studying areas such as divination, martial arts, and astrology. For instance, the punishment for learning and practicing martial arts was as severe as two years of labor camp (Qingyuan, 1934, p. 51).

CONCLUSIONS

The imperial government assumed a position of strict control toward every aspect of the Buddhist community. The controlling position of the government was reflected in the state laws that were enforced by the state officials. According to such laws, the sangha could not accept new members without state permission. It had no right to make decisions about its inner affairs such as the place and time for public ceremonies, forms of social contacts between the members of the sangha and the laymen, the punishment of disciplinary transgressions by its members, or pilgrimages. Even the choice of texts used in the education of the members of the community had to be approved by the emperor and his committees.

To make better sense out of the controlling function of the state, one needs to ask whether the above measures were imposed exclusively on the Buddhist communities. The answer is no. The Song dynasty criminal code, which has been used in this chapter, contains the same laws for the members of Daoist communities as for the members of Buddhist communities (Von Eichhorn, 1968). This means that Chinese lawmakers did not write separate laws for the followers of the Chinese indigenous religion, which was about 2,000 years old by the time the code was written, but automatically extended to the Daoists the laws that had been previously written for the Buddhists.

The fact that the Chinese government did not specifically discriminate against one chosen religion but rather placed all religions under strict political and legislative control is also evident from the history of Christianity in China. Since their early appearance in China, Christian missionaries were forced to follow official regulations similar to those controlling the Buddhists.

Letters by Roman Catholic and Russian Orthodox priests stationed in China during the eighteenth and nineteenth centuries bear witness to this. Many letters contain bitter complaints about Chinese laws. These laws demanded that the missionaries prostrate themselves before the emperor and his high officials, prohibited the missionaries from talking about their religion without permission from state officials, and made it impossible to baptize Chinese people due to the impossibility of obtaining government certificates allowing the Chinese people to accept baptism (Bichurin, 1796; Jensen, 1998; Meskill, 1983; Mungello, 1994; Struve, 1992).

Of course, these demands come as no surprise in light of the restrictions on the Buddhist community. Additionally, it should not be surprising that the followers of the two other world religions spread in China—Islam and Judaism—were eventually subjected to the same government control measures to which the Buddhists, Daoists, and Christians were.

Thus, based on the facts at hand, the Chinese government appears to be a secular political institution that separated itself from all forms of religious ideology and successfully exercised its political and legislative control over the religious communities that associated themselves with such ideologies. The real situation was much more complex than that.

The Chinese government was theocratic in nature. Its political and legislative powers drew from the worship of the spirits of Heaven and Earth, the dynastic ancestors and the *baishen* (the multitude of the spirit-protectors). This worship was observed at all levels of the official government structure, from the emperor to the lowest official (Bodde and Morris, 1967; Ch'u, 1961; Creel, 1961, chaps. 25–28). The strict measures of control imposed by the government against a particular religion, such as Buddhism, Daoism, or Christianity, certainly cannot be explained as mere economical or political necessities of the secular rule. Rather, they must be understood as the expression of the intense religious competition that existed between the official religion of the state and any other religion.

REFERENCES

Bichurin, I. (1796). *Pis'ma* [Letters]. St. Petersburg, Russia: Russkaya Duhovnaya Missiya.

Bodde, D. & Morris, C. (1967). *Law in imperial China*. Cambridge, MA: Harvard University Press.

Buddhism under Mao. (1972). Cambridge, MA: Harvard University Press.

Buswell, R. (Ed.). (1990). *Chinese Buddhist apocrypha.* Honolulu, HI: University of Hawaii Press.

Cambridge History of China (Vol. 3, Sui and T'ang dynasties). (1979). Cambridge, MA: Harvard University Press.

Chan, W. T. (1953). *Religious trends in modern China.* New York: Columbia University Press.

Ch'en, K. (1973). *Buddhism in China.* Princeton, NJ: Princeton University Press.

Ch'en, K. (1976). The role of Buddhist monasteries in T'ang Society. *History of Religion, 15*: 209–231.

Ch'u, T. (1961). *Law and society in traditional China.* Paris: Mouton.

Creel, H. (1961). *The birth of China.* New York: Frederick Ungar.

Gernet, J. (1956). *Les aspects economiques du Bouddhisme dans le société Chinoise du Y au X siecle.* Saigon, South Vietnam: n.p.

Harvey, P. (1990). *An introduction to Buddhism.* Cambridge, MA: Cambridge University Press.

Jensen, L. (1998). *Manufacturing Confucianism: Chinese traditions and universal civilizations.* Durham, NC: Duke University Press.

Kieschnick, J. (1997). *The eminent monk.* Honolulu, HI: University of Hawaii Press.

Meskill, J. (1983). *The banning of Christianity. Introduction to Chinese civilization.* Toronto, Canada: D. C. Heath.

Mungello, D. (1994). *The forgotten Christians of Hangzhou.* Honolulu, HI: University of Hawaii Press.

Nattier, J. (1991). *Once upon a future time: Studies in Buddhist prophecy of decline.* Berkeley, CA: Asian Humanities Press.

Oldenberg, H. (Trans.). (1879). *Pratimoksa.* London: n.p.

Prebish, C. S. (1975). *Buddhist monastic discipline.* University Park, PA: Pennsylvania State University.

Qingyuan tiaofa shilei [Laws and Regulations of the Qingyuan Era Selected According to Categories]. (1934).

Rahula, W. (1966). *History of Buddhism in Ceylon.* Colombo, Sri Lanka: Gunasena.

Snellgrove, D. & Richardson, H. (1968). *A cultural history of Tibet.* London: Praeger.

Spiro, M. (1970). *Buddhism and society: A great tradition and its Burmanese vicissitudes.* New York: Harper and Row.

Sponberg, A. (1982). Report on Buddhism in People's Republic of China. *Journal of the International Association of Buddhist Studies, 5*: 109–117.

Struve, L. (1992). *Voices from the Ming-Qing Cataclysm.* New Haven, CT: Yale University Press.

Suksamran, S. (1977). *Political Buddhism in Southeast Asia.* London: Hurst.

Tambiah, S. (1996). *World conqueror and world renouncer: A study of Buddhism and polity in Thailand.* Cambridge, MA: Harvard University Press.

Tanglu shuyi [The Tang Dynasty Code with Commentaries and Explanations]. (1936).

Tsukamoto, Z. (1948). Hokushu no haibutsu ni tsuite [On persecution of Buddhism by the northern Zhou]. *Toho gakuho, 16*: 29–101.

Tucci, G. (1950). *The tombs of the Tibetan kings.* Rome: Istituto Italiano per il Medio ed Estremo Oriente.

von Eichhorn, W. (1968). Betrag zur rechtlichen stellung des Buddhismus und Daoismus. *Sung: T'oung Pao* (Volume 7).

Weinstein, S. (1987). *Buddhism under the T'ang*. Cambridge, MA: Harvard University Press.

Wright, A. (1951). Fu I and the rejection of Buddhism. *Journal of the History of Ideas, 12*: 88–89.

Wright, A. (1971). *Buddhism in Chinese history*. Stanford, CA: Stanford University Press.

Zurcher, E. (1959). *The Buddhist conquest of China*. Leiden, Germany: Brill.

Zurcher, E. (1981). *Eschatology and messianism in early Chinese Buddhism*. Leiden, Germany: Leiden Sinology.

Part II

Press Freedom in Religious and Secular Societies

Chapter 4

The Problems of Press Freedom in Iran: From the Constitutional Revolution to the Islamic Revolution

Kazem Motamed-Nejad and Naiim Badii

INTRODUCTION

This chapter will examine the problems of press freedom in today's Iran with respect to their historical background during the past century (i.e., from the Iranian Constitutional Revolution of 1906–1909 to the Islamic Revolution of 1978–1979). Since the Islamic Revolution, the number of newspapers and magazines in the Islamic Republic of Iran has increased drastically. Nevertheless, in spite of this quantitative development, some obstacles remain for independent and free activities of newspapers and magazines. The obstacles that have damaged the development of the press are: (1) the continuation of a policy on limitation on free publication (particularly the need to obtain permission from the government for the establishment of a newspaper); (2) the absence of a desirable climate for the press for defending the public interest against governmental policies; (3) the presence of self-censorship; and (4) an unbalanced distribution of government subsidies to the press.

Studies about the problems of press freedom in Iran during the post-revolutionary era, particularly after the end of the Iran-Iraq war in 1988, have become significant. The First Seminar on Studying Iran's Press Problems, held in February 1991 in Tehran, was the first step in analyzing press freedom issues in Iran.

After the May 1997 presidential elections and the start of the Mohammad Khatami's government, a favorable climate for the development of a free, independent, and pluralistic press emerged. As a result, increased attention is being given to the study of the problems of press freedom.

This chapter has four parts. The first part presents the theoretical foundations of press freedom based on Western liberal experiences with an emphasis on

United Nations Educational Scientific and Cultural Organization's (UNESCO) New Communication Strategy for the development of a free, independent and pluralistic press and other mass media. The second part will compare Iranian press underdevelopment to the press situations in Turkey and Egypt to better understand the freedom of press problems in Iran. The third part presents a study of the historical heritage of limitation and press censorship during the authoritarian and dictatorial periods of the pre-revolutionary era and the continuation of its effect on the present time. The fourth part discusses the changes that have taken place during the post-revolutionary era and shows the development of press freedom during the past 20 years and perspectives for an independent, pluralistic press. In conclusion, the recent developments in the growth of press freedom in Iran will be stressed.

THEORETICAL ASPECTS OF A LIBERAL PRESS SYSTEM: FREEDOM, INDEPENDENCE, AND PLURALISM

The foundations of press development and other media of mass communication in Third World countries were developed by UNESCO's Communication Division during the 1940s and 1950s. They were based on the Western liberal press system, with an emphasis on UNESCO's Constitution and art. 19 of the Universal Declaration of Human Rights, stressing the right to freedom of the press and information. For this reason, the early United Nations (UN) report about the condition of mass media in developing countries was entitled *Freedom of Information* (United Nations, 1953).

UNESCO's later efforts to assist in the development of mass communication in various regions of the Third World led to extraordinary regional conferences in the late 1950s and early 1960s. As a result, UNESCO's report was presented to the United Nation's General Assembly in 1961 and set forth criteria and minimum standards for the development of mass communication in developing countries. The report, while stressing freedom of the press and information, suggested a minimum standard of 100 copies of daily newspapers for 1,000 persons, 50 radio receivers for 1,000 persons, 20 television receivers for 1,000 persons, and 20 cinema chairs for 1,000 persons (UNESCO, 1961).

The Importance of a Free, Independent, and Pluralistic Press in UNESCO's "New Communication Strategy"

UNESCO's present communication programs and strategies seek to address world communication inequity and international information imbalance. They also stress, with respect to the New Communication Strategy, freedom of the press and free flow of information within countries and on the global level.

It should be remembered that since the early 1990s, following the downfall of the Soviet Union and other dependent countries in Eastern Europe, UNESCO has offered the New Communication Strategy, and as in the 1950s and 1960s, the issue of press freedom and the free flow of information is one of UNESCO's top priorities.

For this reason, since 1991, in order to achieve the specific objectives of the New Communication Strategy, UNESCO has started new activities. To promote the development of the free, independent, and pluralistic press and other mass media, UNESCO has launched a series of regional seminars around the world.

The first of these seminars was held in the spring of 1991 in Windhoek, the capital of Namibia; the second in the autumn of 1992 in Alma Ata, the capital of Kazakhstan; the third, in the spring of 1994 in Santiago, the capital of Chile; the fourth in the winter of 1996 in Sanaa, the capital of Yemen, and the fifth in the summer of 1997 in Sofia, the capital of Bulgaria. The final declarations of these seminars mentioned the importance of addressing legal obstacles to free press publication and stressed abolishing the requirement of government permission for the establishment of newspapers and other periodicals.

The Three Principles of the Press Freedom System

A look at press freedom in Western countries, where the press system is based on the principles of freedom, independence, and pluralism, helps one better understand the freedom aspect of UNESCO's New Communication Strategy.

1. Freedom of the Press and Information. The first principle of a free press system (i.e., freedom) has its origin in the "Glorious Revolution" of 1688–1689 in England, the United States' Revolution of 1776, the French Revolution of 1789, and the abolition of prior press publication licensing and censorship of the press that was announced for the first time in England in 1695. Article 11 of the Declaration of Human Rights and Citizens of the Great French Revolution (1789), which referred to press freedom as the most valuable freedom for human beings, mentions legal limitation of this freedom, and the first amendment to the Constitution of the United States (1791) states that, "Congress shall make no law . . . abridging the freedom of speech, or of the press."

In Iran, after the Constitutional Revolution of 1906–1909, in accordance with art. 13 of the Constitution of the constitutional Monarchy (approved in 1906) and art. 20 of its amendment (approved in 1907), press freedom was recognized, and the censorship of publications was prohibited for the first time. Also, using the free press concept, the first Iranian press law was approved in 1908, with no requirement for government permission for publication, with an emphasis on limitations for press offenses, and with a requirement for prosecution of press offenses in judicial courts in the presence of a jury.

During the period after the Islamic Revolution of 1978–1979, on the basis of art. 24 of the Constitution of the Islamic Republic of Iran (approved in 1979) and art. 168 of this Constitution, the principle of press freedom was anticipated, and the need to prosecute press offenses in judicial courts in the presence of a jury was stressed. Nevertheless, the first press law after the Islamic Revolution (approved in 1979) and the second press law of this period (approved in 1986) followed the limited reforms of the Iranian press laws during the reign of the Pahlavi dynasty (1941–1979). Therefore, the need to obtain prior permission from the government for publication was preserved, thus presenting an obstacle to press freedom.

2. Press Independence. The second founding principle of a free press is the independence of the press and other communication media, including the impartiality and objectivity of journalists. Independence of the press means political and economic independence of newspapers, magazines, and other communication media from the government and other private economic monopolies. Impartiality and objectivity of journalism are professional endowments and have been practiced since World War I to counter the negative aspects of sensationalism and "yellow journalism."

3. Press Pluralism. The third principle of a free press is the plurality of the press and other communication media, and it is derived from the legal principle of free publication. This principle rejects authoritarian power and the imposition of one thought and stresses the plurality of the press and other mass media, with skeptical optimism about their activities.

The importance of pluralistic mass media has been stressed clearly in the Constitution of the Islamic Republic of Iran. The Constitution's preamble refers to the role of mass media in the evolutionary course of the revolution. Its preamble also refers to the mass media's service in spreading Islamic culture, however, it stresses the importance of encountering different thoughts.

Standards for Measuring the Freedom and Independence of the Press

In the late 1950s, many researchers began measuring the amount of press freedom in different countries of the world. In 1960, Nixon published a study of press freedom in 85 countries. During 1963–1964, he refined the methodology and scale slightly and did another study, in which he classified 117 countries (Nixon, 1965). His studies were limited to print media only, and whereas the rating system was a device for classifying, it was not a device for measuring, since there was an absence of uniform and complete criteria for determining the degree of press freedom in each country.

In 1966, Lowenstein (1972), of the Freedom of Information Center of the School of Journalism, University of Missouri, undertook a worldwide survey of press freedom. In the beginning of the project, the center hoped to continue it on a regular basis, believing that it could provide not only an index but perhaps a predictor of political change in the nations of the world.

1. "Free" Press and "Controlled" Press. Lowenstein started with the following definitions of a "free" press and a "controlled" press:

A completely free press is one in which newspapers, periodicals, news agencies, books, radio and television have absolute independence and critical ability, except for minimal libel and obscenity laws. The press has no concentrated ownership, marginal economic units or organized self-regulation. A completely controlled press is one with no independence or critical ability. Under it, newspapers, periodicals, books, news agencies, radio and television are completely controlled directly and indirectly by government, self-regulatory bodies or concentrated ownership. (Lowenstein, 1972)

2. Press Independence and Critical Ability Factors. Numerous factors were used for measuring press freedom. They were selected on the basis of their overall inclusiveness and comparability. These factors were considered as press independence and critical ability (PICA) factors (Lowenstein, 1972, pp. 131–133; Weaver, Buddenbaum, and Fair, 1985).

A PARADOXICAL PRESS UNDERDEVELOPMENT

A general look at the press situation in Iran shows that during the period after the Islamic Revolution considerable development had taken place in the area of press freedom. In recent years, the number of newspapers and magazines has increased considerably. According to an interview with Bourghani, the Deputy Minister of Culture and Islamic Guidance, there are presently over 800 periodicals published in Iran ("Accelerating development of Iranian press," 1998). This number is almost more than five times the number of periodicals published during the period before the revolution, indicating a quantitative development of the press in Iran. A study of the present content of periodicals shows that in some areas, particularly in the publication of specialized magazines, quality has improved. In the case of art and cultural magazines and political and social magazines, particularly in magazines critical of government policies, a qualitative development can be seen.

In spite of this positive change, the Iranian press has not been able to play a real role in society's development and progress during the post-revolutionary period. In this respect, the necessary motivations to attract readers to daily newspapers, which are the most important social promoters, have not been provided.

Daily Newspapers

A look at the present press situation in Iran, particularly the situation of daily newspapers, indicates the existing paradox between readers' potential use of periodicals and their limited actual use of them.

To understand this situation, an examination of Iran's major socioeconomic indexes is essential. In fact, in 1994, Iran had a population of over 65 million. According to government reports, more than 70 percent of the Iranian population was literate and able to read newspapers ("The literacy movement's," 1995). Iran's economic growth and the purchasing power of most people, compared to other countries in the region, allow access to newspapers and magazines.

Moreover, when comparing UNESCO's 1961 minimum press development standard for Third World countries (100 newspapers per 1,000 persons) with the present press situation in Iran, a large gap is noticeable. Under UNESCO's minimum standard for press development in Third World countries, the 65 million people in Iran need 6.5 million copies of daily newspapers. According to the government's estimates, the total circulation of all daily newspapers in Iran in 1994 hardly passed 1.5 million (Center for Media Studies and Research, Ministry of Culture and Islamic Guidance, 1994). Compared to other countries in the region, the development of daily newspapers in Iran is slow.

To shed some light on the underdevelopment of the Iranian press, a comparison of the present press situation in Iran to that of Egypt and Turkey is relevant. Considering the similar cultural and historical traditions in these three countries, particularly their common experiences with respect to encounters with the West and modernization during the past two centuries, the development of the mass media, particularly the press, which is the oldest medium, should be similar. Furthermore, the publication of printed periodicals was almost simultaneous in Egypt (1828), Turkey (1831), and Iran (1837). In addition, these three countries are similar with respect to their population, their current sociopolitical importance, and their prominent position in the Middle East.

According to data published in UNESCO's 1993 *Statistical Yearbook*, circulation of all daily newspapers and the number of copies per 1,000 persons are higher in Turkey and Egypt than in Iran. According to this data, in 1990, newspapers in Turkey and Egypt had circulations of 4.5 million and 3.5 million, respectively, and the number of copies per 1,000 persons was 71 copies and 57 copies, respectively. During the same period, circulation of Iran's daily newspapers did not reach 1.5 million copies, and the number of copies, per 1,000 persons, was 26.

Also, it should be noted that in 1990, in terms of the number of daily newspapers and the total circulation of copies between Turkey and Iran, the gap is even wider. During 1990, there were 399 daily newspapers in Turkey and only 21 in Iran (see Table 4.1) (UNESCO, 1993).

Nevertheless, during recent years, the number of newspapers in Iran, compared to the period before the Islamic Revolution and even the period during the Iran-Iraq war (1980–1988), has increased drastically. At the beginning of 1995, there were 25 daily newspapers in Iran, of which 17 dailies were published in Tehran.[1] At the threshold of the Islamic Revolution, the number of daily newspapers in the capital barely passed 10.[2]

This situation has been repeated in post-revolutionary Iran. The press blossomed for a short period during the "Spring of Freedom" in the winter and spring of 1979 and again between the autumn of 1979 and the beginning of the Iran-Iraq war, at the end of the summer of 1980. In the spring of 1981, because of new restrictions against publication and the cessation of all non-governmental newspapers, the number of Tehran daily newspapers was reduced to seven.[3] Besides the low number of daily newspapers in Iran, compared to Turkey, the

Table 4.1

Population, Number of Daily Newspapers, Daily Circulation, and Number of Copies per 1,000 Persons in Turkey, Egypt, and Iran

Country	Population	Number of Dailies	Circulation	Copies of Newspapers per 1,000
Turkey	57,326,000	399	4,000,000	71
Egypt	54,688,000	14	3,500,000	57
Iran	57,272,000	21	1,500,000	26

Source: UNESCO, 1993.

poor circulation of Iran's daily newspapers is another index for their underdevelopment. This negative aspect also exists in comparison to newspapers in Egypt.

A quick study of the press changes in Turkey and Egypt during the period following World War II shows the existence of daily newspapers in each country with relatively high circulations of about 1 million copies (Barrat, 1992). However, in Iran, other than during a very short period during the 1978–1979 revolution in which the circulation of each of the two oldest existing Tehran newspapers reached over 1.5 million copies, the circulation of Iranian newspapers never reached that level and presently is between 350,000 to 400,000 copies.

Among the various daily newspapers in Turkey, the *Hurriett*, the leading daily newspaper, has a circulation of 1 million on Sunday (Barrat, 1992). Other major Turkish daily newspapers include *Sabbah, Turkey, Melliat*, and *Meydan*. These four newspapers, respectively, had circulations of 780,000, 785,000, 670,000, and 657,000 in 1991 (The General Directorate of Press & Information of the Turkish Republic, 1991).

In Egypt, daily newspapers have high circulations. The largest Egyptian daily newspapers, all published in Cairo, are *Al Ahram, Al Akhbar*, and *Al Jomhoorieh*, with circulations of 900,000, 800,000, and 650,000, respectively (Barrat, 1992).

However, in Iran, circulations of daily newspapers are much lower than in Turkey and Egypt. In fact, the highest circulation belongs to *Hamshahri*, a four-color daily newspaper owned by the Tehran Municipality, which began publication in January 1992. Since January 1998, *Hamshahri's* circulation has been over 400,000 copies daily. The circulation of *Ettelaat* and *Kayhan*, the two oldest Tehran dailies that continue their publication after the downfall of the

Monarchy, varies between 100,000 to 150,000 copies a day. The circulations of other new Tehran daily newspapers, which started their publications after the Islamic Revolution and particularly after the Iran-Iraq war, range between 10,000 and 50,000 copies.

Non-Daily Newspapers

A comparative study of the press in Iran and Turkey shows that not only do the Turkish daily newspapers have a higher circulation than Iranian daily newspapers, but the Turkish non-daily newspapers and other periodicals also appear to be more developed compared to their Iranian counterparts.

According to data published in UNESCO's 1993 *Statistical Yearbook*, the number of non-daily newspapers and magazines and periodicals in Turkey in 1990 were 872 and 1,325, respectively. In Iran, during the same year, the number of non-daily newspapers was 50, and the number of periodicals was 318.[4]

To clarify the underdevelopment of the Iranian press, a comparative study of some of the socioeconomic indexes of countries (i.e., Turkey, Egypt and Iran) provides interesting results. This review shows the low usage of some means of communication in Iran, even though the economic level and purchasing power of the Iranian people are higher than in Turkey and Egypt.

A comparison among the major development indexes, as reported in the 1994 edition of the *Report on Development in the World*, and *World Report on Human Development*, published by the Banque Mondiale (World Bank) and Programme des Nations Unies pour le Développement (United Nations Development Programme), respectively, shows that Iran's per capita Gross National Product ($2,300) is higher than Turkey's ($1,980) and Egypt's ($640). Similarly, these indexes show that the number of private cars is higher in Iran than in Turkey and Egypt (see Table 4.2). With respect to the utilization of paper and newsprint, Turkey and Egypt use these products twice as much as Iran. Nevertheless, with regard to book publication, Iran is ahead of Egypt and not far behind Turkey. In terms of the number of telephones, Iran is ahead of Egypt but behind Turkey.

All comparisons of the mass communication media (i.e., print, cinema, radio, and television, as well as other communication and cultural indices in Iran, Turkey, and Egypt) indicate the underdevelopment of Iranian mass communication, particularly the print media, despite Iran's economic advantage.

To better understand this paradoxical underdevelopment and to find the principal reasons behind it, a deeper study of the historical experiences, social functions, and fundamental problems of the Iranian mass media, particularly the press, is necessary (Motamed-Nejad, 1977, 1978, 1978–1979, 1995).

A comparative analysis of the content of Iranian newspapers before, during, and after the Islamic Revolution shows the inconsistencies between the real needs of the society, including the country's national interest and the content of newspapers (Badii, 1995; Badii and Atwood, 1986).

Table 4.2
The Socioeconomic Conditions of Turkey, Egypt, and Iran: Some Major
Development Indexes

Country	Pop. (000)	LR%	GNP$	TNPP	NPBPP	NTPP	NCPP
Turkey	57,326	72	1,980	4.7	10.9	20.3	3.6
Iran	57,272	54	2,200	2.0	8.1	4.8	4.7
Egypt	54,688	48	640	4.6	3.0	4.6	2.6

Pop: Population, 1992.
LR%: Percent of literacy rate, 1992.
GNP$: Gross national product in U.S. dollars, 1991.
TNPP: Tons of newsprint per 1,000 persons, 1990.
NPBPP: Number of published books per 1,000 persons, 1990.
NTPP: Number of telephones per 100 persons between 1990–1992.
NCPP: Number of cars per 100 persons, 1990.
Sources: Banque Mondiale, 1994, pp. 172–173; Programme des Nations Unies pour le Dévelop-
   pement, 1994, pp. 109, 176–177.

THE IMPACT OF HISTORICAL LEGACY:
AUTHORITARIAN PRESS CONTROL AND CENSORSHIP

The condition of the press in Iran is a consequence of 150 years of socio-
political conditions. Unfortunately, the press in Iran started as a superficial im-
itation of the West, ignoring Iran's independent development and cultural
identity. In the third decade of the past century, the Turkish Ottmani, Iranian
Qajar dynasties, and Egypt remained independent countries of the East. Their
rulers turned to modernity to strengthen their power and established newspapers
in their countries. In May 1837, the first official governmental authoritarian
Iranian newspaper was published. During the same period, the press in Europe
was passing through the authoritarian and revolutionary stages, and entering the
liberal commercial stage which continues to the present time. In other words,
the press in Iran started with the motivations of the revolutionary press in the
West at the time that the liberal and commercial press was prevailing.

Press Freedom after the Constitutional Revolution

For 70 years, from the time of the establishment of the first newspaper until
the Constitutional Revolution, the government-owned and/or government-
supervised press was the only press in Iran. Following the Constitutional Revolution, in accordance with the first Iranian Constitution with its amendment
and the first Iranian Press Law, freedom of the press was officially recognized.

Freedom for press activities was mentioned in the first Iranian Constitution and its amendment, following the Constitutional Revolution (1906–1909). Under art. 13 of the 1906 Iranian Constitution, newspapers can publish, without any distortion or change in meaning, all discussions of the Majlis (parliament), so all people can be aware of all discussions and reports. Each person considered benevolent may write in a public newspaper so that no issues are kept from the public eye. Hence, all useful matters, such as Majlis debates and the people's reactions to the debates, may be published, provided that their publication does not contradict the essential interests of state and nation. Any person who publishes anything in the press with personal aspiration, libel, or contempt will be legally questioned and punished.

Article 20 of the Amendment of the Constitution of Iranian Monarchy (1907) also stresses freedom of the press. All press, other than that which is misleading and indecent to the respected religion, is free, and any censorship in it is prohibited. Nevertheless, whenever anything is contrary to the press law, its publisher or writer will be punished according to that law. If the writer is famous and residing in Iran, the publisher, printer, and distributor are immune from any harm.

Article 79 of the 1907 Amendment of the Constitution of Iranian Monarchy recognizes the need for trying press offenses before a jury and provides that, in the case of political misdeeds and press, the jury will be present in the court.

The first Iranian press law was approved by the National Assembly (*Majlis Shoraye Melli*) in February 1908. The law was based on the July 29, 1881, French Press Law. The law stressed general press freedom and prohibition of press censorship and restrained the need for obtaining permission for the publication of newspapers. It also set a foundation for press freedom by its treatment of press offenses and by abolishing the requirement that publishers obtain government permission for publication.

Press Controls and Restrictions during the Pahlavi Dynasty

Nevertheless, 10 years after the Constitutional Revolution, and in accordance with a decree approved in 1918 by the council of ministers, the principle of free press publication was limited and contingent upon permission obtained from the council. Later, after the 1921 coup d'etat by Reza Khan and his attempt to capture the Iranian monarchy, the pressure on the press was increased. Hence, in October 1923, the parliament approved the Law of Press Supervision, which provided censorship of newspaper content.

During the reign of the Reza Shah (1925–1941), because of severe government censorship, freedom of the press disappeared. After the Reza Shah fell from power, an appropriate climate for freedom of the press appeared, but it lasted only a short time. Following a public revolt in Tehran in the autumn of 1942, all newspapers were banned, and in accordance with the Revision of the Part of the Press Law, approved in December 24, 1942, the 1908 Press Law was revised, and publishers were required to obtain permission for the publication of newspapers. In later press laws, approved in February 1952 and August 1955, this obligation was preserved. Therefore, during the 37-year reign of Mohammad Reza Pahlavi, the last king of Iran, from September 1941 to January 1979, with the exception of a few short periods in the early 1940s and during the nationalization of the oil industry and national government of Dr. Mohammad Mossadeq between 1951 and 1953, there was intense government control of the press.

PRESS CHANGES FOLLOWING THE POST-ISLAMIC REVOLUTION

The paradoxical underdevelopment of the press in Iran was affected by the negative legacy of authoritarian regimes during the past century and a half. To fully understand the development of the Iranian press, a review of the changes and practice of the press during the post-revolutionary era is necessary.

After the victory of the 1978–1979 Islamic Republic, whose two main slogans were "freedom" and "independence," it was expected that a desirable and an appropriate legal and institutional framework would prevail over press freedom. The first press law during the post-revolutionary era was approved by the Revolutionary Council in August 1979, a few months before the approval of the Constitution of the Islamic Republic of Iran. This was the peak of the "Spring of Freedom," when hundreds of new journals were being published freely. Nevertheless, this law required that publishers obtain a license for the publication of newspapers and magazines from the Ministry of National Guidance. As a result, an oppressive climate prevailed over the press.

The Constitutional Framework of Press Freedom

Later, with the approval of the Constitution of the Islamic Republic of Iran in December 1979, relatively positive principles regarding press freedom emerged. The preamble of the new Constitution provides that the mass media (radio/television) must follow the direction of the evolutionary course of the Islamic Revolution in the service of spreading Islamic culture. In this way, they must bear fruit from the encounter of thoughts and prevent the dissemination of destructive, anti-Islamic characteristics.

The third article of the Constitution of the Islamic Republic of Iran (1979) provides that the government of the Islamic Republic of Iran is responsible for the attainment of the aforementioned objectives for the realization of the following: "2. Raising the level of public consciousness in all areas by the correct use of the press, mass media and other means of communication."

Article 24 of the 1979 Constitution of the Islamic Republic of Iran stresses freedom of the press by providing that publications and the press are free to express matters unless they are injurious to the fundamentals of Islam or public rights. There are a few concerns over this article. The main one is that it mentions press freedom but does not guarantee this freedom. Other countries whose constitutions address press freedom have constitutional guarantees of press freedom that their governments do not feel free to ignore. Another concern is the failure to protect all aspects of press freedom, including the gathering, dissemination, publication, and receipt of news and information. The article only mentions "expression of matters." As a result, only the freedom of publication is protected. In addition, failing to provide for freedom of the press for matters injurious to the fundamentals of Islam or public rights could limit the mentioned freedom and open the way for press censorship and prior restraint.

Article 168 of the 1979 Constitution of the Islamic Republic, regarding the prosecution of press offenses before a jury, provides that investigation of political and press offenses shall be held in open sessions of the Courts of Justice in the presence of a jury. The procedure for appointment of jury members, their legitimacy and jurisdiction and the definition of a political offense, shall be determined by law in accordance with Islamic criteria.

In fact, after the Islamic Revolution of 1978–1979, as in the period after the Constitutional Revolution, press activities were autocratic and contrary to the revolutionary ideals of the new Iranian Constitution. For this reason, only recently have new hopes for a free, independent, and pluralistic press been noticeable.

Perspectives for Promoting a Free, Independent, and Pluralistic Press

After evaluating the positive efforts taken in recent years to provide a desirable climate for the development of the press and other mass media in Iran, evidence of progress exists. Decisions have been made to address the underdeveloped press. Steps have been taken to support and strengthen press freedom and economic independence and to secure the professional independence of journalists and follow the communication objectives and policies established by UNESCO in the 1992 Alma Ata Declaration about "Promoting Independent and Pluralistic Asian Media."

In fact, most of the objectives and recommendations in the Alma Ata Declaration were presented at the First Seminar on Studying Iran's Press Problems, held in the winter of 1991, nearly two years before the Alma Ata seminar. These objectives included legally guaranteeing the freedom of speech, press, and information, abolishing the barriers for establishing new publications, providing support to help the free flow of information, upgrading journalism education and other professional training, developing press and other mass media management principles, guaranteeing the professional independence of journalists through the development of professional associations, supporting the safety and security of journalists, and combatting economic barriers to a diverse and an independent press.

At the above-mentioned seminar, Iranian press problems were considered in

12 areas with 30 papers presented by Iranian researchers and specialists. In this seminar, issues such as providing a desirable climate for freedom of the press, strengthening the legal protection of the press, revising the press laws, and economically supporting the press, including governmental subsidization, were discussed. Also discussed were topics such as journalism education, professional independence, and the management of the press institution. The activities of other institutions such as news agencies and public relation offices, commercial advertising agencies, newsprint printing facilities, and press distribution facilities were analyzed. In addition, important topics such as press and national development, press and national security, press and cultural invasion, and audience research and gratification by the press were reviewed.

After the seminar, neither the government nor media institutions developed any programs or policies to implement the seminar's objectives and recommendations or to resolve the issues discussed. Nevertheless, the indirect effects of the seminar appeared gradually. A few months later, in the autumn of 1991, press litigation before a jury began for the first time in Iran. Although an amendment to the 1907 Iranian constitution stressed the presence of a jury in all press trials, and a jury was again suggested in art. 168 of the new constitution, a jury for a press offense did not occur until 1991.

In 1995, concerned with revision of the present press law, politicians and journalism specialists held open debates about improvements in the publication of newspapers and magazines and the removal of barriers to free publication. A research program was undertaken concerning the "Legal Foundations of Press Freedom" to help lawmakers write the new press law.

Recent debates concerning the need for regulating government subsidies, the importance of journalism associations and syndicates, and studies concerning advertising regulation are all steps toward solving Iranian press problems. The improvement of journalism education, including the availability of bachelor, master, and doctoral degree programs, has propelled journalism education in Iran into a new era.

CONCLUSION

It seems that more than 10 years after the end of the Iraq-Iran war, there was a turning point with respect to the improvement of press freedom conditions in Iran. Prospects for a free, independent, and pluralistic press are brighter than ever.

Between September 1997 and April 1998, the important following developments were implemented by President Khatami's government regarding the development of press freedom:

1. The "Professional Association of Iranian Journalists" was established in October 1997.[5] During the winter and spring of 1998, the association made important efforts in creating better working conditions for journalists, to protect the free exercise of

journalistic activities, to promote juries for press offenses, and to select the best journalists of the year during the press festivals.

2. The composition of juries for press trials was revised. Unlike the past few years, juries now have an independent view regarding press cases. In the press trials during February and March 1998, there were more favorable decisions with respect to journalists criticizing the government than in the past. Also, television channel 5 broadcast press trials before a jury on the same day as the trial.

3. The number of periodicals, particularly newspapers, increased. The increase during the autumn and winter of 1997–1998 was incredible. As of July 1998, there were about 30 daily publications in Tehran.

4. The announcement of the second ''Seminar on Studying Iran's Press Problems'' at the end of May 1998 was another important step taken by the new president toward improving and developing press freedom. The first seminar, held in February 1991 while the present president was Minister of Culture and Islamic Guidance, stressed that the seminar be held biannually to oversee important press issues in Iran, the most important being freedom of the press. However, in recent years, due to a lack of interest by officials of the Ministry of Culture and Islamic Guidance, further seminars were forgotten.

To further the development toward a desirable climate for press freedom in Iran, the need to obtain prior permission of the government for the establishment and publication of newspapers should be removed. There is a possibility that a revision of the present press law, which has the support of the new government, will eliminate this problem, and instead of ''prior permission'' for publication, an ''announcement'' or ''registration'' procedure, or a combination of both, will be chosen.

NOTES

1. Presently, these newspapers include 23 daily Persian newspapers (*Abrar, Abrar Varzeshi, Afarinesh, Akhbar, Akhbare Eghtesad, Jahan Eghtesad, Ettelaat, Farda, Ghods, Gozareshe Ruz, Hamshahri, Iran, Jaméeh, Jomhoori Islami, Kayhan, Kayhan Varzeshi, Kar va Kargar, Khabar, Khabar Varzishi, Resalat, Salam, Sobhe Khanevadeh,* and *Zire Gonbade Kabod*), three English daily newspapers (*Iran News, Kayhan International,* and *Tehran Times*), one Arabic daily newspaper (*Kayhan Al Arabi*), and one Armenian daily newspaper (*Alik*).

2. Among these newspapers, five Persian daily newspapers (*Ayandegan, Ettelaat, Kayhan, Paygham Emrooz,* and *Rastakhiz*), two English dailies (*Kayhan International* and *Tehran Journal*), one French daily (*Journal de Téhéran*), and one Armenian daily (*Alik*), existed.

3. These newspapers include *Ettelaat, Kayhan, Jomhoori Islami, Sobhe Azadegan, Kayhan International, Tehran Times,* and *Alik*.

4. In this study, the circulations of non-daily newspapers and periodicals of Iran and Turkey were not available, because UNESCO's 1993 *Statistical Yearbook* contained no statistical records of this.

5. The ''Syndicate of Reporters and Writers,'' established in 1962 during the Mon-

archy, was the only professional journalism organization in Iran. It terminated its activities two years after the downfall of the Monarchy and, until the establishment of the new journalists association, it made no effort to protect the independence of the profession.

REFERENCES

Accelerating development of Iranian press. (1998, April 20). *Iran*, p. 3.

Badii, N. (1995, Juillet–Décembre). Content characteristics of major Iranian newspapers: A comparative analysis of six Tehran dailies. *Cahiers d'Études sur la Méditerranée Orientale et le Monde Turco-Iranien (C.E.M.O.T.I.)*, *20*: 45–72.

Badii, N. & Atwood, L. E. (1986, Autumn). How the Tehran press responded to the 1979 Iranian revolution. *Journalism Quarterly, 63*: 517–536.

Banque Mondiale. (1994). *Rapport sur le développement dans le monde, 1994: Une infrastructure pour le développement*. Washington, D.C.

Barrat, J. (1992). *Géographie économique des médias: Diversité des Tiers Mondes*. Paris: Litec.

Center for Media Studies and Research, Ministry of Culture and Islamic Guidance. (1994). *Evaluation of present press situation in Iran*. Tehran, Iran.

Constitution of Iran, art. 13 (1906).

Constitution of Iran, Amendment of the Constitution of Iranian Monarchy, arts. 20, 79 (1907).

Constitution of the Islamic Republic of Iran, preamble, arts. 3, 24, 168 (1979).

Constitution of the United States, amend. I (1791).

The General Directorate of Press & Information of the Turkish Republic. (1991, April). *Turkey at a glance*. Ankara, Turkey.

The literacy movement's report on the increase in literates in Iran. (1995, January 18). *Kayhan*, p. 2.

Lowenstein, R. L. (1972). Press freedom as a political indicator. In H. D. Fischer & J. C. Merrill (Eds.), *International communication: Media, channels, functions* (p. 130). New York: Hastings House.

Motamed-Nejad, K. (1977, July–August). *Impact of mass media on Iranian society*. Paper presented at the Advanced Study Seminar of the East-West Communication Institute, Honolulu, HI.

Motamed-Nejad, K. (1978, September). *Communication and Westernization: Mass media and national culture in Iran*. Paper presented at the XI World Conference of the International Association for Mass Communication Research, Warsaw, Poland.

Motamed-Nejad, K. (1978–1979). Information et pouvoir en Iran. *Annuaire du Tiers Monde, 5*: 185–213.

Motamed-Nejad, K. (1995, Juillet–Décembre). Médias et pouvoir en Iran. *Cahiers d'Études sur la Méditerranée Orientale et le Monde Turco-Iranien (C.E.M.O.T.I.)*, *20*: 13–43.

Nixon, R. B. (1960, Winter). Factors related to freedom in national press systems. *Journalism Quarterly, 37*(1): 13–28.

Nixon, R. B. (1965, Winter). Freedom in the world press. *Journalism Quarterly, 42*: 6.

Programme des Nations Unies pour le Développement. (1994). *Rapport mondial sur le développement humain*. Paris: Economica.

UNESCO. (1961). *Mass media in the developing countries: A UNESCO report to the United Nations* (Reports and Papers on Mass Communication, 33). Paris: UNESCO.

UNESCO. (1993). *Statistical Yearbook*. Paris: UNESCO.

United Nations. (1953). *Freedom of information, 1953: Report submitted to United Nations Economic and Social Council* (Document No. E./2426). New York: S. P. Lopez.

Weaver, D. H., Buddenbaum, J. M., & Fair, J. E. (1985, Spring). Press freedom, media and development, 1950–1979: A study of 134 nations. *Journal of Communication, 35*(2): 104–117.

Chapter 5

The "Monkey Trial" in the Land of the Bible: Modern Techniques of Religious Censorship—The Case Study of Israel

Yehiel Limor and Hillel Nossek

INTRODUCTION

In October 1998, an agreement between Israel and the Palestinian Authority was signed in the White House. This agreement, which was signed by Israeli Prime Minister Benjamin Nethanyahu, Palestinian leader Yasser Arafat, and U.S. President Bill Clinton, was intended to be an additional step toward the realization of a Middle East peace settlement.

The signing of the agreement, which contained many compromises on the part of Israel, was accompanied by numerous protests on the part of religious and right-wing circles in Israel, which opposed any agreement that would involve handing over territories in the West Bank to the Palestinians. These circles even threatened to act toward bringing down the government, which relied on a shaky coalition in which the religious parties were an important component.

The signing ceremony in the White House was held on a Friday afternoon and was concluded only minutes before the beginning of the Jewish Sabbath. Jewish law forbids travel, writing, and the use of electric appliances on the Sabbath. At the end of the ceremony, the Israeli media requested an interview with Prime Minister Nethanyahu, but he refused to hold a press conference so as not to desecrate the Sabbath. This refusal was unusual, since the prime minister, like his predecessors, had in the past given interviews on the Sabbath to the electronic media.

The refusal to be interviewed was the result of pressure from religious groups that were furious that, due to the time difference between the two states, the ceremonial signing of the agreement in Washington had taken place after the Sabbath had already begun in Israel. This pressure resulted in the actual censorship of a statement by the prime minister for 24 hours. The direct victims were the media and, through them, the entire Israeli public.

Six years earlier, PepsiCo began to market its products in the Israeli market. This penetration into a new market required extensive marketing and advertising groundwork, particularly since Coca-Cola products had been sold in Israel for years and led the soft drink market. PepsiCo's advertising campaign, designed to penetrate the Israeli market, was based on a series of drawings illustrating the stages of the evolution of mankind from primordial monkey to modern man. The campaign angered the ultra-orthodox community, because the theory of evolution stands in contradiction to the Jewish belief that the world was created 5,000 years ago and that man was created by God. Announcements were posted in ultra-orthodox areas calling for a boycott of Pepsi Cola. The threat had the desired effect. The company's management panicked, and because the orthodox and ultra-orthodox sectors provide a large potential clientele for soft drinks, the campaign was withdrawn and replaced with a new one that did not annoy the ultra-orthodox population.

In 1996, Benetton was forced to renovate a billboard showing a black horse crouching over a white horse after orthodox circles vehemently protested the public display of pornography. At the same time, Israeli fashion companies replaced bus stop posters, in which models exposed their arms or legs, after ultra-orthodox extremists set fire to one bus stop after another.

The cancellation of media interviews on the Sabbath, boycott threats, and even setting fire to bus stops are only three manifestations of religious censorship in twentieth-century Israel. There are various aspects to this censorship that combine religious belief with politics and economics. This chapter focuses on one aspect of religious censorship—its use against the mass media. It also examines religious censorship in a historical, social, and political perspective and analyzes the influence of religious censorship on the structure of the media and their performance.

In addition, this chapter explores whether the case of religious censorship in Israel is idiosyncratic or if its implications traverse sectoral and geographical borders. In other words, can the Israeli case serve as a case study for other democratic societies in which struggles between two sectors of the population, religious and secular, are taking place or may take place? These two sectors, in Israel as in other states, are not homogenous. It is possible to find a broad spectrum of ideas, outlooks, and beliefs within each of them, from the ultra-orthodox to the ultra-secular. A broad spectrum of opinions is accepted in a democratic society, but censorship, by its very essence, stands in contradiction to the basic values of democracy. Its existence becomes more problematic when it replaces the methods of negotiation and mutual persuasion that are so essential to democracy.

THEORETICAL BACKGROUND

Censorship has existed since the fear arose that ideas contain a force capable of undermining any establishment, political or religious. A broad sociological definition states that censorship is "a form of surveillance: a mechanism for gathering intelligence that the powerful can use to tighten control over people or ideas that threaten to disrupt established systems of order" (Jansen, 1991, p. 14).

Censorship of any kind inherently contradicts liberal and democratic values whose purpose is to enable freedom of expression and free, unmonitored activity of the market of ideas and opinion. This is particularly true when censorship is directed toward the mass media. It is no wonder that censorship is virtually synonymous with non-democratic regimes. The normative theory (McQuail, 1994) adopted the basic categorization of relations among the state, society, and the mass media and laid the groundwork for a multidimensional examination of the structure of the media and their performance, including the various constraints to which they are subjected. The term structure, according to McQuail's definition, refers to aspects that include, among other things, the media's freedom from external controls. The term *performance*, according to the same definition, "refers to the manners in which the media carry out their chosen or allotted informative or entertainment tasks" (1994, p. 121).

Siebert, Schramm, and Patterson (1956) identified two models of government in which censorship is a controlling mechanism used systematically by the government—the authoritarian model and the totalitarian model. Censorship, albeit in a less rigid form, is also one of the central components of the developmental model of government (McQuail, 1992), which is characteristic of Third World states in the first stage of development following liberation from colonial occupation.

The accepted model of government in democratic states, the social responsibility model, rests upon liberal tradition and should be free, at least apparently free, of the control of any kind of censorship. The social responsibility model is based on the self-monitoring of the mass media, in other words, self-censorship, the purpose of which is to ensure the peace and security of society and the balance between various democratic values, including freedom of expression. Codes of practice or codes of ethics, which are accepted by the media in many states, are prominent, institutionalized expressions of the existence of this internal censorship. However, self-censorship is not the only form of censorship directed toward the media. Censorship is used against the media in a multitude of spheres, albeit frequently in a latent and an indirect form.

From a historical perspective, it is possible to divide censorship into three basic categories—religious censorship, political censorship, and moral censorship (Jensen, 1995). This chapter suggests an additional category, security censorship, which must be distinguished from political censorship (Limor & Nossek, 1995). From the mass media's point of view, each type of censorship

Table 5.1
Categorization of Various Patterns of Censorship

Type of censorship/ Form of implementation	External	Agreement	Self-imposed/Internal			
			Institution	Medium	Organization	Individual
Religious	A1	A2	A3a	A3b	A3c	A3d
Political	B1	B2	B3a	B3b	B3c	B3d
Moral	C1	C2	C3a	C3b	C3c	C3d
Security	D1	D2	D3a	D3b	D3c	D3d

can be implemented in three ways. First, censorship may be external, imposed by laws, orders, or other techniques of imposing pressure (see boxes C1, D1, A1, and B1 in Table 5.1). Second, censorship may be by agreement, various arrangements of cooperation between the government or other bodies and the media, the purpose of which is to prevent the publication of forbidden or harmful material (see boxes A2, B2, C2, and D2 in Table 5.1). Finally, censorship may be internal self-censorship, a self-imposed restriction on the part of the media.

Internal self-censorship can be implemented on four levels—the institution (see boxes A3a, B3a, C3a, and D3a in Table 5.1), the medium (see boxes A3b, B3b, C3b, and D3b in Table 5.1), the organization (see boxes A3c, B3c, C3c, and D3c in Table 5.1) and the individual (see boxes A3d, B3d, C3d, and D3d in Table 5.1). The first level of censorship, the institution, is exemplified by the decisions of the Press Council in Israel, the highest authority of Israel's media establishment (Caspi & Limor, 1999). The second level of self-censorship, the medium, is demonstrated by the internal censorship mechanism of the American movie industry and the complaints committee of the British press. In all of these cases, on both the institutional and the medium levels, internal control mechanisms were established to ward off the implementation of external controls. The third level of self-censorship, the organization, is exemplified by a newspaper, broadcast station, or publisher that determines an editorial line or advertising policy and promises that, through self-monitoring, there will be no deviation from this line. The fourth level of self-censorship, the individual, is demonstrated by a journalist, radio or television broadcaster, or author who internalizes institutional or organizational norms and acts accordingly, thus neutralizing the need for the existence of other control mechanisms, internal or external.

While the existence of political or security censorship and the manner of its implementation may be instructive regarding the nature and essence of a political regime in a particular society, the existence and methods of implementation of religious censorship and censorship on moral grounds demonstrate the nature of society and the focal points of cultural wars. From the perspective of media-society relations, the existence of religious censorship may shed light on the level of the institutionalization of relations between religion and the state and society. Religious censorship and the methods and means of its implementation can also serve as a scale of the status of the media in society. The acceptance of the burden of external censorship (see box A1 in Table 5.1) may show that the media are not sufficiently immune to external pressure. Religious censorship implemented by agreement (see box A2 in Table 5.1) may indicate that, in the spirit of social responsibility, the media demonstrate sensitivity toward groups and sectors in the public at large. On the other hand, censorship by agreement may indicate weakness on the part of the media. The agreement, which is a compromise, bears witness to the media's inability to withstand external pressure. Internal self-censorship on the levels of the institution (see box A3a in Table 5.1), the medium (see box A3b in Table 5.1), the organization (see box A3c in Table 5.1), and the individual (see box A3d in Table 5.1) may bear witness to normative behavior that internalizes the values of social responsibility but may also illustrate capitulation to external pressure. Media that implement self-censorship out of capitulation do not usually tend to admit as much, as such a confession is also an admission of weakness.

While history reveals that technological developments have left their marks on cultural processes and even on culture wars, the technological innovations of the modern age pose a new type of challenge for any type of censorship and may be a factor in the acceleration of the development of culture wars. The globalization of the media leads to the globalization of media content (Hamelink, 1994; Sreberny-Mohammadi, 1991) and poses a real threat to insular cultures and societies. Direct satellite channels are, by definition, global media that appeal to various audience types "regardless of national borders and historical and cultural features of various societies" (Nossek & Adoni, 1996, p. 54). Although many technological innovations of the mass media reached Israel late compared to other Western states, from the early 1990s onward, cable channels have taken their place alongside terrestrial television channels, thus enabling the reception of satellite broadcasts originating in countries throughout the world. Also, preparations for the reception of satellite broadcasts (DBS) have begun in Israel, and computers with Internet access have become common in Israeli households.

To societies and communities that are attempting to preserve their unique tradition and culture, global media content contains a threat in the fields of news, entertainment, and advertising. The news, which is distributed throughout the world on CNN, SKY, or the BBC, exposes these societies to information that their leaders had previously been able to prevent from being spread. Entertainment programs, distributed worldwide, import threatening foreign values. Advertisements present both visual and substantial stimuli that are perceived as a danger to the existing norms.

On the other hand, modern technologies enable insular societies to establish community media systems that offer their community members alternative media content and provide a platform from which to condemn the contents pre-

Figure 5.1
The Israeli Case: The Media Institution versus the Religious Institution,
Combined with the Political Institution

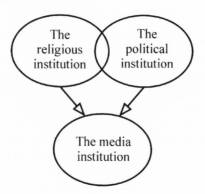

sented on the general or global channels. A salient characteristic of this intra-sectarian communication, particularly in communities such as the orthodox and, more so, the ultra-orthodox, is that it is rarely broadcast outside of the community, and its content, which is internally controlled, is unknown to the public at large. Secular local and community media, on the other hand, attempt to adopt pluralistic characteristics in order to reach all of the sectors, including the religious.

The social responsibility model in democratic states in which there is a separation between religion and state creates a triangle whose three points are the state, the religious institution, and the media institution. The media institution and the organizations that comprise it are exposed to pressure from the other two institutions as well as pressure from other institutions in society. In the Israeli case, owing to the identification of the political establishment with the religious establishment, the picture is different from that in states in which there is a separation between religion and state (see Figure 5.1). As a result, the mass media find themselves facing a system of controls that has dual interests and compounded power.

The interaction and mutual sympathies between the religious institution and the political institution empower the religious sector and thus give it far greater fields of action than that existing in states in which there is a clear-cut separation between religion and state. The initial basis for Jewish religious censorship may be in the Ten Commandments, one of which orders, "Thou shalt not make unto thyself a graven image." Like the Christian church, whose censorship mechanisms have been widely discussed (Grendle, 1977; Menache, 1990; Putnam, 1967), Judaism also imposed strict censorship for generations (Carmilly-Weinberger, 1977). From this aspect, there is nothing new in the attempt to impose religious censorship in modern Israel. However, a more accurate examination reveals new patterns of manifest modern censorship, as well as latent censorship. Israeli society is adopting modern techniques, not only for self-preservation but also to spread its influence over other sectors.

RELIGION AND STATE IN ISRAEL: HISTORICAL AND SOCIAL BACKGROUND

When the State of Israel was established in 1948, the Declaration of Independence determined that the new state would be democratic and Jewish. Linking together democracy and religion laid the groundwork for constant tension between them. This tension has accompanied the state throughout its existence. Similar tension exists in many democratic states, but the case of Israel is much more complicated. While many democratic states inserted clauses in their constitutions separating religion and the state, there is no such separation in Israel.

In fact, the decision not to draw up a constitution immediately upon a declaration of independence can be seen as an additional expression of the opinion of both the religious and secular communities that, as Ravitzki (1997) put it, "the rival camp is doomed to diminish, to fade away, and possibly even to pass from the face of the earth." In other words, as long as each of the two communities believed that the life expectancy of its rival was limited, each had no interest in institutionalizing and perpetuating its relations with the other. The practical expression of this perception was the status quo, which was based on the lifestyles that had been accepted in the British mandatory period, which preceded the State of Israel. The status quo defined the rigid borders between the secular camp and the religious camp (Friedman, 1990), and it was implemented in a number of areas, including family law (the determination that the rabbinate is the only body authorized to perform marriages and divorces), funerals (the rabbinate is responsible for carrying out funerals), education (the recognition of the existence of separate educational systems for the orthodox and ultra-orthodox sectors), the Jewish dietary laws (all national and public institutions, even the army, must observe these dietary laws and "keep kosher"), and the Sabbath (public services, including public transport, were not operative on the Sabbath, with rare exceptions).

The partners to the status quo agreements, the secular sector and the religious sector, were both part of the Zionist consensus embracing the vast majority of the Israeli public. The term *secular* requires further definition. In Israel, the secular public includes those who have traditional leanings, however partial (e.g., different levels of observance of the dietary laws, not traveling on the Sabbath, or synagogue attendance on the High Holidays).[1] Similarly, the religious public includes liberals as well as those who lean toward the orthodox pole. The groups that did not adopt the Zionist ideology, the extreme left, communists in the secular camp, and the ultra-orthodox in the religious camp, were marginal ones in the society and had little strength or influence.

The secular sector, which was the banner-bearer of the Zionist idea, was willing to adopt the satus quo, not only out of the desire to draw the religious sector closer to it but also in an attempt to prevent an open rift in the newly established state. The religious sector agreed to the status quo, which it saw as a compromise, mainly because its social and electoral power was much weaker than that of the secular sector. In the first elections following the establishment of the state, the orthodox and ultra-orthodox received 16 out of the 120 seats in the Knesset, the Israeli parliament. Furthermore, the religious sector believed that it was possible to combine the values of democracy, Zionism, and Judaism, thus leading to the development of religious Zionism, which attempted to combine democratic ideas with Halakhic perceptions while accepting all the obligations required of citizens in a democratic state.

The status quo between the two camps did not include the public cultural sphere. This was particularly evident in regard to radio broadcasting. Although the radio was a government body,[2] it broadcast on Saturday, the Jewish Sabbath. The explanation for this was that *Kol Yisrael*, the Israel Broadcasting Station, was a continuation of the mandatory broadcasting station, which broadcast on Saturday, and the status quo justified the continuation of an existing situation. In other fields of cultural consumption, such as cinemas, theaters, museums, and nightclubs, no all-inclusive decision was made. These fields remained under the jurisdiction of each municipal authority.

The mass media map of Israel was limited and static for many years. The first important change came in 1968 with the introduction of a single television channel. The channel's introduction was accompanied by great fears regarding the negative effects that it might bring and posed a threat to the religious sector. If the television channel were to broadcast on Saturday, it may tempt traditional and even religious people to watch, thus breaking the Sabbath prohibition against using electricity. To the religious sector, the introduction of the new medium caused a change in the status quo. The secular camp saw television as nothing more than an additional communication medium, like radio, which worked in the framework of the Israel Broadcasting Authority. Therefore, television, like radio, should broadcast on Saturday. A coalition crisis developed around the question of television broadcasts on Saturday. To resolve the crisis, the government forced the hands of the representatives in the Broadcasting Authority's plenum, which decided that the new medium would not operate on the Sabbath. A private citizen then appealed to the High Court of Justice and won a temporary court order to run the television station on Saturday, thus setting a precedent. Since then, it has continued to run on the day of rest (Caspi & Limor, 1999).

The Israeli advertising industry also was limited in its scope and activities for many years. There were few billboards, and these were placed predominantly in places rarely frequented by the orthodox community. This situation gradually changed. As economic activity expanded and as the economy adopted the marketing strategies of the United States and other Western states, billboards became more prominent and more bold in order to attract maximum attention.

For many years, the cultural discourse between the secular and religious sectors was part of the political discourse between them. The religious camp formed itself into a political party and ran in the elections to the Knesset. Parliamentary representation awarded the religious camp electoral weight, and as this weight increased, the religious representatives were able to increase their demands. These demands were related not only to the rights and privileges of the religious camp's constituents but also to altering the lifestyle of the secular sector.

The Six-Day War of 1967 altered the physical map as well as the spiritual map of the State of Israel. At the end of the war, Israel found itself controlling extensive territories, including the West Bank, which had previously been held by Jordan. The occupation of the West Bank turned the historical dream of Greater Israel into reality and fired the imagination of those who saw the occupation as the first stage toward the renewal of the historical heritage of the greater Jewish state and maybe even the Jewish kingdom. The occupation of the territories brought in its wake a deep rift in the Israeli public, one that has continued to divide it for decades. On one side were the hawks, supporters of the undivided Land of Israel. Some of the hawks were captives of messianic and religious fervor, and others believed that the occupied territories were a security asset that could not be relinquished. On the other side were the doves, the majority of whom were left wing and secular, who believed that *realpolitik* requires the return of the territories and that the occupied Palestinian population had the right to self-determination.

The political rift divided the Israeli public in two. Neither of the two large parties, the left-wing labor party nor the right-wing Likud party, succeeded in gaining a clear-cut majority. Therefore, the party that formed a government required coalition partners. The religious parties acted as the main partner, a role which gave them political power which only increased as the large parties became increasingly dependent upon them in order to preserve the coalition. In parallel, the electoral strength of the orthodox and ultra-orthodox sectors increased, and in the 1996 elections, they received 23 seats in the Israeli parliament, a 50% increase over the first elections in 1949. This increase in political power played a role in religious censorship, both manifest and latent.

The Six-Day War delineated not only new physical boundaries for the State of Israel but also raised once again, and with greater intensity, the debate on the state's religious nature. Two Jewish groups that had previously played a limited role in this debate, the ultra-orthodox and the Reform Jewry, joined the public discourse. This is of great importance, because these two groups relied on large Jewish constituencies outside of Israel. These constituencies attempted to motivate Israeli groups, mainly by pouring in money in order to change legislation regarding religious matters.

Religious censorship has been implemented for many years, mainly internally, to prevent the infiltration of undesirable content from the secular world. A control committee comprised of rabbis determined what may and may not be published in the orthodox and ultra-orthodox sectors' press (Levy, 1989; Michelson, 1990), and ultra-orthodox families were not allowed to have radios in their homes. The accelerated development of the mass media map, which began in the 1980s, provided a rich variety of new media channels, both print and electronic. The 1991 Gulf War, which exposed the State of Israel to the threat of Iraqi missile attacks, led to the cancellation of the prohibition of radio set ownership among the ultra-orthodox, because the radio served as the source of information regarding missile attacks. These developments, as well as technological innovations in the field of mass communication, posed a threat to the orthodox and ultra-orthodox sectors. While in the past internal censorship had sufficed, the orthodox and ultra-orthodox sectors were now forced to impose external censorship in order to protect their community from the content of the mass media.

Another explanation for the change in the policy of the orthodox and ultra-orthodox sectors is related to the rise in the power of liberal activist groups promoting the concept of a civil society. The struggle of these groups to separate the civil-Israeli identity from the Jewish identity, the expansion of cultural activities on the Sabbath and the High Holidays, the steady increase in the number of people driving their private vehicles on Saturdays, the creation of secular frameworks to deal with marital issues, the increasing number of secular funerals, the abolition of theater censorship, and the intensification of the struggle for freedom of expression led to a strategic change in consciousness. According to Ravitzki (1997), the present conflict between the religious sector and the secular sector is an expression of the development of a new consciousness according to which "the other represents a stable and vital phenomenon, which has a continuation and will have children and children's children" (1997, p. 5). In other words, from the moment the religious camp realized the secular camp was not transient, but was rooted and stable, it was necessary to formulate a new strategic perception to deal with this threatening and dangerous rival. This change in strategic perception was expressed in the transition from defensive, internal censorship to offensive, external censorship. The Israeli political reality gave the religious parties great power and also laid the groundwork for the religious struggle that is part of the broader one over the Jewish identity of the State of Israel. As will be demonstrated later, the means employed in this struggle include political means, economic means, and even the use of physical violence.

The struggle over the identity of the State of Israel moves between two poles (see Figure 5.2), the democratic pole and the theocratic pole. Religious censorship reflects the self-perception of the religious sector regarding its place in the secular state, the respect the religious sector gives to the secular sector, and the intensity of the cultural war between the two sectors.

RELIGIOUS CENSORSHIP: CATEGORIZATION OF PATTERNS OF ACTION

Religious censorship has many faces. Table 5.1 proposes three categories of censorship—external censorship, censorship based on agreement, and internal self-censorship. This chapter focuses on external religious censorship.

Figure 5.2
The State of Israel: Between Democracy and Theocracy

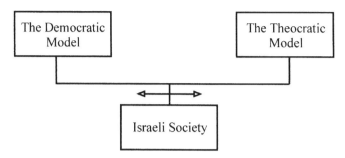

Any attempt to examine external censorship directed at the mass media requires identification of the levels of analysis of censorship activity. This chapter proposes nine levels of analysis of censorship activity.

The first level of analysis is the constitutional one. Does the censorship act by power of legislation that enables the institutional imposition of restrictions on religious grounds, or is its activity not anchored in the framework of a law?

The second level of analysis is the legal one. Does the religious censorship limit itself solely to activity in the legal framework, or does it include the use of illegal action?

The third level of analysis is the level of transparency. Is the censorship imposed openly, or in a latent manner?

The fourth level of analysis is the level of institutionalization. Is the censorship activity carried out in a formal manner, or are informal means used?

The fifth level of analysis is the tactical level. Is the censorship implemented directly or indirectly?

The sixth level of analysis is the level of target. Who is the target toward whom the censorship or the pressures aimed at implementing the censorship are directed?

The seventh level of analysis is the level of pressure. Are the pressures that are intended to bring about censorship imposed on the political, economic, legal, or other levels?

The eighth level of analysis is the level of content. Is the censorship directed toward news, entertainment, cultural, or advertising content?

The ninth level of analyis is the level of the medium. Is the censorship directed toward all of the media, one medium, some of the channels, or one specific medium?

These criteria contribute to the examination of religious censorship and its patterns of action and make it possible to place religious censorship in a social, cultural, and political context. For example, formal, open activity aimed at bringing about a change on the constitutional level demonstrates the status and power of the religious sector. The successful implementation of an economic boycott aimed at bringing about a change in the contents of the media shows the extent of the religious sector's power and, more significantly, the degree of its unity. Illegal censorship activity, particularly when it does not meet with a firm response on the part of the authorities, demonstrates the weakness of the government and its inability or unwillingness to enter into confrontations with subcultures in the society and in the state.

HOW RELIGIOUS CENSORSHIP IN ISRAEL WORKS

Censorship is a tool that various groups use to achieve their goals. Since the implementation of censorship is a tactical act, it is not always carried out in an open and a public manner. In many cases, it is implemented in indirect, latent ways. Using the above criteria, this chapter examines religious censorship in Israel through cases that reveal the variety of issues in which censorship is implemented and the patterns of its operation.

In regard to the constitutional level of analysis, there is no legislation in Israel that provides for restrictions on the media on religious grounds. The legislative activity of the representatives of the orthodox and ultra-orthodox sectors in the Knesset focuses on issues such as conversion, observance of dietary laws and the Sabbath, rabbinical courts, and religious education. Nevertheless, religious representatives initiated one noteworthy attempt at legislation that would have a direct bearing on the functioning of the media. In 1997, a Knesset member from an ultra-orthodox party proposed a private bill to amend the Defamation Law. The proposed amendment would have protected the religious community by making it illegal to state the religious affiliation of arrested crime suspects.

At the legal level of analysis, many activities aimed at bringing about media censorship are performed in a legal framework. Legal demonstrations, letters to newspaper editors, activities of religious pressure groups, pressure from religious representatives in public bodies that oversee the media, and appeals by and to Knesset members are just some examples of legal actions. On the other hand, there also are numerous documented cases of illegal activities, including the stoning of buses bearing immodest advertisements (Arbelli, 1998), threats against companies that distribute billboards because of an advertisement showing a woman, which the religious oppose on principle (Alon, 1997), ultra-orthodox riots in a museum in the town of Holon in order to prevent the opening of an exhibition on Saturday (Saban, 1997), and sticking sleeves onto posters in which women appeared with bare arms (Sigan, 1997).

At the transparency level of analysis, it is not difficult to find numerous documented cases of overt censorship, including boycott threats and setting fire to bus stops. Naturally it is difficult to find documented cases of covert censorship, but one such example is the secret agreement signed between a billboard company and a committee of rabbis. In the agreement, the company agreed to refrain from placing billboards carrying messages or pictures that would offend the religious in ultra-orthodox neighborhoods and to permit the ultra-orthodox to spray black paint over such posters inadvertently placed in these neighborhoods (Galanti, 1995).

At the level of institutionalization, there are many cases of censorship activity carried out through informal channels and means. Such cases are inherently difficult to document. One documented case of this type was a decision of a rabbi, who had been one of the most popular entertainers in the country before he turned religious, to cancel his television show. The rabbi made this decision due to pressure from the street in the ultra-orthodox community rather than because of an official ruling by the rabbis or leaders of his community (Zaltzman, 1997). It must be noted that the ultra-orthodox community does not watch television, and the show was meant to serve as a bridge between the ultra-orthodox and secular sectors. There are numerous cases of formal censorship activity. In one such case, following appeals from members of his own religious party, the Minister of Education postponed the airing of a television program on homosexual youth on educational television, over which he had jurisdiction (Kashti, 1997). Jewish religion regards homosexuality as a severe sin. Another example of formal censorship is the appeal by the Israeli Minister of Transport to the bus companies to refrain from using advertisements that may offend some of the public. The minister, a member of a religious party, is responsible for granting licenses to public transport lines and for subsidizing them. The minister claimed, ''I wouldn't define this as censorship, but rather, as culturally humane'' (Danielli, 1998).

At the tactical level of analysis, there are many cases where religious censorship is implemented directly against the media. One such case was the appeal by an ultra-orthodox association to cancel the broadcast of a drama on television because it contains a scene in which the ultra-orthodox are seen beating a girl (Segev, 1995). In other cases, censorship is levied indirectly, as in the above-mentioned case in which an ultra-orthodox faction of the government threatened a coalition crisis if a broadcast on homosexual youth was not cancelled (Eichner, 1996). Another example of indirect censorship is the cessation of a program on sex, broadcast on the local Jerusalem radio station, after the city's Council for Religious Affairs threatened to withdraw the kosher license of the hotel in which the station's studio is located (Pfefer, 1997).

At the level of the target, religious censorship aimed at influencing the functioning of the media is directed at various targets. An example of pressure levied against an advertiser is the appeal by ultra-orthodox circles to a textile company to withdraw a campaign in which new styles of underwear were presented (Gaoni, 1998). An example of pressure on the channel is the case in which a television channel was only allowed to film the Jewish New Year's prayers of the ultra-orthodox on the condition that none of the camera crew were Jewish (Rahat, 1997). Examples of pressure on message distributors include setting fire to newspaper stands selling secular newspapers in ultra-orthodox neighborhoods and opposition to the installation of cable television in a town in the south of

Israel, in which the majority of residents were religious and contended that "cables are a greater danger to the Israeli family than drugs" (Allouche, 1995).

At the level of pressure, the importance of the orthodox and ultra-orthodox parties in the coalition government gives them the ability to use political means in order to impose religious censorship. An example is the leader of the ultra-orthodox Shas political faction in the Knesset's warning to the government that the operation of the cable television's shopping channel on Saturdays may come back to haunt them in the elections (Ilan, 1995a). Censorship through economic means also is common. In September 1998, the Israeli cellular telephone company, Cellcom, removed billboards that showed a man and a woman embracing one another. Within a few days, these billboards were replaced with new ones featuring a father embracing his son. The pictures of the man and the woman were removed in response to the call by a group of ultra-orthodox rabbis "not to join and not to make new deals with Cellcom, until the abominable advertisements, which alienate the chosen people from the holy land, are removed" (Zaltzman & Harsonki, 1998). Another example is the threat by religious leaders to initiate a consumer ban of a popsicle company in response to an advertisement for a new popsicle. This advertisement included a variation on a scene from the movie *Basic Instinct* (Ilan, 1995b).

At the level of content, religious censorship is levied against all of the media content, the news, entertainment, culture, and advertising. An example of censorship of the news is the physical assault on a news crew that was covering the prayers at the Western Wall (Somech, 1998). An example of censorship of advertising billboards is the 1995 removal of posters showing dancer Pina Baouche dancing in a long white gown with bare arms (Dayan, 1995). Censorship in the field of entertainment is illustrated by the case in which representatives of ultra-orthodox parties threatened a coalition crisis if a series of items in a popular television show was not removed (Zaltzman, 1996a). The reason for the removal was that the items discussed chapters of the Bible from a satirical perspective and were therefore blasphemous. Censorship in the cultural arena is demonstrated by the demand of ultra-orthodox politicians that dancers in the *Bat-Sheba* dance troupe wear modest attire rather than dance suits in a festive performance, broadcast live on television in honor of Israel's fiftieth Independence Day. The dancers refused and cancelled their participation in the performance.

At the medium level, religious censorship may be directed toward the communications media in general, toward a specific medium, or toward a specific media organization such as a newspaper, a radio station, or a television channel. An example of censorship at this level of analysis is the struggle, headed by the ultra-orthodox daily newspaper *Yated Ne'eman*, calling for a ban on companies that advertise on television on the Sabbath. The newspaper noted that these companies not only desecrated the Sabbath themselves but also led the general public to do so by providing the financial basis for the operation of broadcast television on the Sabbath. The newspaper claimed that, without advertisements, the channel would have to terminate its Sabbath broadcasts. Indeed, some large companies gave in to the pressure and stopped airing their advertisments on Saturdays (Ilan, 1995c).

Sometimes the representatives of a medium or an entire media sector acknowledge the existence of such censorship, as in the confession of a senior advertiser that members of the creative department of the advertising agency claim that their creative ability has been ''virtually castrated'' for fear of the reactions of the religious sector (Blumenkrantz, 1994). Another example is the recommendation by the advertising committee of television channel 2 to remove a McDonald's cheeseburger advertisement, since the mixing of milk and meat, which is forbidden by Jewish dietary laws, may offend the ultra-orthodox community (Zaltzman, 1996b).

DISCUSSION

In 1992, PepsiCo was forced to remove newspaper advertisements that reflected the evolutionary progression from primordial monkeys to modern man after ultra-orthodox circles threatened a general boycott. ''The monkeys affair'' was not the only incident in which religious censorship was used against PepsiCo. The following year, the company sponsored a performance in Israel by the rock group Guns N' Roses and announced its intention to do the same for Michael Jackson. In response, the dietary committee of the ultra-orthodox sector announced its intention to revoke the kosher label on the company's products. The label was not returned until a year later, when PepsiCo agreed ''not to sponsor performances and events which oppose the pure Jewish values'' (Cohen, 1998).

These two cases exemplify the dozens of documented multidimensional and multifaced censorship cases presented herein. Although some of the censorship activities described above may be seen as attempts to protect the orthodox and/or ultra-orthodox communities from the infiltration of foreign influences, some are clearly not cases of protective censorship but offensive censorship. In other words, these cases show a conscious, deliberate attempt to shape the contents of the discourse in the secular public space. The Pepsi boycott is a clear-cut example of offensive censorship. Drawings of monkeys would not have been accepted for publication in the newspapers of the orthodox and ultra-orthodox communities, and the ultra-orthodox do not attend rock concerts.

The manifest, direct operation of religious censorship is an indication both of the increasing awareness of the orthodox and ultra-orthodox sectors of their political and economic power and of the religious sector's willingness to use its power to promote particular interests. Religious censorship is a concrete expression of Ravitzki's (1997) definition of the development of the awareness that ''the other [secular sector] represents a stable and vital phenomenon, which has continuation and children's children'' (p. 5). The use of censorship against the secular sector through the media is a deliberate attempt to alter the status quo and to gradually obliterate the existing boundaries between the two sectors. The boundary of the cultural space, in contrast to other areas of the status quo, is in the form of an unwritten code. Therefore, a victory on the part of religious censorship would redesign this code and the cultural space it governs. While censorship can be viewed as a mechanism of brute force, it is a replacement for dialogue and negotiation, which are nonexistent in Israel.

The threats of political and economic brute force that accompany the use of religious censorship have rarely been executed. In many cases, the threat of using political or economic force was enough, and there was no need for actual sanctions. The capitulation of the secular sector, including the media, is no coincidence. It reflects the Israeli identity crisis that the secular population of Israel is undergoing. This crisis is causing mental and intellectual paralysis in the secular sector, which has difficulty in presenting ideological alternatives to those proposed by the religious sector.

Religious censorship presents the Israeli media with a dilemma that is not unique to Israel. The media in many Western states, including Israel, suffer from the problem of low credibility, and they face criticism from religious groups and others for leaning toward sensationalism, adopting the style of the yellow press, and harnessing journalistic ethics to the service of media corporations and media barons. Even if the media resist religious censorship that stems from pure ideological motives, they find it difficult to do so when the religious sector packages its contentions in moral-social claims such as the protection of minors, the purity of the family, opposition to the use of drugs, or general humanistic values.

The case of religious censorship in Israel reveals the weakness of the mass media and their inability or unwillingness to combat the intense pressure put upon them. In Israel, as in other democratic states, the market economy rules the mass media. When an audience group is not satisfied and threatens to damage circulation or ratings, the media are willing to bend their professional values. Even public broadcasting, which used to be the symbol of professionalism, is exposed to similar economic pressure, as well as direct political pressure, and gives in to it. The orthodox and ultra-orthodox sectors have identified this weak point of the mass media, and in order not to harm business, the media are willing to do "monkey business."

NOTES

1. It should also be noted that the accepted scale for religiosity in Israel is based on the subjective definition of the respondents. This definition creates a continuum that classifies the adult Jewish population in Israel into four principal subgroups: from "ultra-orthodox" at one end of the continuum (4.5%) to "orthodox" (13%), "traditional" (33%, including 4% who define themselves as "secular believers"), and "secular" (49%) (Herman & Ya'ar-Yochtman, 1998).

2. The radio was government owned until 1965, when the Israel Broadcasting Au-

thority was established. This is an independent authority, modeled after the British Broadcasting Corporation (BBC).

REFERENCES

Allouche, Z. (1995, January 25). "The cables war" in Netivot: Will they corrupt the youth or contribute to their education? *Yediot Aharonot*, p. A11.

Alon, G. (1997, December 23). Rubinstein and Arbel ordered the opening of an investigation against an ultra-orthodox committee "for the prevention of pornographic advertising." *Ha'aretz*, p. A6.

Arbelli, E. (1998, March 3). Ultra-orthodox stoned a bus with an "immodest" advertisement. *Ha'aretz*, p. A4.

Blumenkrantz, Z. (1994, June 6). Creativity is castrated because of the ultra-orthodox. *Ha'aretz*, p. C5.

Carmilly-Weinberger, M. (1977). *Censorship and freedom of expression in Jewish history*. New York: Sepher-Hermon Press with Yeshiva University Press.

Caspi, D. & Limor, Y. (1999). *The in/outsiders: The media in Israel*. Cresskill, NJ: Hampton Press.

Cohen, B. (1998, June 5). It didn't start with Bat-Sheba. *Yediot Aharonot*, p. 14.

Danielli, Y. (1998, September 25). Minister Yahalom demands "internal censorship" of bus ads. *Ma'ariv*, p. A4.

Dayan, S. (1995, September 17). Pina Baouche: Without shoulders and arms. *Ma'ariv*, p. B17.

Eichner, A. (1996, October 20). Ultra-orthodox: TV show on homosexuals—scandalous. *Yediot Aharonot*, p. A21.

Friedman, M. (1990). The State of Israel as a religious dilemma. *Alpayim, 3*: 24–68 (in Hebrew).

Galanti, Y. (1995, April 9). Secret agreement: "Postermedia" permits the ultra-orthodox to paint over bus-stops with abominable advertisements. *Ma'ariv*, p. A12.

Gaoni, Y. (1998, September 14). The committee for the prevention of abominable advertising demands the cancellation of the Delta "Punchtonim" underwear advertising campaign. *Haaretz*, p. C5.

Grendle, P. (1977). *The Roman Inquisition and the Venetian press, 1540–1605*. Princeton, NJ: Princeton University Press.

Hamelink, C. J. (1994). *Trends in world communication—On disempowerment and self-empowerment*. Penang, Malaysia: Southbound.

Herman, T. & Ya'ar-Yochtman, Y. (1998). *The peace process and the secular-orthodox rift*. Tel Aviv, Israel: Tel Aviv University, the Steinmetz Center.

Ilan, S. (1995a, March 26). MK Benizri: The operation of the shopping channel on the Sabbath will harm the government in the '96 elections. *Ha'aretz*, p. A6.

Ilan, S. (1995b, May 25). Na'amat and the orthodox are initiating a ban on Whitman products due to a popsicle advertisement. *Ha'aretz*, p. A8.

Ilan, S. (1995c, June 5). Numerous companies announced that they would stop advertising on Channel 2 on Saturdays. *Ha'aretz*, p. A1.

Jansen, C. S. (1991). *Censorship: The knot that binds power and knowledge*. New York: Oxford University Press.

Jensen, C. (1995). *Censored: The news that didn't make the news and why*. New York: Four Walls Eight Windows.

Kashti, O. (1997, April 8). The Education Minister: Homosexual behavior—a moral flaw. *Ha'aretz*, p. A8.

Levy, A. (1989). *The ultra-orthodox*. Jerusalem: Keter (in Hebrew).

Limor, Y. & Nossek, H. (1995). Military censorship in Israel: Anachronism in a changing world or a model of coexistence between press and government in democracy. In M. Lemhstedt & L. Poethe (Eds.), *Leipziger jahrbuch zur buchgeschichte* (Vol. 5) (pp. 281–302). Weisbaden, Germany: Harrassowitz Verlag.

McQuail, D. (1992). *Media performance*. London: Sage.

McQuail, D. (1994). *Media theory* (3rd ed.). London: Sage.

Menache, S. (1990). *The Vox Dei—Communication in the Middle Ages*. New York: Oxford University Press.

Michelson, M. (1990). The ultra-orthodox press in Israel. In D. Caspi & Y. Limor (Eds.), *Mass media in Israel—A reader* (pp. 218–232). Tel Aviv, Israel: The Open University (in Hebrew).

Nossek, H. & Adoni, H. (1996). The social implications of cable television: Restructuring connections with self and social groups. *International Journal of Public Opinion Research, 8*(1): 51–69.

Pfefer, A. (1997, November 28). The Religious Council censored Radio Jerusalem. *Kol Ha'ir*, p. A19.

Putnam, G. H. (1967). *The censorship of the Church of Rome and its influence upon the production and distribution of literature (1906)*. New York: Benjamin Books.

Rahat, M. (1997, September 30). Channel 2 cannot film the celebrations at the grave of the rabbi from Breszlaw. *Ma'ariv*, p. A16.

Ravitzki, A. (1997). *Religious and secular in Israel: A culture war?* Jerusalem: The Israel Democracy Institute (in Hebrew).

Saban, E. (1997, December 22). Ultra-orthodox riots in the Holon Arts Center; Attempt to prevent a happening. *Ma'ariv*, p. A18.

Segev, E. (1995, December 5). The ultra-orthodox leverage association demands the cancellation of episodes in the series "Sitton." *Ha'aretz*, p. B5.

Siebert, F., Schramm, W., & Patterson, R. (1956). *Four theories of the press*. Urbana: University of Illinois Press.

Sigan, L. (1997, July 6). The land of the long sleeves. *Ha'aretz*, p. B3.

Somech, A. (1998, August 3). Dozens of ultra-orthodox attacked a Channel 1 television crew covering the prayers at the Western Wall. *Ha'aretz*, p. A3.

Sreberny-Mohammadi, A. (1991). The global and the local in international communications. In J. Curran & M. Gurevitch (Eds.), *Mass media and society* (pp. 118–138). London: Edward Arnold.

Zaltzman, A. (1996a, November 11). Kopatsch or the coalition. *Ma'ariv*, p. B6.

Zaltzman, A. (1996b, October 15). Recommendation: To remove the cheeseburger ad from the TV because it "offends the ultra-orthodox community." *Ma'ariv*, p. A12.

Zaltzman, A. (1997, June 23). Uri Zohar leaves TV show due to ultra-orthodox pressure. *Ma'ariv*, p. A13.

Zaltzman, A. & Harsonki, Y. (1998, October 7). Cellcom gave in to the ultra-orthodox— Its billboards will come down. *Ma'ariv*, p. A21.

Chapter 6

Who Speaks for China? State Control over the Discourse on Opium

Alan Baumler

Opium has been an important issue for all Chinese governments of the twentieth century. All Chinese governments with any pretensions to nationalist legitimacy were expected to have some program for eliminating this scourge. However, all Chinese governments before 1949 were deeply involved in the opium trade themselves, and they profited from it both financially and politically. This presented a golden opportunity for critics of these governments, but it was an opportunity that they were never able to take advantage of. This chapter will examine the various efforts of Chinese states to control critics of its opium policies.

Opium had been commonly smoked in China and throughout Asia for hundreds of years, and opium taxes had become a mainstay of Chinese and colonial governments. In the twentieth century, however, opium taxes gradually went out of favor, and governments began the process of suppressing the opium trade. There were several reasons for this change. The opium trade could be hard to control and tax, and as governments grew more sophisticated and powerful, they were able to call on other forms of revenue besides commercial taxes such as that on opium. New ideas about opium also played a role. Under the influence of the germ theory of disease, the concepts of drug abuse and drug addiction were developed. These ideas held that opium use would inevitably destroy both the user and society. Drug control thus became a key issue for all modern states. Non-medical use of opium and its derivatives was banned in the metropolitan countries and was gradually reduced in the colonies.

China was part of these trends, but for the Chinese, opium was a more important, more difficult issue than it was for the colonialists. For the Chinese, the goal of purifying the nation was not just a matter of good government but one of national survival. China's repeated defeats in the last century could be tied to the opium trade, and all Chinese governments promised to take action to eliminate this trade. This was more difficult in China than elsewhere. Chinese governments were heavily dependent on opium, and the disorder of the twentieth century only made it more attractive as a revenue source. It is impossible to determine how much of government revenues at various levels came from opium, but it was often substantial. The national government estimated that it received 9 percent of its revenue from opium in 1928 (*China Yearbook*, 1929–1930, p. 656). Liu Xiang, the warlord of Sichuan, was getting at least a fifth of his revenue from opium in the early 1930s (Zhou, 1997, p. 115), the amount to which he publicly admitted. The real figures are no doubt much higher. Opium was particularly appealing to local governments that had few other sources of revenue, and the problem was thus very hard for the central government to control. All of this money made government officials quite ambivalent about opium suppression. Ordinary Chinese could also be ambivalent about the trade, since so many of them profited from opium or smoked it. The process of opium suppression in China would thus be a halting and a complex one.

Despite this, it was inevitable that China would eventually suppress opium. By 1911, elimination of opium had become one of the necessary tasks for the creation of a new China. No Chinese government ever denied this goal, but all were also financially dependent on opium. A classic example of this ambivalence is a 1924 speech given by Sun Yat-sen. According to Sun, no Chinese government that based itself on the will of the people could possibly be involved in the opium trade. Sun also claimed, however, that the opium problem was too complex to be fully dealt with before China was reunified (Sun, 1961, chap. 2, p. 881). In fact, when Sun was making this speech, his government was deeply involved in marketing opium in Canton and would continue to do so. This was typical of all Chinese governments. All were involved in the opium trade in some way, and all claimed to be opposed to it in principle. It is easy to read Sun's speech as a farce, since he was simultaneously selling and condemning opium. This was in fact how foreigners often viewed China's opium policy, but inside China, things were different. The usual solution to this dilemma was to sell opium under the guise of an opium monopoly theoretically aimed at the gradual elimination of opium but in practice aimed at producing revenue. As all Chinese governments were involved in the opium trade, none could be criticized for this. Good governments were those who used opium only as a temporary expedient to finance Chinese national salvation. Bad governments were those who wanted the money for selfish reasons. As Chiang Kai-shek's government put it:

Inasmuch as the income derivable from opium tax has long been the chief source of revenue from which the monthly expenses of Hupeh Provincial Government, and the Hupeh Dyke Construction and the emergency expenses of the anti-Communist campaign within the three provinces are drawn, it has been designated as proper government revenue as distinguished from illegitimate extortion for selfish purposes so characteristic of the former militarist regime. (Marshall, 1977, p. 21)

The key to this program was trust. As long as potential critics trusted the government to not become addicted to opium revenue, this dichotomy made it possible for governments to have their cake and eat it too. In practice, no Chinese government was able to convince the Chinese public and foreign observers of its pure motives with regard to opium. As a result, the governments faced the potential for truly devastating criticism. No Chinese government could possibly weather charges that it was selling opium. As a result, the governments made strenuous and usually successful efforts to control the discourse on opium, turning the focus toward those parts of the opium problem where the government could take pride in its actions.

INTERNATIONAL CRITICISM

China's international standing was of vital importance both in itself and for domestic reasons (Kirby, 1997). Throughout the Republican period, China was under the threat of imperialist domination by Japan. China's only hope for victory over Japan was foreign support and intervention, either on the national level or from bodies such as the League of Nations, thus the good opinion of foreigners was vital to China. Inside China, foreign opinion also was vital. For most Chinese, China's success or failure in creating a modern nation would ultimately be judged by foreigners, and making China look good in foreign eyes was one of the important duties of any Chinese government. Chinese opium policy therefore strove to avoid subjecting China to international humiliation. This was no easy task, as by the twentieth century it was assumed by foreigners that Chinese governments were entirely untrustworthy on the topic of opium. As American diplomat Miles Lampson put it, "I instinctively mistrust Chinese sincerity in all such matters" (Walker, 1991, p. 59).

Around the turn of the century, all governments began passing laws to put dangerous drugs under state regulation and to ban the non-medicinal use of drugs entirely. Since drugs were relatively easy to smuggle, to make this system of controls work it had to be international. A system of international drug control was set up, beginning with the Hague Treaty of 1912. At first China was enthusiastically in favor of this movement. China was one of the main destinations of the international flow of drugs and one of the largest producers, thus it had to be involved in international control efforts. This was China's first opportunity to deal with the world powers on a basis of equality, and China jumped at the chance. It was also an opportunity for China to criticize the world powers for their deep involvement in the opium trade, especially their sale of opium to Overseas Chinese in their colonies.

China soon began to find these conferences less pleasant. For the world powers, dealing with the domestic drug trade was a fairly easy matter. In their Asian colonies, it was more difficult, since the opium trade was a key financial support of all of the colonies. Still, the role of opium was gradually reduced, and after World War II, the opium monopolies were completely abolished. In China, the situation was more complex. After the death of Yuan Shikai in 1916, China entered the warlord period, and the central government in Beijing had almost no power to force local militarists to do anything, especially not to end the trade in opium, one of their most important sources of revenue. China was thus failing completely in its international obligation to end the opium trade, and international opium conferences were a series of humiliations as China tried to explain away its obvious failures.

China began to break with the treaty system beginning with the 1924 Geneva conference, which led to a treaty signed by most of the world powers, but not China, in 1925. The Geneva conference was intended to give teeth to earlier agreements by limiting the worldwide production of opium and setting up an international body to see that treaty provisions were carried out. The chief problem with controlling the opium trade was that opium was fairly easy to smuggle, and unless the international flow of narcotics was reduced, local efforts to control the trade could not succeed. Thus China's problems with controlling opium were no longer merely domestic matters, but had to be looked into by the world powers. China had no hope of being able to control opium production as the world powers wished, and thus it could not hope to live up to the requirements of the new system. China walked out of the conference but could not simply deny that it was interested in opium suppression, which would be disastrous for its reputation internationally and domestically. Instead, China went on the offensive, criticizing the Geneva plan's willingness to tolerate opium sales. Under the Geneva treaty, the European powers agreed to gradually eliminate their opium monopolies over a period of 15 years, beginning from the date that the League certified that production had been eliminated in the major producing countries, which in practice meant Persia and China (Walker, 1991, p. 37). Thus the foreigners could go on selling opium to Overseas Chinese indefinitely. The Chinese heatedly charged that this was a smokescreen for continued opium sales to colonial subjects. By this point, opium sales of any sort were hard to defend, and while the international opium control bodies were critical of China, the provisions of the treaty gave the Chinese an opening for a propaganda offensive against the international opium system.

The first part of the offensive lay in putting the foreigners on the defensive. The Chinese government emphasized the growing role of opium derivatives, especially morphine and heroin, in its drug problem and the role of foreigners in bringing these to China. China did not produce these drugs; they were distributed by foreigners using the protection of the foreign concessions (Chinese Government Opium Suppression Committee, 1930, p. 6). This attack had much merit. First, this was a trade that the Chinese government had little financial stake in and could therefore criticize freely. Second, it was true that refined drugs were a growing problem and that this problem often was connected to foreigners, an issue that put the foreigners on the defensive. Foreign governments might not condone the trade, but many foreign criminals, especially Japanese, did take advantage of their extraterritoriality. The Chinese government also called attention to the plight of the Overseas Chinese, who were being exploited by European colonial opium monopolies. The Chinese were thus trying to shift the focus of the debate and implicitly absolve themselves of guilt for failing to control opium. Indeed, the government specifically stated that unless the foreigners were willing to live up to their obligations under the 1912 Hague Treaty, China would consider it a dead letter (Chinese Government Opium Suppression Committee, 1930, p. 23). These two issues, refined drugs and the Overseas Chinese, became the center of China's opposition to the international system.

China's international propaganda campaign had a domestic side as well. The government also was trying to control domestic opinion about opium, and it would attempt to channel Chinese impressions in the same direction as foreign ones. In addition, the government needed to prove to the Chinese people that it was dealing with the foreigners successfully and not allowing China to be humiliated on the opium issue. All of these issues came together in the campaigns against the League of Nations' planned inspection of the opium situation in China.

In 1929, the League of Nations sent a Commission of Inquiry to Asia for the purpose of determining how successful various states were in living up to their treaty obligations. This presented a dilemma for China, since even a cursory inspection would prove that China's claims that its opium problem was under control were sheer sophistry. Attacking the League inspection team became one of the centerpieces of Chinese propaganda. In some respects, the inspection was a godsend for the Nanjing government. It gave a clear foreign target for anti-opium propaganda, and it exemplified the worst of international opium policy. The inspectors were to ensure that states were living up to their treaty obligations. Therefore, the inspections of the European colonies were simply to ensure that the monopolies were running efficiently, not to encourage their elimination.

Furthermore, the inspections were not charged with investigating the refined drug situation. The Chinese government could and did charge that this was nothing more that a whitewash, letting the foreigners off the hook the same way the 1925 Geneva agreement had. This international propaganda campaign had at least some success. By attacking the colonial opium monopolies, the Chinese won the favor of the Americans, the only colonial power with no opium monopoly, and the Americans continued to stand by the Chinese in their opposition to the Geneva system. The Commission of Inquiry also was unable to visit China, or even the International Settlement in Shanghai, because of Chinese opposition. This was an important victory for Nanjing, because it meant that the League would be dependent on the Chinese government for information about the opium situation in China. Other sources of information were available, but the Chinese government was moving to control these as well.

DOMESTIC CONTROL

The chief target of the campaign against the Commission of Inquiry was Chinese public opinion, not foreign diplomats. The government wanted to drive perceptions of the drug problem toward refined drugs and the role of foreigners and away from opium and the role of the Chinese government. The affair also gave the government an opportunity to stand up to foreign bullying and to counter the embarrassing charge that the Chinese were a race of opium addicts. Opposition to the inspection became a major part of the government's anti-opium work and propaganda (Dier, Record Group 2, File 1415).

A good example of this line of criticism comes from an anti-opium publication of the Zhejiang provincial Guomindang. The publication gave most of its attention to the international context of the opium problem and the problem of refined drugs. The League of Nations came in for special criticism. The publication pointed out that the League's opium policies could be seen as a great act of international brotherhood, aimed at eliminating the scourge of opium, but that they could also be seen as part of a great plot to profit from addicting the Overseas Chinese to opium (Zhongguo Guomindang Zhejiang sheng zhixing weiyuanhui xuanchuan bu, 1930, p. 33). As late as 1924, the Crown Colony of Hong Kong received 21 percent of its total revenues from opium sales, and other colonies were on a par with this. Obviously colonial governments had a vested interest in selling as much opium to their Chinese subjects as possible. Their protests that smuggled opium from China was making suppression impossible were nonsense. They were worried about opium from China because it cut into their profits (p. 47). Implicitly, the foreigners had no grounds to criticize what China was or was not doing about opium.

Perhaps the most interesting part of the Zhejiang attack on the Commission was that Zhejiang had always been critical of Nanjing's connection to the opium trade (Baumler, 1997, p. 166). Apparently that now would be pushed into the background by the foreign threat. Even more significantly, the Anti-Opium Association (described later) joined in the attacks on the inspections, although never as strongly as the government would have liked. Had the inspection team come to the International Settlement in Shanghai, it would have been met by some of the most important members of the Association, who would have expressed their opposition to the inspection and given the inspectors photos of foreigners selling drugs, presumably to prove that the drug problem was primarily created by foreigners (Zhonghua guomin judu hui, 1931, p. 184). As it happened, the inspectors did not come to Shanghai, yet the Association carried on the war against the role of foreigners in the opium trade. Garfield Huang (Huang Jiahui), the most visible of the Association's leaders, was sent on a tour of Southeast Asia to inspect opium conditions there. He reported that the colonial opium monopolies, which in theory were supposed to be controlling and gradually eliminating the opium trade, were in fact aimed entirely at producing revenue. The colonialists were perfectly aware of the dangers of opium and forbade it to their own people, but they were more than willing to profit from selling it to the Chinese (*China Weekly Review*, 1930). These critiques could just as well have come from the government, but it is significant that they came from what had been two of the most strident critics of Nanjing's opium policies. The campaign against the Commission of Inquiry was a key turning point in bringing these formerly critical groups under governmental control.

Nanjing needed to control organizations such as the Anti-Opium Association in part because it was capable of upsetting China's international position. Chiang Kai-shek could see to it that the foreigners received no dangerous information about China's opium trade from official sources.

[There] may be cases when our actual work in suppression does not come up to the standards originally provided by the Suppression Program, which will quite likely arouse misunderstanding from foreign nations. In order to avoid misunderstanding all material on statistics in relation to opium and drug suppression should be scrutinized by the Military Affairs Commission before they are published. (Walker, 1991, p. 101)

He could not, however, prevent foreigners from getting information from other sources, and thus these sources needed to be controlled. Thus there were international benefits to domestic control. Domestic control was also important in and of itself, and in many respects, these domestic benefits were far more valuable. The two most dangerous organizations that Nanjing had to control were the Anti-Opium Association (*Judu hui*), and the Anti-Opium Commission (*Jinyan weiyuanhui*).

Chiang Kai-shek's government was never very powerful and was constantly trying to subdue an array of challenges to its power. The most potentially dangerous critics were the residual warlords, who had theoretically accepted the authority of the central government but in fact remained independent and quite powerful. Since most of these were as deeply involved in the opium trade as the Nanjing government, they were unable to openly criticize Nanjing's policies. However, the warlords were able to take advantage of criticism by others, the most important critic being the Chinese Anti-Opium Association (*Zonghua guomin judu hui* [AOA]). The AOA was largely an organization of Shanghai Christians and, despite heroic efforts, it was never able to spread much beyond this base. It was quite effective for awhile, despite lacking a mass or national following. The Association was an official communicating body of the League of Nations and thus was immune to many of the tactics that the government sometimes used against domestic critics. It was based in Shanghai, the center of the modern media in China, and its members were well-connected, respected individuals. Besides receiving dues, it also received funds from overseas, giving it financial independence. Most important, the issue of opium itself gave the Association protection. The government could not be seen as attacking a group that opposed opium. In 1927 and 1928, the Association led a campaign against the Nanjing government's planned national opium monopoly. The key to the

Association's success was its ability to mobilize popular opinion. It collected statistics and information about the opium problem throughout China and published them in its own periodicals. It conducted lecture campaigns and radio broadcasts, sponsored anti-opium plays and movies, and held a nationwide anti-opium day once a year. All of these things made the Association the natural center of anti-opium activity and made its interpretation of the opium problem an authoritative one.

The Association's untouchable position and good connections made it a natural rallying point for the many critics of Chiang Kai-shek's regime, and the opium issue was a fine medium to use to attack the government. In 1927–1928, the Association led the campaign to force the government to abandon its plans for an open national opium monopoly (Baumler, 1995). The government was forced to abandon its plans, but it began to take immediate and effective steps to muzzle the AOA.

The Association had been able to discomfort the government, in part because in 1928 the Nanjing government was still newly established and had many rivals. By 1929, most of these had been subdued, and the Association was more isolated. More important, the government began to systematically subvert the Association's position. In March 1928, the central government sent representatives to meet with the officers of the Association to work out an agreement for cooperation between the two. The government agreed to pass laws requesting the gradual elimination of the opium trade and to call a national anti-opium conference to meet in November. The government also agreed to set up an Anti-Opium Commission (*Jinyan weiyuanhui*), which would report to the Ministry of the Interior rather than the Ministry of Finance, as earlier opium control offices had. The head of the new commission was to be Zhang Zhijiang, a Christian with a strong record on opium and some ties to the AOA.

The Association was happy with these actions at first, but as time went by, it became apparent that it had been hoodwinked. The National Anti-Opium Conference was held in 1928, but it had no power to do anything but recommend actions to the government, which ignored them. Regular national conferences were supposed to be called in the future, but they never were. The new Anti-Opium Commission was created, but it also did little. The Association managed to preserve its independence, but it did transfer its Inspectorate, responsible for compiling statistics on opium use around the country, to the Commission, and the Inspectorate's members were put on the government payroll. The Association had lost one of its key powers, control over China's opium statistics. It had put its faith in the government's goodwill, and it was giving up important powers and getting little in return.

The government also began to compete with the Association for control of public opinion. The Association was encouraged to shift its annual Anti-Opium Day to the same day as the government's, and the government also began to compete with the Association in propagandizing the people. The Association had created Anti-Opium Day (*Jinyan jie*) in the 1920s, and it became one of the keys to its successful propaganda campaign. Although the mass of the Chinese people could not maintain a fervor against opium all year, they could certainly do so for one day, and by 1927, Anti-Opium Day was a major affair, with mass meetings, posters, plays, and speech contests in schools all over China. Newspapers could be counted on to publish a good deal on the opium problem, and politicians would be chastised for their failings throughout the year. This public attention made it easier to found new branches of the Association and probably brought in donations as well. Anti-Opium Day was central to the Association's control of the discourse on opium, and the government gradually took this over as well (Baumler, 1995).

Part of the attempt to change the discourse on opium was connected to the international control system, shifting attention to refined drugs and to the foreigners and foreign concessions. Much of it also was purely domestic but used basically the same tactics, not denying the opium problem entirely but focusing on those parts that put the government in the best light. The Nanjing government's direct involvement in the opium trade centered on the Hankou Special Tax Office. Hankou was a key Yangzi river port, and from here the government could control both market access for upstream opium suppliers and access to opium for downstream opium distributors (Baumler, 1997, p. 212). Not surprisingly, government anti-opium propaganda did not mention the Hankou office and instead focused on the two other ends of the trade—the West China warlords who produced the opium and the people who smoked it. The warlords were an obvious target, since they were enemies of the regime who supported themselves by selling opium. The smokers are more interesting, as a 1935 speech by Du Yuesheng shows. The speech emphasizes the importance of registering and curing opium users as the key to opium suppression (Shanghai shi jinyan weiyuan hui, 1935, p. 3). In theory, this had always been a part of the government's opium suppression policies, but it was rarely carried out. What made this so appealing was that registration and cure were primarily the responsibilities of local governments, and if they were not being carried out, Nanjing could hardly be blamed. In any case, as long as there was demand for opium, there would be supply, and until opium smoking was eliminated, it probably was best that this opium be provided by the government. This was not a point Du made directly in his speech, but since he was a member of the Shanghai Anti-Opium Committee and was also widely known as China's biggest opium merchant, it is not a hard subtext to bring out.

By the early 1930s, therefore, the government had made enormous strides in taking over the discourse on opium. It had shifted its focus to problems such as refined drugs and the West China warlords that could not damage Nanjing's legitimacy. It also had rehabilitated Du Yuesheng. Du probably got himself appointed to the Anti-Opium Committee because it tickled his sense of humor, but the fact that the government was willing to appoint him shows how confident it had become in its position. No Chinese government was ever entirely innocent on the topic of opium, so the question became one of intentions; the government might be dealing in opium, but as long as it was for a good cause and the ultimate goal was elimination of the trade then it was acceptable. By shifting the debate to topics such as heroin and the international treaties, which the government sincerely opposed, it was able to build up its credibility on opium, allowing it to associate with the likes of Du Yuesheng. However, this credibility was not enough. Nanjing had to move further to control the actual organizations that threatened it, the Anti-Opium Association and the Anti-Opium Commission.

THE DECLINE OF THE ANTI-OPIUM ASSOCIATION

The Association had experienced considerable success in forcing Nanjing to change its policy, but as early as the Jiangan case, it had begun to lose faith in the government's goodwill. In the 1929–1935 period, the Association would continue to push for a stricter opium policy, usually with no success. It also would try to encourage the type of mass enthusiasm that it had used so effectively in the 1927–1928 period, thus going over the head of the government. This would prove to have no effect, and the Association was faced with a choice between open and hopeless dissent and grudging acceptance of the government, and by choosing the latter, it accepted the lapdog role that Nanjing found useful.

The last national campaign of the Anti-Opium Association was the national anti-opium campaign of 1929. The Association organized anti-opium activities in most of the major cities of China in succession during the spring and summer of 1929. Part of the goal was to fulfill the Association's duties under the 1928 agreement (i.e., to spread the message of opium suppression to the people and encourage them to follow the government's lead). Another motive may have been to create a nationwide climate of opinion such as that in Shanghai, which had enabled the Association to affect government policy, hopefully dragging Nanjing back to a more activist policy. The campaign had limited success on the first objective and none at all on the second.

The campaign was intended to spread around the country the enthusiasm that the Association had created in Shanghai in 1927 and 1928. This would be done by organizing multiday anti-opium shows along the lines of the anti-opium week in Shanghai. If local anti-opium groups lacked the initiative to organize an anti-opium week, the Association would do so for them and create or revitalize local branches. The Association claimed 400 local branches, but since that the Hangzhou branch was formed only when the Association's exhibition arrived in May 1929, this seems to be an exaggeration (*China Weekly Review*, 1929a, 1929b). The initiative and most of the planning for the shows came from the Shanghai office of the Anti-Opium Association. It set the dates for the shows and sent out the advance men to organize them. Posters would be put up a few days before the group arrived, and local newspapers would be asked to publicize the shows. The program would last five to 10 days and would feature educational displays, dramatic performances, speech and essay contests for the students, opium burnings, and finally, a mass rally, where the assembled populace would be addressed by Association leaders from Shanghai and various local dignitaries. The Association visited larger cities throughout the Yangzi delta and in the Southeast and Northeast.

The tour's rhetoric was predominantly educational. There was some criticism of morphine smuggling out of the Kuangtung Leased Territory during the campaigns in Manchuria, but there was little other criticism of government policy. In his announcement of the campaign, Garfield Huang stressed the importance of the displays of photographs and pictures assembled at the Association's Shanghai office in bringing the message of opium suppression to the common people in an easily understood visual form. Simple messages aimed at common people were the whole rationale behind the existence of the Association under the 1928 plan. The Association was supposed to be educating the common people to obey, not rousing the educated to dissent. The Shanghai office and Garfield Huang had already been quite critical of the Nanjing government and its opium policies, but in 1929, the Association was still carrying out the role that it had agreed to in 1928—educating the people.

The Association also attempted to use the campaign to extend its permanent organization into the provinces. It would send representatives to the targeted cities well in advance and have them recruit local public organizations, sometimes 30 or 40 of them, to organize a committee to make preparations for the local campaign. These organizations would then form the membership of a local branch of the Anti-Opium Association. In compiling its annual reports on the opium problem, the Association relied on data from local branches and correspondents (often missionaries). In 1929, many new branches were either formed or reactivated, the most important being the Zhejiang branch, organized in Hangzhou in December 1929 (*Zhejiang sheng juduhui zongbaogao*, 1935, p. 1). The goal was to give the organization real national reach, but beyond Zhejiang, the provincial and local branches vanished almost as quickly as they appeared.

The new campaign also had very limited results in reducing the opium trade. Propaganda had been able to whip up enough support among the literate classes in Shanghai to force changes in the government, but in the provincial cities, the level of public awareness and activism was far lower. The Association managed to turn out good crowds but never to influence provincial policy or create self-sustaining local movements. It does not seem to have even made an attempt to influence rural people. It did not influence provincial or local policy, and the effects of the campaign on the opium smokers themselves were minimal. In most cases, these effects faded almost immediately. In May 1930, the British consul in Harbin reported that the sole remaining effect of the previous summer's campaign in Mukden was that the city's opium dealers were a bit less open in posting prices on the streets (*The opium trade*, 1974, chap. 27, p. 37).

Without government support, the Association simply could not maintain a national anti-opium movement, so it began to specialize. Although it may not have been a conscious decision, the Association began to specialize in foreign issues, including the Overseas Chinese, publishing, collecting statistics, and occasionally complaining about opium problems in specific parts of China, usually Anhui and Fujian, the two opium-producing provinces closest to Shanghai. All of these things were, of course, quite acceptable to the government.

The foreign focus was natural for an organization of Shanghai Christians, and although there would continue to be branches outside of Shanghai, the Association slipped back into its position of being predominantly a Shanghai organization (Zhonghua guomin judu hui, 1931, p. 177). The Association represented China at various international meetings (usually Christian rather than government) and tried to maintain good relations with the League of Nations. When the Far Eastern Inspection came to Shanghai over the protests of the Nanjing government, the leaders of the Association expressed their private misgivings, but the Association did not oppose the visit (Zhonghua guomin judu hui, 1931, p. 184). It also kept in touch with Christian and anti-opium organizations in Japan and other countries.

The Association took an interest in and received support from Overseas Chinese organizations. As early as 1926, it was obtaining money from a wealthy Chinese New Yorker to make anti-opium movies (Zhonghua guomin judu hui, 1931, p. 156). This relationship continued until 1928 (p. 170). The Association kept in contact with anti-opium organizations in the Philippines, Vietnam, and the Dutch East Indies. It sent representatives to various places to report on the opium situation, received Overseas Chinese opium activists, and in 1930 sent an anti-opium tour overseas (p. 191).

These activities gave the Association international connections and stature, protected it from any government attempts to break it up, and also probably provided some money, however, it could not revive the anti-opium movement inside China. To do that, the Association focused on publishing and information gathering. It published monthly magazines in both Chinese and English, a biweekly opium update, plays, reports, and posters. All of these things would have been useful in conjunction with a government campaign against opium, but they were of little use without it. The Association also compiled national statistics. These statistics were based on provincial and local figures, but since most provinces were either passive about suppression or were actually involved in the trade, their statistics were worthless. The journals and publications kept the issue in the public eye, both in China and abroad, but beyond this they could do nothing.

The Association made some feeble attempts to revive its national reach. The anti-opium exhibition was intended to stir up popular enthusiasm, but without some way of making use of this enthusiasm, it accomplished nothing. The Association tried on several occasions to revive its local branches so that they might lead the local campaigns, but with little success. Many of the Association's local branches had been converted into official anti-opium organizations, after which time they became useless (Zhonghua guomin judu hui, 1931, p. 189). Many others simply stopped functioning. Only in the Zhejiang province, where the government remained actively involved in opium suppression, was the Association able to keep functioning. The Association also made an effort to collect its own information, sending out inspectors to collect information and trying to get district magistrates to send opium suppression data directly to it, but it was unable to do much in this regard either. The Association was increasingly unhappy with the government's opium suppression policy, but there was very little it could do other than complain, unless it was willing to break with the government entirely. In September 1929, the Association's Chinese language magazine published an attack of the government's opium policy. It pointed out that opium was being grown and smoked all over China, that officials were either ignoring or participating in the trade, and that none of the resolutions of the national conference had been carried out (*The opium trade*, 1974, chap. 27, p. 13). Despite this, the Association did not break with the government or accuse it of more than negligence. The Association had been pushed into a powerless situation from which it was unable to escape. There were no important political rivals to Chiang Kai-shek to whom the Association could turn, there was no way to bring public pressure to bear on the government, and there was no mass movement that it could organize to bring pressure.

The toothlessness of the Anti-Opium Association was revealed in 1933, when Huang Jiamin, a Shanghai lawyer, tried to form a *zhonghua minzong midu she* (Chinese People's Anti-Drug Society). Huang and his respectable, middle-class associates wanted to help the government in stopping the foreigners and warlords from flooding Shanghai and China as a whole with opium and drugs. Huang and his associates planned to do this primarily through public education. They also would collect statistics and report to the government violations of the drug laws. Huang applied to have his organization registered in October 1933, and he spent the next year being investigated and harassed. Chiang Kai-shek himself took considerable interest in the case. Huang was told that the appropriate organization for anti-opium activities was the Anti-Opium Association, and that if he wanted to do something about opium, he and his friends should join the Association. Huang replied that the Association's dues were too high, and that, in any case, there was no reason that there could not be two anti-opium organizations, just as there were countless anti-famine groups. Despite this, Huang's petitions were repeatedly rejected. His organization was never officially registered and seems to have folded some time in 1934 (Dier, Record Group 33, File 96).

Huang's description of what his organization intended to do is almost a carbon copy of the activities of the Anti-Opium Association, which explains the government's hostility to it. The "anti-government" role that the Association had flirted with in 1927–1928 was still open to others, and Nanjing would pay very close attention to any attempt to create a new anti-opium organization. The original Association had little power, but its position was comfortable enough that its leaders were unwilling to openly challenge the government. It served as the equivalent of a yellow union. Even the attempted monopoly of 1931 was not enough to force the Association into open opposition. It was thus quite useful to the government and continued to exist. The Association gradually faded away, and by 1937, having lost most of its support and financing, it wound up its affairs (*China Weekly Review*, 1937).

THE FAILURE OF THE ANTI-OPIUM COMMISSION

As the Anti-Opium Association was slowly disintegrating, its official homologue, the Anti-Opium Commission, was doing nothing. The delegates at the National Anti-Opium Convention had envisioned the Commission as the central organ for opium suppression in the government. This would provide coherence (rather than having bits of opium policy run by different branches of government), and most important for the reformers, it was not under the Ministry of Finance but the Interior Ministry. What exactly the Commission was supposed to do was not made clear in 1928, and Nanjing never gave it any real power. The Commission served as a clearinghouse for opium cases, compiled statistics and reports, and made suggestions to the Executive Yuan. After 1935, a new anti-opium commission with many of the same powers would serve as the center of an active anti-opium movement, but the 1929–1935 version had almost no impact, since it only had the power to make recommendations to other branches of government, most of whom then ignored them.

Particularly in its first few years, the Commission received many complaints about opium and drug trafficking from both the Anti-Opium Association and private citizens. Although the opium trade was only semiclandestine at this point, people were still arrested for dealing in opium and drugs, either because they did not have proper arrangements with the police or because they had been betrayed. Some of these cases received considerable publicity, and many were referred to the Commission for action. However, by about 1931, the number of these appeals had dropped drastically as it became clear that the Commission was not going to do anything about them.

The Commission's first weakness was its lack of information. It had no way of determining the facts in any case. In some cases, it relied on the newspapers for accounts of important drug cases, but usually it would pass a case on to the appropriate provincial or local government for investigation and action (Dier, Record Group 2, File 1431). Since it often was just this government that was being accused of wrongdoing, this was not going to accomplish much. It was, however, the only way the Commission could gather information. Since the Commission had no executive power, it had to pass on any requests for action to local governments in any case.

Given its inability to find out what was going on and its lack of power to do anything about it, the Commission had no hope of carrying out its mission, and most of its members became aware of this. As early as 1929, the Anti-Opium Association accused the Commission of failing to carry out its duties and of turning China back into the international laughingstock that it had been before the 1928 Anti-Opium Conference (Dier, Record Group 2, File 1424). At the end of 1930, many of the remaining opium activists were purged or left the Commission voluntarily. In December of that year, Zhang Zhijiang was removed as head of the Commission. He had always been excessively enthusiastic, and the star of his patron, Feng Yuxiang, was fading. He was replaced by Liu Ruiheng. Liu was Minister of Health until that ministry was abolished in 1931. It was replaced by the National Health Administration (*wei sheng shu*), also headed by Liu. This gave him the public health credentials that he needed for the job. He also had been a classmate of T.V. Soong's at Harvard (Yip, 1995, p. 47). Soong was Minister of Finance, Chiang Kai-shek's brother-in-law, and a leading proponent of drawing revenue from opium. Early in 1931, Li Jihong, later head of the Hankou Special Tax Office, was added to the Commission. Some important national politicians, Chiang Kai-shek, Feng Yuxiang, and Li Zongren, had been members of the Commission at first, but most had left by 1929. The Commission was losing all of its committed, powerful members and was replacing them with nonentities and monopolists. This probably was part of the abortive run-up to the monopoly plan of 1931, but with these people in charge, it was even less likely that the Commission would even carry out its ordinary duties.

In 1932, Liu complained that the job of the Commission was impossible. Much of the poppy land was in areas outside of government control, but even in areas under Nanjing's authority, the Commission had no power. All provinces were to have stopped collecting opium taxes by this point, but in Hebei, Suiyuan, Shaanxi, Henan, Anhui, and Fujian the opium tax had simply been renamed. In Shanxi, Gansu, Yunnan, Guizhou, Sichuan, and Rehe—all provinces that had traditionally relied on opium taxes—suppression had not even been announced (Dier, Record Group 2, File 1435).

In November 1933, Liu received a joint complaint from the Henan party branch and a local doctor active in opium work about the level of opium activity in China. Liu agreed that the situation was bad. The Western provinces were still growing poppy, and Hunan, Hubei, and Henan were still openly collecting opium taxes. Unfortunately, Liu's role was only advisory, and his advice usually fell on deaf ears. He compared opium to the *likin* tax, which the government had abolished despite the revenue it brought in because of its harm to the nation. Opium was thousands of times worse than *likin*, but the government could not see what was right in front of its face. Liu suggested that this exchange might be made public, putting the failure of the Commission in the public eye, but it apparently never was (Dier, Record Group 2, File 1428).

CONCLUSION

The attempts of the nationalist government to control the discourse on opium between 1927 and 1935 would have to be called a success. The basic goal of the campaign was to carry out a policy of profiting from the opium trade as a "temporary" expedient. This was a policy that had to be positioned properly both internationally and domestically. This was done in part by controlling the discourse on opium and in part by controlling the institutions that dealt with opium. Internationally, Nanjing attempted to turn the focus of international drug policy toward refined drugs and the colonial opium monopolies. This was not a complete success, but China was at least able to blunt some criticism of its activities. More important, by keeping the League's representatives out of China and by taking control of the organizations that gave it access to information about opium in China, the government was able to reduce the League to relative powerlessness. The two most important of these organizations, the Anti-Opium Association and the Anti-Opium Commission, were also tremendously important domestically. By nullifying them, Nanjing was able to avoid potentially disastrous criticism of its actions. Nanjing also shifted the domestic discourse on opium toward more congenial topics such as the refined drug trade and the western warlords. None of these efforts was ever more than partially successful. One critic of the nationalist regime claimed that its opium policies led to ''the degeneration of the virtue of the party-state'' (Wakeman, 1995, p. 259). Whatever long-term loss of public confidence and increased cynicism that Nanjing's polices may have caused, in the short run its handling of the discourse on opium allowed it to flout one of the key principles of Chinese nationalism with remarkably little fuss.

REFERENCES

Baumler, A. (1995, November). Playing with fire: The nationalist government and popular anti-opium agitation in 1927–1928. *Republican China, 21*(1): 43–91.

Baumler, A. (1997). Playing with fire: The nationalist government and opium in China 1927–1941. Unpublished doctoral dissertation, University of Illinois, Urbana–Champaign, pp. 212–213.

China Weekly Review. (1929a, March 9), p. 68.

China Weekly Review. (1929b, May 4), p. 415.

China Weekly Review. (1930, August 30), p. 485.

China Weekly Review. (1937, August 14), p. 372.

China Yearbook (1929–1930), Shanghai, China.

Chinese Government Opium Suppression Committee. (1930). *Traffic in Opium and Other Dangerous Drugs: Annual Report 1929*. Nanjing, China.

Dier lishi dangan guan [Number Two Historical Archives]. Nanjing, China.

Kirby, W. C. (1997, June). The internationalization of China: Foreign relations at home and abroad in the republican era. *China Quarterly*, 150: 433–458.

Marshall, J. (1977, July–September). Opium and the politics of gangsterism in nationalist China, 1927–1945. *Bulletin of the Committee of Concerned Asian Scholars, 8*(3): 19–48.

The opium trade. (1974). (Vols. 1–5). Wilmington, DE: Scholarly Resources.

Shanghai shi jinyan weiyuan hui. (1935). *Jinyan zhuan kan* [Anti-opium special issue]. Shanghai, China.

Sun, W. (1961). *Guofu quanji* [The collected works of Sun Wen, father of the nation]. (Vols. 1–6). Taipei, Taiwan: Kuomindang Central Executive Committee.

Wakeman, F. (1995). *Policing Shanghai 1927–1937*. Berkeley, CA: University of California Press.

Walker, W. O. (1991). *Opium and foreign policy: The Anglo-American search for order in Asia*. Chapel Hill, NC: University of North Carolina Press.

Yip, K. C. (1995). *Health and national reconstruction in nationalist China: The development of modern health services, 1928–1937*. Ann Arbor, MI: Association for Asian Studies.

Zhejiang sheng juduhui zongbaogao [Comprehensive report of the Zhejiang province anti-opium association]. (1935).

Zhongguo Guomindang Zhejiang sheng zhixing weiyuanhui xuanchuan bu. (1930). *Judu yundong congkan* [The anti-opium movement].

Zhonghua guomin judu hui. (1931). *Judu yundong zhinan* [Guide to the anti-opium movement].

Zhou, Y. (1997). *Nationalism, history and state building: Anti-drug crusades in China, 1924–1997*. Unpublished doctoral dissertation, Duke University.

Chapter 7

Pluralism and Prior Restraint on Religious Communication in Nigeria: Policy versus Praxis

Bala Musa

INTRODUCTION

Religion occupies a significant, sensitive place in the sociocultural and political life of Nigeria. Chesterton said that early American society was "a nation with the soul of a church" (Mead, 1985, p. 48). Similarly, Nigeria is a country with the heart of religion, the only difference being that Nigeria's heart pulsates with the irregular rhythm of a multiple belief system. Religion underlies the African worldview. Moemeka (1983) stated that, in Africa, religion is a way of life. Mbiti (1990) opined that "Africans are notoriously religious, and each people has its own religious system with a set of beliefs and practices." According to Mbiti, "Religion permeates into all the departments of life so fully that it is not easy to isolate" (p. 1). He believes that, "African peoples do not know how to exist without religion" (p. 2). His investigation showed that each of the over 3,000-person groups in traditional African society has a religious system of beliefs, ceremonies, rituals, and priests. Sanneh (1996) argues that the rapid spread of Christianity, Islam, and other foreign religions in West Africa should be seen as a function of the people's strong religious quest rather than as a result of spiritual or religious imperialism.

As in all other African countries, Traditional African Religion was the prevalent form of worship in Nigeria prior to the introduction of Islam and Christianity. Islam was introduced into northern Nigeria in the mid-1300s by Muslim missionaries from Mali. However, the first major wave of Islamic evangelization in the mid to late fifteenth century was the massive migration of Arabic traders from North Africa, the Fulani from Mali, and "itinerant Muslim scholars from the University of Timbuktu" (Ifemesia, 1972, p. 94) to Kano during the reign of Ya'qub (1453–1463). By the end of the sixteenth century, Islam had become the state religion of the Hausa, Kanuri, and Fulani ethnic groups due to the conversion of their rulers. However, the second and most significant expansionist cum evangelistic effort that gave Islam its major boost was the nineteenth century Islamic *jihads* (religious wars), led by Usman Danfodio (Hunwick, 1972).

Christianity first came to the region presently called Nigeria through Portuguese businessmen in the early 1400s (Ryder, 1972). For about a century, most Christian evangelistic activity was limited to the islands and surrounding coastal areas. Though commerce was the primary motive of the earliest explorers, "Proselytizing zeal was never wholly absent from the policies" of the Portuguese in this area (p. 225). There were a few sporadic conversions at this period. Concerted and systematic evangelization came after the end of the slave trade through the efforts of missionary organizations such as the Church Missionary Society (CMS), the Sudan Interior Mission (SIM), and Baptist, Methodist, and Catholic missions.

The patterns and routes of entry of Christianity and Islam into the region created separate geoethnic regions within which each religion has dominance. Islam came from the Middle East, through North Africa, and across the Sahara Desert to the northern part of Nigeria. Thus northern Nigeria has been the stronghold of Islam in the country. Although Christianity also originated in Palestine, the vehicle and route of its arrival in sub-Saharan Africa were Europeans and North Americans. The result has been that while the North is predominantly Muslim, the South, particularly the Southeast, is essentially Christian. The Southwest and the Middle Belt have been the contested grounds for both religious groups. With religious boundaries coinciding with ethnic and political boundaries, it is almost impossible to separate religion from politics in the country (Kukah, 1993; Musa, 1995a, 1996; Usman, 1987).

THE STATE AND RELIGION: A WORLDVIEW—LIFEVIEW DILEMMA

The Constitution of the Federal Republic of Nigeria states the resolve of the people "To LIVE in unity and harmony as one indivisible and indissoluble Sovereign Nation under God," while also stating categorically in § 10 that, "The Government of the Federation or of a State shall not adopt any religion as State religion."

The apparent contradiction of these provisions, that of the nation being under God yet secular, is more than rhetorical. It underscores the inherent dialectics between the worldview and lifeview of the people in the area of religion. It reflects the dilemma that religion poses to policy makers, as well as the conflicting expectations of citizens regarding its place in public and private life. It poses the question: What is the appropriate balance between objectivity at the national level and passionate devotion at the communal and individual level? The former calls for tolerance and cooperation, while the latter favors hegemony and proselytizing, sometimes forcefully, as an act of devotion. This conflict has consistently plagued the process of nation-building as the founders and builders of the Nigerian state struggle to find a proper framework for the interplay between the atheistic, polytheistic, and monotheistic systems that coexist in the society. This quest for a workable formula for civil society has sent the architects of the nation back to the drawing board 10 times since the unification of the country in 1914.

The 1979 Constitution cited above is the eighth constitution adopted by and experimented on by the country. Under British colonial rule, the Constitution was drawn and redrawn five times in less than a half-century. Named after the Colonial Governors, these moribund constitutions included the Lugard Constitution (1914), the Clifford Constitution (1922), the Richards Constitution (1946), the McPherson Constitution (1951), and the Lyttelton Constitution (1954).

Since independence, the country has created and jettisoned the Independence Constitution (1960), the First Republic Constitution (1963), the Second Republic Constitution (1979), and the Fourth Republic Constitution (1989) (Kirk-Greene, 1997). Following the former military ruler's sudden death in 1998, the constitution he signed into law in 1995 was put forth for revision. Different groups are again agitating for changes that would suit their interests.

These constitutions define not only the political structure but also the social, religious, economic, and other spheres of national life. Debates over the appropriate status of religion in the Nigerian constitution and the nation are often the most animated sessions on the floors of the constitution drafting bodies. In April 1978, Proceedings of the Constituent Assembly ground to a halt when 93 Muslims, led by Shehu Shagari, who later became the president, walked out of the meeting in protest against the House's rejection of their proposal for a Federal Sharia Court of Appeal (Ibrahim, 1997). Gilliland (1986) asserts that, "One of the most critical and polarizing debates was a religious one that nearly brought down the Assembly. No issue that came before the Assembly raised the deep feelings of the two worlds, Islamic and Christian, like this proposition" (p. 187). This scene was repeated in the drafting of the Third Republic Constitution in 1989.

The wording of the 1979 Constitution is loaded with fundamental assumptions concerning the cohesion and stability of the state. These include the sovereignty, unity, and oneness of the nation as well as a belief in God. Experience has proven that such claims are both simplistic and costly to the process of nation-building. While sovereignty, unity, oneness, and nationhood are the ideals to which the country aspires, they do not reflect the existing reality. In reality, Nigeria is a pluralistic state comprising many people and sociocultural groups having numerous, and sometimes conflicting, allegiances that tend to detract from these national objectives. Failure to posit national cohesion as an ongoing process rather than an existing resource amounts to attempting to advance into the tertiary stages of statecraft without the necessary foundation. "In each case, after the constitutional mechanics have declared [Nigeria] fit for the road, [Nigeria has] discovered that no sooner has [it] set out on [its] journeys than the political engines begin to malfunction'' (Kukah, 1996, p. 7). Often the religious chamber is one of the earliest to exude fumes and signal for attention. The thesis here is that the problem lies in the improper alignment between the ideal of national unity and the reality of sociocultural pluralism, including religious pluralism. The unity, oneness, and sovereignty of the nation have continually been tested by the incidences that threaten to erode them. The civil war, Nigeria's membership in the Organization of Islamic Countries (OIC), and the reactions to the annulment of the 1993 presidential election are just some of these cases. The manipulation of religion (Islam by Libya, Iran, and Saudi Arabia and Christianity by Britain, Rome, and the United States) to expand political influences in Nigeria, also have served to undermine the country's sovereignty (Haynes, 1996).

Why are the relations among the numerous religious traditions in Nigeria volatile? The answer may be found in the doctrines and philosophies of the various religious groups vis-à-vis the state, pluralism, and religious freedom, which includes the freedom to hold, change, and propagate one's beliefs. A brief analysis of the status of religion in the state as reflected in Traditional African, Christian, and Islamic religions will provide an understanding of the varying expectations of the diverse groups as well as the issues that arise from them.[1]

TRADITIONAL AFRICAN RELIGION

The relationship between state and religion in Traditional African Religion is very nebulous. It varies from one culture and context to another. In their premodern forms, some societies were theocratic while others were monarchical. Even among theocratic groups such as the Kutebs of Taraba State, where the *Kukwen* (communal priests) wielded more influence than the *Ukwe* (chief), religion was not totalitarian (Gilliland, 1986). This is because Traditional African Religion is neither evangelistic nor exclusionist. It does not discourage other belief systems from flourishing within its domain. As mentioned earlier, each clan has its own religious system. None tries to convert people from other groups. In fact, the relationship between religion and the soul of each community is such that adherents of each local religious practice go to great lengths to keep others outside their fold. They see their progress, security, and welfare so linked to religious observance that to expose the religion to outsiders poses a security threat to the community. In other words, most African religions are occultic and secretive. Membership is usually based on kinship, which is in keeping with the collectivist and communal life of the people.

Religion in the African tradition is secretive but not private. People do not choose which form of religious practice to subscribe. For instance, passage rites such as birth, adolescence, marriage, and death have religious undertones and are not optional for members of a particular clan (Mbiti, 1990). Also, African religions are not exclusive, in that membership in a particular religious cult does not prevent one from belonging to several others. This means that conversion attempts in Traditional African Religion are not geared toward calling one out or separating one from a particular group and aligning with another. In other words, they have maximum religious tolerance (Miranda, 1994), which accounts for the preponderance of religious syncretism in the country. The implication of this worldview is that while there is minimal dichotomy between the sacred and the secular in Traditional African Religion, its relationship with the state is neither hegemonic nor totalitarian. Contrary to Mead's (1985) view that the origins of religious pluralism can best be traced to the Christian tradition of tolerance and rational conversion, history shows that Traditional African Religion was highly pluralistic.

CHRISTIANITY

Although both Christianity and Islam are haunted by the history of the crusades and *jihads* in Europe, the Middle East, and North and West Africa, many scholars are quick to showcase Christianity as the model of religious tolerance and pluralism in the modern world (Mead, 1985). Some argue that this tolerance is not only recent but that it reflects a Western tradition of modernity and secularism (Siddiqui, 1997). Earliest Christian missionary activity in Nigeria was associated with colonial expansion, but coercion was not used as a tool for conversion (Gilliland, 1990). This gives Christianity the image of a world religion that is nontotalitarian. Nigerian Christians have essentially adopted the Western concept of separation of state and religion. They often advocate a secular state, which to them means official neutrality in the sphere of religion and the absence of any state religion.

This posture, which Ilesanmi (1997) notes is rapidly changing, is also embedded in the transcendence theology of the early missionaries. Until recently, most devout Christians made strict distinctions between sacred and spiritual activities on the one hand and secular and mundane affairs on the other hand. This made them shy away from worldly things. Religion had no place in state matters, and a good Christian could not conceive of becoming a politician. More Christians are now embracing dominion theology and are beginning to engage popular culture. Still, the community favors religious neutrality, as articulated in the philosophy of a secular state. The Catholic Bishops of Nigeria, in their submission to the Constitutional Review Committee in 1986, described a secular state as one where "there is no official religion, but in which religion as such may nevertheless be treated with respect; and religious bodies and their activities are seen as purely social agents within the communities" (Catholic Bishops of Nigeria, 1986, p. 9). To them, that was "the only viable 'modus vivendi' " for the survival of the country (p. 9). Some regard that stance as a defense against Muslims using their control of federal power to impose a national religion.

ISLAM

While Christians have been advocating that Nigeria remain a secular state, Muslims agitate that the Constitution declare the country a religious state (Mbadinuju, 1987; Ngokwe, 1984). Muslims argue that in Islam there is no distinction between the secular and the religious. " 'Secularism' is a concept completely foreign and opposed to the Islamic theory of the state. In fact the State exists for the main purpose of protecting and furthering the religion" (Coulson, 1957, p. 49). This gives the impression that the Islamic vision of the state is unitarian rather than pluralistic. That is partly the source of anxiety among non-Muslims in Nigeria concerning the call for a religious state, which is compounded by the totalitarian practices of Islamic states such as Iran, Saudi Arabia, Sudan, and Pakistan.

The Islamic Conference, in its 1972 Charter, expressly endorsed the International Bill of Human Rights and the Universal Declaration of Human Rights as "the basis for fruitful co-operation amongst all people" (Mayer, 1991, p. 14). Many Muslim scholars opine that the contemporary classic view among Muslim nations, that a Muslim state must be totalitarian, is more political than religious (Al-Nabhan, 1974; Siddiqui, 1997). Making a case for religious freedom in the Islamic state, Abu (n.d.) says:

Freedom of religion in its Islamic context implies that non-Muslims are not compelled to convert to Islam, nor are they hindered from practicing their own religious rites. Both Muslims and non-Muslims are entitled to propagate the religion of their following as well as to defend it against attack or seditious provocation (*fitnah*), regardless of whether such action is launched by their co-religionists or by others. (p. 190)

Similarly, Uthman (1401/1908) observes:

No power of any kind in the Islamic state may be employed to compel people to embrace Islam. The basic function of the Islamic state, in this regard, is to monitor and prevent the forces which might seek to deny the people their freedom of belief. (p. 91)

The Qur'an only forbids evil speech, not differences of opinion: "God loves not public utterance of evil speech except by one who has been wronged (IV: 148).

According to Kamali (1997), the Qur'an supports freedom of opinion (*Hurriyyat alra'y)* and freedom of expression (*Hurriyyat al-bayan*) (p. 5). He adds that "the *Shari'ah* encourages freedom of expression in a variety of ways including the promotion of good and prevention of evil (*hisbah*), sincere advice (*nasihah*), consultation (*shura*), personal reasoning (*ijtihad*), and the freedom to criticize government leaders."

According to Mayer (1991), Islamic nations such as Algeria, Egypt, Iran, and

Iraq were even more eager to ratify the International Bill of Rights than were non-Muslim nations like the Vatican, China, Angola, and Belize. However, the experiences of many of the former countries reveal the yawning gap between constitutional provision and political practice, a situation that also applies to Nigeria.

CONSTITUTIONAL PROVISION AND PRACTICE OF RELIGIOUS FREEDOM

As a member of the United Nations (UN) and the Organization for African Unity (O.A.U.), Nigeria subscribes to the U.N. Article on Human Rights as well as the African Charter on Human and Peoples' Rights of the O.A.U. (Nguema, 1990), both of which specify the protection of such fundamental liberties as freedom of conscience, religion, and expression. They also protect the individual and corporate freedom of association and assembly. Moreover, § 24 of the Constitution of the Federal Republic of Nigeria (1979) states that:

(1) Every person shall be entitled to freedom of thought, conscience and religion, including freedom to change his religion or belief and freedom, either alone or in community with others and in public or in private, to manifest and propagate his religion or belief in worship, teaching, practice and observance.

(2) No person attending any place of education shall be required to receive religious instruction or to take part in or attend any religious ceremony or observances if such instruction, ceremony or observances relate to a religion other than his.

(3) No religious community or denomination shall be prevented from providing religious instruction for pupils of that community or denomination in any place of education maintained wholly by that community or denomination.

(4) Nothing in this section shall invalidate any law that is reasonably justifiable in a democratic society—

(a) in the interest of defense, public safety, public order, public morality or public health; or

(b) for the purpose of protecting the rights and freedom of other persons, including their rights and freedom to observe and practise their religions without the unsolicited intervention of members of other religions.

It would seem from this that religious freedom is fully protected in Nigeria. Unfortunately, "constitution-gazing," as Markoff and Regan (1987) rightly observe, "is a perilously inaccurate way of discovering, much less predicting, a nation's politics" (p. 164). The remainder of this discourse examines this dissonance in the Nigerian context, with particular attention to prior restraint on religious speech. The term *speech* is used here in a broad sense to include verbal communication, use of the mass media, posting of religious banners, religious education, and other forms of religious communication. Prior restraint connotes the chilling effects of a hostile environment on the individual's ability to express his or her views or exercise his or her rights. Prior restraint may result from official laws and policies, the intimidating attitudes and actions of others, or one's principles toward self-restraint. If any of these factors produce an inertia or frustrate the individual or group from engaging in the pursuit of activities as they otherwise would choose to, this can be considered a form of prior restraint (Mincberg, 1993). In other words, anything that directly or indirectly excludes or discourages the practice and/or propagation of one's faith can be construed as a form of prior restraint.

Despite the explicit constitutional provisions in favor of religious freedom, every religious group in Nigeria experiences some form of discrimination and prior restraint in the practice and propagation of its faith. The groups that are most marginalized from public expression are the ones regarded as cults. The oldest ones in this category, such as the Ogboni fraternity, are generally viewed as forms of Traditional African Religion. As mentioned earlier, the federal government, under the administration of the late General Murtala Muhammed, a Muslim, banned public servants from belonging to such groups. Newer groups that are regarded as cults, mostly new age movements of Western and Eastern origin that are prevalent on college campuses and among youth, have also been outlawed and thus excluded from public discourse. The government justified its action by the many atrocious ritual murders and inhuman practices associated with these groups. These cults have neither denied the government's allegations nor contested what may be regarded as a violation of their constitutional rights. These groups' nonclandestine modes of operation may be the product of their extreme pluralism, since most of their members publicly profess to belong to mainstream religions.

As evangelistic groups, Christians and Muslims are more vocal in propagating their faiths. They also are more sensitive and reactive to anything that seeks to restrict them in this pursuit, which is why cases of prior restraint involving these groups make it to the news media or courts more frequently. On some occasions, the federal government has prevented Muslims and Christians from holding public religious gatherings. This usually follows incidents that are perceived to pose a religious threat. Most of the time, it is a checkmate situation where one group tries to restrict the activities of the other(s) in regions considered one's stronghold, without any regard to the constitutional rights of the other(s) to flourish without hindrance. State and local governments are most guilty of this. They use their political machinery to stifle religious speech by banning public preaching, denying permission to hold public rallies and processions, failing to protect places of worship, denying access to the public media, refusing to allocate land and public facilities for religious meetings, disrupting religious gatherings, arresting and detaining preachers, and declaring or making certain communities and language groups inaccessible to members of other religious groups (Kukah, 1992).

This suppression of religious freedom is merely a reflection of the lack of other forms of societal freedom and fundamental human rights. Kukah (1996) states that religious freedom cannot be guaranteed in the absence of other rights.

The fact that Nigeria's human rights records are not commendable naturally flows into the sphere of religion. At the moment, many leaders of thought are either in detention as political prisoners or in exile. There is a thin line between religious freedom and other rights. If, as Boven (1991, p. 447) suggests, "religious liberty gets its full meaning only in the broad context of human rights," it is naive to expect religious freedom in a society that does not guarantee the right to peaceful assembly, protection from arbitrary arrest, or the right to freely enter and exit the country.

Coupled with the disregard for constitutional rights is the culture of judicial restraint in the Nigerian legal system. Okonkwor (1983) and Obilade (1979) observe that the Nigerian courts are more inclined toward judicial restraint rather than judicial activism in their interpretation of the rights and liberties of citizens. Aggrieved parties also find it difficult to secure the desired justice because of conflicting structures in the system. Conflicts arise in the interpretation and application of the statutes, depending on whether cases are being tried under the customary law, common law, Shari'a law, martial law, or a judicial tribunal.

FORMS OF PRIOR RESTRAINT

Cases of prior restraint on evangelization in Nigeria date back to the colonial days. The British colonial policy of Indirect Rule favored the isolation of the various states, kingdoms, and ethnic groups that would later form the nation of Nigeria. The Indirect Rule policy was designed to minimize contact between different groups. In the bid to foster good relations with the Muslim traditional rulers in Nigeria, Christian missionaries were prevented from evangelizing Muslim communities in the north. Clarke (1986) noted that:

The colonial government, though not anti-Christian missionary *per se*, was for a number of reasons extremely reluctant to allow Christian missionaries to work in the main Islamic centres of northern Nigeria such as Kano, Sokoto, Katsina, Bauchi, and Maiduguri. (p. 109)

This gave rise to not only political but also religious zoning of the country. Although such physical restraint no longer exists, it has created a territorial psyche that gives communities the audacity to deny others an equal right to exist in their enclaves. This is evident in the policies and responses of various governments and communities toward religious pluralism.

EDUCATION

For about a century, Arabic literacy and Qur'anic education thrived in the Islamic strongholds that now constitute northern Nigeria, while Western and Christian education spread in the south. The restriction and exclusion of either system of belief and thought from the other's domain was initially a logistic reality. However, when the physical barriers disappeared, the religious authorities chose to maintain the separation for strategic reasons as a means of protecting their wards from being indoctrinated by the other group(s). The subsequent influence of Christian education in the north as an evangelistic tool justifies this perception. The fact remains that, until today, the educational system was structured in favor of prior restraint on religious communication.

With the introduction of the Universal Primary Education program in 1975, the government took over most schools, which were hitherto run by religious groups. In the south, prayers were eliminated from schools. In the Muslim-controlled states, where Western education was seen as a tool of Christian evangelization, the measures to restrict Christian activities were more far-reaching. School prayers were stopped; the students who wanted to organize prayer sessions were denied the use of school facilities. Christian Religious Studies was dropped from schools' curricula from the elementary to college levels. Christian parents have protested against the imposition of Qur'anic education on their wards, and the Islamic states do not permit Christians to establish and run schools of their own.

Kukah (1992) lamented how

in states like Kano, the state government has refused to allow broadcasts of Christian programmes on the state television and radio. It insists that all children in primary schools be taught Islamic knowledge, while denying Christians the right to teach Christian religious knowledge in schools. (p. 199)

MASS MEDIA

Whereas there is freedom of ownership of the print media, the government has, until recently, reserved the exclusive right to own and operate the electronic media. Now that the electronic media is being privatized, the decree establishing the National Broadcasting Commission forbids the licensing of religious broadcasting stations. The decision not to license these stations may be due to the volatile religious atmosphere in the country, the abuse of religious speech in the past, the excessive politicization of religion, and the constant use of the mass media to heighten religious tensions (Musa, 1990, 1995b; Usman, 1987). However, the fact remains that such a policy constitutes a form of prior restraint.

PROPERTY

Another form of prior restraint on evangelizing communities, which has survived from the colonial era until the present, is the prohibition against siting religious buildings in some quarters. This is most pronounced in Islamic communities, which are the least tolerant of pluralism. In inner cities such as Kano, Sokoto, Katsina, and Maiduguri, no religious buildings are allowed other than mosques (Clarke, 1986; Walsh, 1993).

Table 7.1

A Conceptual Framework for Tolerance and Freedom of Expression

	High	Proselytizing	
Low	Islam	Christianity	High
Pluralism	Shintoism	A. T. R.	Pluralism
	Low	Proselytizing	

INTEGRITY

Between 1982 and 1992, there were several Christian-Muslim clashes. Many of these were so violent that thousands of lives were lost, and worship places and property worth millions of dollars were destroyed. In 1990 and 1991, in the Kaduna and Bauchi states, religious confrontations occurred that were borne out of mutual suspicion and intolerance between Christians and Muslims. Mention also must be made of the intrareligious riots in Kano, Yola, and Katsina. Such religiously motivated attacks create a feeling of insecurity and vulnerability in the minds of minority religious groups, leading to inertia in the propagation of their beliefs.

CONCLUSION

Although the Nigerian Constitution guarantees all citizens the right to practice and propagate their religions in an atmosphere devoid of interference, the experiences of those seeking to present their faith in the public arena have fallen far below expectation. Most often, minority groups find that the Constitution is unable to protect them from mental and physical violation. Although the Constitution declares the country a secular one, the actions of the various governments reflect anything but neutrality. The attitudes and reactions of the religious groups toward ''non-believers'' also are dictated by their belief systems rather than the legal tenets of noninterference. Proselytizing and pluralism are significant factors in religious aggression. Religious aggression has been the highest among Christianity and Islam. Table 7.1 shows the amount of proselytizing and pluralism involved in each religion. High pluralism accounts for the reactionary and acquiescent attitudes of Christians and Traditional African Religionists.

For Nigeria to be a truly secular state where religious pluralism and freedom flourish, the government must not only be neutral in its dealings with the various religious groups, it must be active in defending those whose freedom of worship is violated. The gulf between the constitutional guarantee of religious freedom and the practical violation of such rights must be bridged. Also, states must eliminate policies that marginalize religion from public schools and the mass media. Above all, those interested in securing the freedom to practice their beliefs must recognize that such liberty can only be attained within the larger framework of other human rights, which as of now are not respected in the country.

NOTE

1. It is impossible to catalogue all of the religious affiliations of the over 104 million people in Nigeria. While paying particular attention to Traditional African Religion, Islam, and Christianity as the dominant three religious groups in the country, one cannot deny the existence of other groups. To do so would be as fallacious as saying that Hausa, Ibo, and Yoruba are the only ethnic groups in the country. The Nigerian state recognizes the existence of other religious affiliations. The Oyo state government recently prosecuted the leader of the Guru Maha Raji Movement in Nigeria over land ownership and corruption. The Ancient Mystical Order Rosae Crucis (AMORC) and Rosicruscian Society sued the Evangelical Churches of West Africa (ECWA), the publishers of *Today's Challenge*, for libel. The Murtala Muhammed regime banned public servants from participating in the Ogboni cult. The federal and state governments have had a running battle with campus cults. These examples affirm the presence of numerous other religious groups. However, the national dialogue has been dominated by the three mainstream religious bodies, which in turn contain many shades and variations within their ranks.

REFERENCES

Abu, Zahrah M. (n.d.). *Tanzim al-Islam li'l-Mujtama*. Cairo: Matba'at Mukhaymar.

Al-Nabhan, M. F. (1974). *Nizam al-Hukm fi'l-Islam*. Kuwait: Jami'at al-Kuwait.

Boven, T. (1991). Advances and obstacles in building understanding and respect between people of diverse religions and beliefs. *Human Rights Quarterly, 13*: 437–452.

Catholic Bishops of Nigeria. (1986). *Christian/Muslim relations in Nigeria: The stand of the Catholic Bishops*. Lagos, Nigeria: Catholic Secretariat.

Clarke, P. B. (1986). *West Africa and Christianity*. London: Edward Arnold.

Constitution of the Federal Republic of Nigeria, §§ 10, 24 (1979).

Coulson, N. J. (1957). The state and the individual in Islamic law. *International and Comparative Law Quarterly, 6*: 49–60.

Gilliland, D. S. (1986). *African religion meets Islam: Religious changes in northern Nigeria*. Lanham, MD: University Press of America.

Gilliland, D. S. (1990). First conversion and second conversion in Nigeria. *Mission Studies, VII-2*(14): 131–150.

Haynes, J. (1996). *Religion and politics in Africa*. London: Zed Books.

Hunwick, J. O. (1972). Islam in West Africa A.D. 1000–1800. In J.F.A. Ajayi & Espie (Eds.), *A thousand years of African history* (pp. 113–131). New York: Humanities Press.

Ibrahim, O. F. (1997). Religion and politics: A view from the north. In L. Diamond et al. (Eds.), *Transition without end* (pp. 427–447). London: Lynne Reinner.

Ifemesia, C. C. (1972). The peoples of West Africa around A.D. 1000. In J.F.A. Ajayi & Espie (Eds.), *A thousand years of African history* (pp. 39–54). New York: Humanities Press.

Ilesanmi, S. O. (1997). *Religious pluralism and the Nigerian state*. Athens: Ohio University Center for International Studies.

Kamali, M. H. (1997). *Freedom of expression in Islam*. Cambridge, MA: Islamic Texts Society.

Kirk-Greene, A. (1997). The remedial imperatives of the Nigerian constitution, 1922–1992. In L. Diamond et al. (Eds.), *Transition without end* (pp. 31–53). London: Lynne Reinner.

Kukah, M. H. (1992). The politicisation of fundamentalism in Nigeria. In P. Gifford (Ed.), *New dimensions in African Christianity* (pp. 183–206). Nairobi, Kenya: All Africa Conference of Churches.

Kukah, M. H. (1993). *Religion, politics, and power in northern Nigeria*. Ibadan, Nigeria: Spectrum Books.

Kukah, M. H. (1996). *Religion and the politics of justice in Nigeria*. Lagos, Nigeria: Constitutional Rights Project.

Markoff, J. & Regan, D. (1987). Religion, the state and political legitimacy in the world's constitutions. In T. Robin & R. Robertson (Eds.), *Church-state relations: Tensions and transitions* (pp. 161–182). New Brunswick, NJ: Transaction Books.

Mayer, A. E. (1991). *Islam and human rights: Tradition and politics*. Boulder, CO: Westview Press.

Mbadinuju, C. C. (1987). *Law and religion in Nigeria*. Onitsha, Nigeria: Topprint.

Mbiti, J. S. (1990). *African religions and philosophy*. Portsmouth, NH: Heineman Educational Books.

Mead, S. E. (1985). *The nation with the soul of a church*. Macon, GA: Mercer University Press.

Mincberg, E. (1993). A look at recent Supreme Court decisions: Judicial prior restraint and the First Amendment. *Hastings Law Journal, 44*: 871–979.

Miranda, E. O. (1994). Religious pluralism and tolerance. *British Journal of Religious Education, 17*: 19–34.

Moemeka, A. A. (1983). Socio-cultural environment of communication in traditional Nigeria: An ethnographic exploration. *Communicatio Socialis, 16*: 332–334.

Musa, B. A. (1990). The mass media and socio-political crisis in Nigeria. In N. Alkali et al. (Eds.), *African media issues* (pp. 148–157). Enugu, Nigeria: Delta Publications.

Musa, B. A. (1995a). *Prior restraint on choice of language and approach for evangelism in Nigeria*. Paper presented at the annual Religious Speech Communication Association Convention, San Antonio, TX.

Musa, B. A. (1995b). *Trends in popular culture and freedom of expression in West Africa: Implications for 21st Century society*. Paper presented at the annual Speech Communication Association Convention, San Antonio, TX.

Musa, B. A. (1996). *The bloc-press phenomenon and conflict management in Nigeria: Implications for nation-building*. Paper presented at the annual Speech Communication Association Convention, San Diego, CA.

Ngokwe, I. B. (1984). *Religion and religious liberty in Nigerian law*. Roma: Pontificia Universita Lateranense.

Nguema, I. (1990). Human rights in Africa: The roots of a constant challenge. *Human Rights Law Journal, 11*: 261–299.

Obilade, A. O. (1979). *The Nigerian legal system*. London: Sweet & Maxwell.

Okonkwor, R. C. (1983). Nigeria's sedition laws—Their effect on free speech. *Journalism Quarterly, 60*: 54–60.

Ryder, A.F.C. (1972). Portuguese and Dutch in West Africa before 1800. In J.F.A. Ajayi & I. Espie (Eds.), *A Thousand years of African history* (pp. 217–236). New York: Humanities Press.

Sanneh, L. (1996). *Piety and power: Muslims and Christians in West Africa.* New York: Orbis Books.

Siddiqui, A. (1997). *Christian-Muslim dialogue in the twentieth century.* New York: St. Martin's Press.

Usman, Y. B. (1987). *The manipulation of religion in Nigeria, 1977–1987.* Kaduna, Nigeria: Vanguard.

Uthman, F. (1401/1908). *Huquq al-Insan Bayan al-Shari'ah al-Islamiyyah wa'l-Fikr al-Qanuni al-Gharbi.* Beirut, Lebanon: Dar al-Shuruq.

Walsh, J. (1993). *Religious riots in Nigeria.* Birmingham, England: Centre for the Study of Islam and Christian-Muslim Relations.

Chapter 8

Latvian Legal and Liturgical Legacy: First Transgressions and Turmoil, then Technology and Tolerance

Riley Maynard

The Baltic country of Latvia contributes an interesting perspective to a study of religion, law, and freedom. It is a country of quick changes, brutal repression, and a proud return to a free democracy. Its long history is filled with military takeovers, bloody protests, and extreme fluctuations in governing structures. Latvians have felt the iron boots of tyranny from the Teutonic Knights and the German Nazis. They have battled troops from Tsarist Russia and the army of the Soviet Union. Until 1991, Latvia had experienced only 20 years of independence.

The country's origins go back to 2500 B.C., and the capital city, Riga, was founded in 1201. Like its Baltic neighbors Lithuania and Estonia, Latvia became a battleground for armies invading from virtually all directions. The flags of Poland, Sweden, Russia, and Germany flew over the country for hundreds of years. The rise of Latvian nationalism began in the 1860s, sparked by folk writer Krisjanis Valdemars and folk song collector Krisjanis Barons.

The more modern history of the country can be traced to 1905, when 50,000 workers protested the Tsar's rule. The Tsar's military killed 80 of the protesters and executed 2,000 more a few months later. During World War I, Latvia was captured in 1917 by the Germans, but a revolt started, which led to a Latvian declaration of independence on November 18, 1918. The country was admitted into the League of Nations in 1921. This began a reign of self-rule that lasted only about 20 years.

A particularly grim period for Latvia began on June 17, 1940, when Soviet troops invaded the country. The Soviet atrocities became more numerous and more brutal by the day, with frequent murders, mass deportations, and placement of thugs into positions of power. All semblance of religious, legal, and cultural freedoms was ended by the military victors, and many institutions considered quite innocuous by Western standards were abolished. The Boy Scouts, Girl Guides, 4-H, YMCA, YWCA, Red Cross, and Jewish National Foundation all were abolished, and all of their property was seized by the government. All religious worship was banned, forcing many churches and their members into an underground status.

The Soviets' rule was short-lived and came to an end when the Nazis invaded in July 1941. At first the German troops were welcomed by some Latvians as a liberating force, but the Nazis duplicated much of the Soviet brutality, in addition to murdering 90 percent of Latvia's Jewish population. Latvian youths were conscripted into the German army, and some ended up fighting their brothers and fathers when the Soviets retook the country in 1944.

From 1944 until 1991, the Latvians were prohibited from religious worship, with such activities considered illegal by the Communist government. Bibles and religious implements were strictly forbidden and had to be smuggled into the country and passed about surreptitiously. Entire biblical texts were typed on manual typewriters with carbon copies for small-scale duplication purposes.

Informers and KGB agents followed anyone suspected of attending religious services. If the churchgoers were discovered at worship, they were punished by imprisonment or through loss of jobs and status. Even children were not immune to penalties, and they could be expelled from schools or ostracized by their peers.

The hundreds of churches scattered across Latvia were relegated to similar fates. Some of the more fortunate congregations had their buildings survive as concert halls or meeting places. Other places of worship met with more ignominious ends, being used for storage for grain, trucks, or machinery. To permit large vehicle entry, the Communists destroyed entire walls and gouged huge holes into the temples. Many churches were demolished altogether, their rubble serving as a grim reminder of official Soviet policy.

The struggles for Latvian political and religious freedoms began concurrently, once again proving the links between these societal elements. Latvians began a series of political protests in the late 1980s. Interestingly, the first Christian newspaper began at about the same time. In 1988, *Svetdienas Rits* (Sunday Morning) started publication as part of the Latvian Evangelical Lutheran Church. On January 21, 1991, special Soviet troops attacked the Interior Ministry building in Riga, killing five people and injuring 10 others. By August of that year, the Communist Party collapsed, and the parliament restored the pre-World War II independence. America recognized Latvia's independence on September 2, 1991, and the country was admitted into the United Nations on September 17. In 1993, the Christian Charity Fund established ''DIALOGS,'' an ecumenical organization that disseminated Christian news from all denominations. The last Soviet troops pulled out of Riga on April 30, 1994, and U.S. President Bill Clinton visited Riga on July 6 of that same year. In 1995, the Christian Charity Fund opened a photo exhibition in Riga that displayed photos of over 700 Latvian churches. President Guntis Ulmanis opened the exhibition, with archbishops and clergy of many denominations in attendance. The exhibition has since toured 67 towns and cities in Latvia to total crowds estimated at 400,000 people. This is quite impressive, considering the country's population is just over 2 million persons.

Latvians are now trying to make their democracy work but are still aware of the close presence of their former oppressors, the Russians. Latvian authorities granted citizenship only to pre-war citizens and their dependents, denying such status to Latvian-born Russian immigrants. Many of these same Russians had their property seized and given back to the descendants of native Latvians. One Latvian resident found himself the owner of six properties since he was the sole survivor of several families. The Russian-speaking immigrants were allowed to apply for citizenship, but the process was slow, permitting by June 30, 1996, the naturalization of only 2,133 citizens out of 3,685 candidates. The former Soviet Union states added to the uncertain status of these immigrants by denying them reentry into their former countries. Since these people were born in Latvia, they were considered Latvians by Russia. About 700,000 Russian-speaking people were left in a state of uncertainty. They are subjected to shabby treatment by Latvians and are the victims of prejudice in many social and political activities. For instance, although Latvians were taught how to speak the Russian language in their schools, many of them refuse to talk to Russians who cannot speak Latvian.

Latvia is undergoing sweeping changes in its social, political, economic, and religious foundations. The Soviet-style economy is gone, and a wave of capitalistic renovation and transformation is rapidly occurring. One can walk down virtually any commercial street in Riga's central city and see building construction, new stores, street vendors, and Western-style entrepreneurial activity. There is a McDonald's restaurant just across the street from the Freedom Monument area where President Clinton spoke in 1994.

Such vast changes in a country's civilization are not without their victims. Just as marketplace successes dot the city's landscape, so do the failures—the homeless, the destitute, and the economic casualties. Beggars of all ages are a common sight throughout Riga, and the new government is overwhelmed by the sheer numbers of the disenfranchised. Political and social agencies are struggling to meet the demands of pensioners, disabled persons, and unskilled workers.

Church officials, missionaries, and religious proselytizers poured into Latvia to meet the challenges of a country whose spiritual needs had been neglected or suppressed for decades. The exact numbers of native and immigrant worshipers were difficult to determine. Ilmars Mezs of the United States Information Service has been conducting ethnic research for that agency since Latvia's democratization. He explained that some congregations tend to exaggerate their numbers. "Some church people in small towns will tell you they have 1,000 members, but you find out the town only has 700 residents" (personal interview by author, October 14, 1997).

After years of research efforts, governmental sources have estimated the total number of church members in Latvia to be 777,654. This total breaks down to the following denominations:

1. Lutherans   324,380
2. Catholics   225,436
3. Russian Orthodox   190,515
4. Old Believers   22,478
(another Russian Orthodox faction)
5. Baptists   6,056
6. Jewish   5,000
7. Adventist   3,789

Latvia's religious denominations are not without their controversies and dissensions. Juris Calitis is the pastor of Riga's St. Savior's Church, formerly of Lutheran affiliation but now an Anglican church. He thinks the Latvian Lutheran church is inflexible, which has caused some churches and their members to withdraw and join other denominations and sects. "Catholic and Baptist churches are growing. Many of them are feeding off the shrinking of the Lutherans" (personal interview by author, December 16, 1997). Calitis opines that church membership will continue to expand in Latvia. "I think it's going to grow. The question is whether it will be the Roman Catholics or Lutherans."

The Latvian government finally devised a strategy for determining the number of churches and denominations practicing religion in the country. After 1995, churches had to apply for recognition under new procedures. Based on similar canons in other Baltic states, the laws set out a four-part process:

1. Applicants may apply to be recognized by the government as a religious organization if they have 10 persons as members.
2. Applicants may then be recognized as a nontraditional church if they have 10 religious organizations; such churches can then make their own decisions on schools, monasteries, and so on.
3. Applicant churches must register with the government every year for 10 years. After 10 years it is not necessary to register annually.
4. Applicants' status will be changed from a nontraditional status to that of a traditional church after 25 years.

Ringolds Balodis, the government's director of associations and religious departments, said that such measures were not meant to discourage new religions but more to find out how many churches were operating in Latvia. Nonetheless, he and his department were threatened with the wrath of various gods from several organizations. "Nobody pressures you like new religions," he said (personal interview by author, November 14, 1997).

The Christian Charity Fund has begun a new exposition, "Come and See." There are such religious artifacts as Latvian editions of the Bible, ranging from 1685 till the present. Visitors can read Christian periodicals and prayer, sermon, and hymn books. Other memorabilia include Bibles in many different languages as well as Bibles and Bible studies on computers. The Christian Charity Fund's use of digital media, though somewhat new to Latvia, is not unique. Many churches and religious organizations are using computers to spread the word, both to their members and to a lay audience.

There are now hundreds of thousands of religious practitioners in all areas of Latvia, and they have a genuine need for communication. Just as religious devotees have rushed to fill the spiritual void, so have communicators stepped in to solve the information shortage. Media of every type are vigorously distributed throughout every portion of the country. Radio, TV, print, and digital media are taking Latvian religion to new audiences. In addition to the indigenous Christian media listed in Tables 8.1 and 8.2, there is also the European Christian Channel, a satellite entry from Vienna, Austria. American televangelist Kenneth Copeland is telecast on Latvian Independent Television, although the dubbing is in Russian, not Latvian.

This proliferation of religions and media is not universally admired. Ivars Kupcis of the Christian Charity Fund sees negative aspects. Kupcis, the Fund's History Department Director, says, "Communications make the new religious movements popular, but it mainly happens in a negative sense. Many people who read in national newspapers of strange activities of different sects become afraid of all religions" (personal interview by author, September 29, 1997).

As Latvia acquires more experience in governing a democracy, its citizens will likely demand more political, legal, and religious freedoms. The expansion of religious and secular media is continuing, but one must wonder how many different media 2 million people can support.

What does the future hold for religious media in Latvia? Kupcis thinks the secular and religious media have similar destinies. "The process of professionalizing is happening in the mass media of Latvia today. Professionals replace amateur journalists. I'm sure that it also will be the main change in religious media in the next few years" (personal interview by author, September 29, 1997). Such a trend will benefit the consumers. More professionalism means better coverage of religious, political, and legal issues and improved responses to the public.

Table 8.1
Religious Mass Media in Latvia: Print Media

TITLE	MEDIUM (Magazine/ newspaper)	PUBLISHER	TARGET AUDIENCE	PUBLISHING SCHEDULE	STAFF (est.)
Svetdienas Rita (Sunday Morning)	Newspaper of Latvian Evangelical Lutheran Church	Latvian Evangelical Lutheran Church	Lutherans and others	Bi-weekly	6
Solis	Christian Newspaper	Ecumenical Society of Christian Information	Catholics and others	Weekly	7
Katolu Baznicas Vestnesis (Catholic Church Messenger)	Newspaper of Riga Deanery of Latvian Roman Catholic Church	Riga Deanery of Latvian Roman Catholic Church	Catholics	Bi-weekly	5
Katolu Dzeive (Catholic Life)	Religious Social Magazine	Headquarters of Riga Deanery (Latvian Roman Catholic Church)	Catholics	Monthly	9
Ejiet un Maciet (Go and Teach)	Religious-Educational Magazine	Roman Catholic Seminary of Riga	Catholics	Monthly	6
Grecinieku Piestatne (Wayside for Sinners)	Newspapers	Riga St. Joseph's Church (Jacobians)	Catholics and others	Bi-weekly	6
Lutera Draudzes Zinas (Luther's Church News)	Magazines	Riga Luther's Church	Lutherans	Monthly	3

Table 8.1 (continued)

Laba Vests (Good News)	Christian Educational Magazine	Latvian Baptist Church	Baptists, Lutherans, and others	Bi-monthly	6
Baptistu Bestnesis (Baptist Herald)	Magazine	Latvian Baptist Church	Baptists	Monthly	5
Gaismina (Light)	Christian Magazine for Sunday Schools and Families	Union of Latvian Baptist Church Sunday Schools	Children of Christian Sunday Schools	Monthly	3
Latvian Luteranis (Latvian Lutheran)	Newspaper of Augsburgbas Apliecibas Instituts Ltd.	Augsburgbas Apliecibas Instituts Ltd.	Selected Lutherans	Bi-monthly	9
Mantomums (Heritage)	Magazine of Lutheran Theology	Lutheran Heritage Foundation	Selected Lutherans	Monthly	4
Adventes	Magazine	Baltic Union of Seventh Day Adventists	Adventists	Monthly	3
Atspulgs (Reflection)	Youth Magazine	Baltic Union of Seventh Day Adventists	Adventists	Monthly	3
Pilseta Kalna (City on the Mountain)	Youth Magazine	Baltic Union of Seventh Day Adventists	Adventists	Monthly	3
Grauds	Newspaper of Grobina Lutheran Deanery	Liepaja St. Anne Lutheran Deanery	Lutheran Church	Monthly	6

Table 8.2
Religious Mass Media in Latvia: Radio-TV

MEDIUM & TITLE	SCHEDULE	FREQUENCY OR CHANNEL	STAFF
Christian Radio of Latvia	Broadcasts 24 hours a day	101.8 FM (104.7 FM in Talsi, and 104.6 FM in Liepaja)	N/A
Christian TV "Emmanuel"	Telecast every Sunday at 2:00 P.M.	Latvian Independent Television	3
Lutheran Hour (Radio)	Broadcast Saturday at 8:00 P.M.	99.5 FM	5
TV	Telecast on Sunday (various times)	Latvian television	16
	Christian news stories (telecast bi-weekly)	Latvian television	16

REFERENCES

http://www.latnet.lv/WWWsites/society/religion.htm.
> Denominations listed on this site:
> *Baltic Union Conference of Seventh Day Adventists.* A brief information about Seventh Day Adventists in the Baltic countries: history and current activities. In English, Estonian, Latvian, Lithuanian, and Russian.
> *Hare Krishna.* History, philosophy and answers to questions.
> *In God We Trust.* Christian exchange with information, help, and advice.
> *Latvian Bible Society.* Information about the Society and the new Bible translation into Latvian.
> *St. John's Church.* Architecture of the building.

Muiznecks, N. (Ed.). (1997). *Latvia: Human development report.* Riga, Latvia: United Nations Development Programme.

Other Sources

Balodis, R. Director, Department of Associations and Religions, Republic of Latvia. Personal interview, November 14, 1997, Riga, Latvia.

Brikse, I. Chairperson, Department of Communication, University of Latvia in Riga. Personal interview, September 3, 1997, Riga, Latvia.

Calitis, J., Pastor, St. Savior's Church. Personal interview, December 16, 1997, Riga, Latvia.

Duze, D. Producer, Latvian Independent Television. Personal interview, September 16, 1997, Riga, Latvia.

Duzis, G. Producer, Latvian Independent Television. Personal interview, September 16, 1997, Riga, Latvia.

Elftmann, G. First Secretary for Press and Cultural Affairs, U.S. Embassy. Personal interview, November 13, 1997, Riga, Latvia.

Kupcis, I. Director, Department of History, Christian Charity Fund. Personal interviews, September 29, 1997 and October 21, 1997, Riga, Latvia.

Mesz, I. Ethnic and Cultural Information Officer, United States Information Service. Personal interview, October 14, 1997, Riga, Latvia.

Mozers, M. Professor, Department of Communication, University of Latvia. Personal interview, September 24, 1997, Riga, Latvia.

Stengrevica, E. International Acquisitions Assistant, Latvian Independent Television. Personal interview, September 15, 1997, Riga, Latvia.

Streips, K. Radio journalist and professor, Department of Communication, University of Latvia, Riga. Personal interview, December 17, 1997.

Part III

Journalism, Advertising, and Ethical Issues

Chapter 9

Professional Ethics and Sociopolitical Mobilization of Muslim Journalists: A Study of Communication, Ethics, and the Islamic Tradition

Hamid Mowlana

INTRODUCTION

A number of studies on international communication over the last several decades reveal two essential characteristics. One is the ethnocentric orientation of mass communication systems of the highly developed and industrialized nations and the second is the "asymmetric" circulation of information in the world. These two characteristics dominate the world mass media system and indeed are responsible for uneven treatment of events, imbalances in news and information, and unequal distribution of power in the world system.

It is precisely here that a need for a professional code of ethics among Muslim journalists around the world seems imperative and their creation of a network of professional world associations both timely and inevitable. The fact that until now there has been almost no such associations at the international level illustrates the low priority given to information and news among Islamic countries. It also indicates a century-long inattention to the lack of growth in media organizations, which is, in part, a consequence of decades of repression, colonialism, and government control.

From the Islamic Revolution in Iran to the occupation of Afghanistan by the former Soviet Union, from the Persian Gulf War to the tragedy of Bosnia, the last two decades have witnessed profound and worldwide revolutionary movements of an Islamic nature as well as systematic and continuous conflicts that have embraced Muslim lands. The developments in the Islamic world not only have been reported during this period with a good deal of bias, distortion, and ethnocentrism by non-Muslim media, but also the great portion of what has been reported has been provided mainly by the Western media and journalists.

Research shows that 99 percent of world events do not come to the attention of readers simply because they are eliminated and considered unimportant or irrelevant by the media. The Islamic world, in particular, has been on the receiving end of a good share of this modus operandi. For example, consider six levels of the so-called common selections of news in mass communication: (1) sources of production of information and news; (2) journalists and correspondents; (3) central offices of news agencies; (4) local newspapers and editorial offices; (5) mass media editors; and finally (6) recipients, meaning readers or viewers. It has been reported empirically that 98 percent of news and information is eliminated in the second through the sixth levels, with 92 percent elimination from the second through the fifth levels, not to mention the elimination resulting from the process of selectivity on the part of readers and viewers. This Darwinian law of selectivity, once translated and applied to events and developments in the Islamic world (which constitutes one-fourth of the world's population), can indeed have enormous impact on individual and collective perceptions about Islam and its followers. The crucial question is not how strongly the control is exercised but instead by whom, under what conditions, and for what purpose.

A CALL FOR A WORLD ORGANIZATION OF MUSLIM JOURNALISTS

A cursory look at the list of existing media and journalist associations around the world quickly shows how the media are organized and mobilized on the basis of nationality, regionalism, ethnicity, and even religious premises and are among the most active non-governmental organizations around the world. Yet today, remarkably, there are no professional associations of Islamic journalists that can set professional and ethical criteria for news reporting, protect the rights of individual Muslim journalists, and promote the journalistic education and training of young men and women. These aspiring journalists represent a major human resource for Islamic culture and civilization.

Why is it important for Islamic journalists to have a network of associations binding their professional mission? The answer lies in the very core of Islamic political culture, for Islam is not only a religion but also a total way of life for millions of people around the world. Unlike other major cultural systems, Islam transcends geographical as well as racial and ethnic boundaries and strives for universality of humankind. In short, the sociocultural elements inherent in the Islamic community of *ummah* provide a common ground and outline a need for the type of news reporting that is vital to understanding events in the world community. Such a network of Muslim journalists, media associations, and professional organizations also can play an important role as vanguards and promoters of professional aims within the existing systems of international organizations. A network of professional associations thus not only can enhance the exchange of information among various geographical areas known as the

Islamic world but also can stimulate the ongoing mobilization of journalists and their common interests.

What should be the tenets underlying the formation and mobilization of such networks of associations? It must be recalled that news values in the Islamic world differ considerably from the general news values in the non-Islamic world and, more specifically, the West. For example, the concept of so-called "hard news," common in the Western media with its "five Ws" syndrome of "what, when, where, why, and who," is promoted as universal. The real problem is that the recipient of such "five Ws" news is never allowed to conceive of news as a whole but only in fragments, because the structure of the whole is at odds with what is considered "hard facts." The priorities given to news values in the West, such as human interest, proximity, novelty, consequence, and prominence, are totally different from those valued in Islamic contexts.

For example, the notion of proximity in the Western media primarily is a geographical as well as a spatial concept. To apply this concept in its orthodox sense to the Islamic world would eliminate news coming from distant places such as Indonesia, China, Africa, or Latin America when the media and their audiences are located somewhere in the United States or Middle East. Proximity in an Islamic context is neither geographical nor spatial but rather cultural— that is, events of the Islamic community or *ummah* are and must be relevant to the entire Muslim world, regardless of nationalities and countries. The factors of human interest or prominence are by themselves not adequate justification for the reporting of news in the Islamic context. News and information for the *ummah* are social commodities and not cultural industries.

One of the disadvantages arising from Western reporting of the contemporary Islamic world is that news of both cooperative and conflict-filled natures is treated not in an Islamic context but in the generic journalistic culture that has prevailed for decades in Europe and in the United States. Thus a major result is incomplete presentation, if not actual and chronic misrepresentation, of events in the Islamic world as they occur. This reductive refinement of the concept of information and news has been a gradual process extending over several decades and indeed has been responsible for a good deal of misperceptions and even bias. This in itself has provided a kind of journalistic "fundamentalism," which claims universalism, into which issues such as "Islamic fundamentalism" are unfairly lumped.

In a changing and volatile world—where values and ideas are constantly in transition and where internal and external events of nations are becoming more unpredictable, leading to profound political, economic, and cultural transformation—Muslim journalists around the globe must define their own informational and cultural territories and their own professional and ethical standards. One of the weaknesses in the world of Islamic media is the fact that there is a low level of participation of either individuals or associations in regional and international gatherings and conferences. Correspondingly, the power of the West—that is the European and American journalists and media—resides in the fact that these media are systematic and constant participants in a variety of international conferences, symposia, and seminars as well as in international and regional organizations. It is through this process of participation and professional acculturation that individuals can hope to contribute to the process of decision making and learn how to influence the agenda of international organizations.

This is well illustrated by an example from the Persian Gulf War of 1990–1991. During this international political crisis, journalists and correspondents from the major Islamic countries opposing the intervention of the United States and the coalition forces not only were not allowed to be part of the news pool or to cover the countries involved in the war, but also the stream of information coming from the war front was controlled and manipulated, either by the governments involved or by the Western news sources. The existence of a strong professional association of Muslim journalists would have made a definite difference in that it could have exerted pressure collectively to obtain at least part of the privileges extended to other groups and voiced the Muslim journalists' grievances on professional and institutional levels for the whole world to hear. Additionally, on the "home front," the existence of such Islamic professional journalistic associations could give proper recognition to the coverage of events such as the annual *hajj* (pilgrimage) as a major religio-political and sociocultural occurrence and counteract its trivialization through non-Muslim media channels.

An underlying premise of such a network of professional associations is the Islamic worldview, which considers news and information as a process of distribution of knowledge. In short, from the Islamic perspective, mass media organizations and their personnel are engaged in a delicate endeavor centering around both the production and distribution of knowledge. This is because facts by themselves do not have meaning in Islam but, once placed in a proper Islamic social structure, they constitute information leading to knowledge.

A number of concepts comprising the worldview of Islam could be the informational and social basis of such a network of journalists. They include, among others, the concept of *tawhid* (unity of God), the concept of *ilm* (knowledge), the meaning of *taqwa* (fear of God), the process of *adl* (justice), the notion of *ijma* (consensus), the process of *shura* (consultation), the doctrine of *amanat* (public interest), and last but not least the *ummah* (the larger Islamic community).

DEFINITION OF TERMS

A social system is a process of interaction of individuals within a larger unit called society, which exhibits the property that Ibn Khaldun, an Islamic thinker, called solidarity (*assabieh*), a term also employed later by Durkheim in his works. A social system is not the value itself but a system of values and actions of individuals that is associated by symbolic meaning. On the other hand, values are instruments of maintaining the cultural integrity and cohesion of society, serving to legitimize the modes of more concrete actions (Kroeber & Parsons,

1958). Here arises the question of cultural systems and how they interact with problems of conceptualization, theorization, and practices of information and communication. What impact do cultural settings have on the studies of communication? What communication theories and practices do they foster?

The Islamic world consists of a vast and diverse geopolitical area stretching from Indonesia and the Pacific Ocean in the east to Morocco and the Atlantic coast in the west from central Asia and the Himalayas in the north to the southern African nations and the Indian Ocean. As one of the major religions of the world, Islam encompasses one-quarter of the world's population—over a billion people. From the death of the Prophet (SAAS) (572–632 A.D.) and the period of the first four Caliphs (632–661 A.D.) to the end of World War I and the demise of the Ottoman Empire, the Islamic community has been a major world power. In the context of decolonization and increasing numbers of sovereign nation-states, the Islamic world politically, economically, and often culturally began to integrate into the existing sphere of the Western-dominated modern world system. The contacts between the Islamic world and the West in the nineteenth and twentieth centuries increased the absorption of many Islamic countries into quasisecular political entities ranging from hereditary monarchies to modern Western and/or military-style republics. This also resulted in pronounced conflicts between modern secularism and the Islamic tradition of Al Shari'a, the canonical law of Islam.

In order to understand current journalistic practices in the Islamic world and to assess their future direction, it is necessary to examine a number of the fundamental principles upon which the Islamic communication framework has been built and to understand how Islamic societies have come under constraints as a result of global political, economic, and cultural developments over the last century. The central foci of analysis will be the fundamental principles of Islamic ethical methods in communication and the objectives and aims of social communication. The term *social communication* is used here in its broader sense to include all kinds of communication in an Islamic context, including journalism and mass communication. This understanding of social communication should help clarify the function of some of the modern institutions of communication in contemporary Islamic societies.

A distinction should be made between the Islamic term *social communication* or *tabligh* (propagation) and the general concepts of communication, journalism, propaganda, and agitation, commonly used in contemporary literature. The word "communication" comes from the Latin *communico*, meaning "share," and it is essentially a social process referring to the act of imparting, conveying, or exchanging ideas, knowledge, or information. It is a process of access or means of access between two or more persons or places. Also implicit in this definition is a notion of some degree of trust without which communication cannot take place. In its reductive approach (mathematical, technical, and some scientific analysis), communication is associated with the concept of information linking the process with chance events and various possible outcomes. This "atomic" view gives emphasis to quantitative and linear aspects of the process and not to its cultural and cognitive meanings (Cherry, 1961; Kirshenmann, 1970; Shannon & Weaver, 1961; Wiener, 1961, 1967). Journalism, as defined in the West, is the collection, writing, editing, and publishing of news, opinions, and commentaries through newspapers, magazines, broadcasting, and other modern media.

The term *propaganda* is a Western concept and was used for the first time by a committee of Cardinals (founded in 1622 by Pope Gregory) of the Roman Catholic Church having the care and oversight of foreign missions. Propaganda comes from the Latin word *propagare*, and it originally meant propagating the Gospel and establishing the Church in non-Christian countries. The contemporary use of the term *propaganda* in its political, sociological, and commercial contexts, however, dates back to the beginning of the twentieth century. Since World War I, its definition has evolved to connote an instrument of persuasion and manipulation of individuals and collective behavior in national and international scenes (Lasswell, Lerner, & Speier, 1980).

Thus according to French sociologist Jacques Ellul, "Propaganda is a set of methods employed by an organized group that wants to bring about the active or passive participation in its action of a mass of individuals psychologically unified through psychological manipulations and incorporated in an organization" (1965, p. 61). In a somewhat similar fashion, Lasswell (1942) has defined propaganda as "the manipulation of symbols as a means of influencing attitudes on controversial matters" (1942, p. 106). This follows the common definition of propaganda as spreading ideology, doctrine, or ideas and the common definition of agitation as an instrument for arousing people to spontaneous action. The Communist position on propaganda and agitation differs methodologically from that of Lasswell's. As defined by Vladimir I. Lenin, "A propagandist presents many ideas to one or a few persons; an agitator presents only one or a few ideas, but he presents them to a mass of people" (Lenin, 1935–1939, p. 85).

Note that contemporary propagandists, therefore, do not need to be believers in an ideology or a doctrine. Here propagandists are people in the service of the State, the party, the political or commercial campaign, or any other organization that is ready to use their expertise. Propagandists are technicians, bureaucrats, and specialists who may eventually come to despise the ideology itself.

Propagation, on the other hand, is the dissemination and diffusion of some principle, belief, or practice. The Islamic word for propagation, *tabligh*, means the increase or spread of a belief by natural reproduction; it is an extension in space and time, the action of branching out. Social communication, journalism, and *tabligh* in an Islamic context have an ethical boundary and a set of guiding principles. In a broader sense, *tabligh* is a theory of communication and ethics. This theory of communication and global community integration is well stated by Ibn Khaldun in *The mugaddimah* (An Introduction to History). Here he cites "truthful propagation" (*tabligh*) and group cohesion (*assabieh*) as two fundamental factors in the rise of world powers as States and large communities

(Khaldun, 1967, pp. 123–127, 301–316). Thus journalism as the production, gathering, and dissemination of information, news, and opinion is an extension of *tabligh* in its broadest sense.

COMMUNICATION AND ETHICS: THEIR BOUNDARIES AND FRONTIERS

A study of social communication in Islamic society in the early days and certainly before the rise of the modern nation-state system has a unique element to it (Balagha, 1971; Mutahhari, 1982). This is because it was rooted in oral and social traditions and in the notion of *ummah*, or a greater Islamic community. Also the geographical entities now called Islamic countries were not heavily influenced by Western methods, conduct, and regimes in conflict with the major tenets of Islam. With the exception of the Islamic Republic of Iran, which is founded on the Islamic notion of the state, the remaining Islamic countries have state systems that are a mixture of the modern and traditional monarchical or republican systems. Thus their legal and ethical codes are heavily influenced by non-Islamic frames of reference. In many current analyses, great confusion arises from the failure to make a distinction between a nation-state and an Islamic state. It should be emphasized that while the nation-state is a political state, the Islamic state is a *muttagi*, or a religio-political, ''God-fearing'' community or state. The ecological terrain of social communication in an Islamic community emphasizes intrapersonal and interpersonal communication over impersonal types, social communication over atomistic communication, and intercultural communication over nationalism.

Moving from the process of social communication to the definition of ethics, it must be emphasized that the boundaries of the study called ''ethics'' vary from culture to culture. For the purposes of the present study, a method of ethics is defined as any rational procedure by which we determine what an individual human being as a person and as a member of a community ought to do as a ''right'' action by voluntary means. By using the word ''individual'' as a member of a community, this definition does not make a distinction between ethics and politics. From an Islamic perspective, the study and conduct of politics cannot be separated from the methods of ethics; the need is to determine what ought to be and not to analyze what merely is. Consequently, the conception of ethics here essentially deals with the Islamic perceptions of conduct as an inquiry into the nature of the unity of God, humankind, and nature, and the method of attaining it (Mutahhari, 1985).

Since the Enlightenment, the West gradually divorced religion from secular life. Ethical conduct of everyday life was left to an individual's conscience, as long as the individual's actions did not conflict with the perceived public morality. In Islam, this separation of the religious from the secular sphere did not materialize, and if attempts were made by the late modernizers to do this, the process was never completed. Thus throughout Islamic societies, not only did religion encompass the person wholly but it also shaped the conduct of the individual in general through the application of Islamic socioreligious ethics. In short, whereas modern ethics in the West became predominately social in nature, in Islamic societies ethical power remained social as well as religious. As the Qur'an says: "The noblest of you in the sight of Allah is the best of you in conduct" (49:13). In the Islamic tradition, the term *adab* means discipline of the mind or every praiseworthy conduct by which a person excels.

Until the nineteenth century, Islamic canonical law, Al Shari'a, provided the main if not the complete legal underpinnings of social and economic conduct in Muslim societies. The intimate contact between Islam and modern Western industrial countries, coupled with the process of colonization of substantial parts of Asia and Africa, introduced a number of Western standards and values to these societies. Thus, at the beginning of the twentieth century, with the introduction of modern means of communication, transportation, and technologies, the fields of civil and commercial transaction proved particularly ripe for change and for new methods of conduct.

The first foothold of European law, criminal and commercial, in the Islamic countries (particularly in the Ottoman Empire) was advanced as a result of the system of Capitulations. This system ensured that the European citizens residing in the Middle East and in a large part of Africa would not be governed by the Islamic laws and codes of ethics but by their own laws and traditions. Furthermore, the reform movements such as the Tanzimat in the Ottoman (1839–1876) and the Constitutional in Iran (1906–1911) were indeed direct translations of French and other European codes that tended to establish secularism and injected rules of conduct that were particularly European. In Egypt, that process, from 1875 onward, went even further in the adaptation of European laws, including commercial and maritime law, and it included the enactment of civil codes that were basically modeled on French laws and that contained only a few provisions drawn from Shari'a.

For example, in the fields of journalism and media practices, many Islamic countries adopted the concepts, norms, and legal codes of the West without considering the broader notion of laws and ethics in Islam. It should be remembered that the body of Islamic laws and ethics is classified according to a scale of values: obligatory (*vajeb*); recommended (*mostahab*); permitted (*mobah*); disapproved (*makroh*); and prohibited (*haram*). There is unanimity among the various schools of Islamic jurisprudence in matters such as prohibited and obligatory categories, and the differences are usually regarding the disapproved or undesirable and recommended categories. This is the difference of degree called *"ikhtlaf"* and not the difference of categories or extremes referred to as *"iftragh."* The existence of a unanimous standard is unique to Islamic jurisprudence. The Western study of law and ethics does not fulfill these conditions.

COMMUNICATION AND ETHICAL THINKING AND PRACTICES IN ISLAMIC SOCIETIES

The current ethical thinking and practices in Islamic societies, especially as they might relate to community, communication, and social interactions, are usually based on two different but important dimensions: normative religious ethics as explained in the primary source of Islam, the Qur'an and the traditions (*al-sunna*) of the Prophet and the *Imams*.

Normative secular ethics range from the Greek tradition of popular Platoism to the Persian tradition of giving advice to sultans and wazirs about government and politics to the more contemporary ethical frameworks introduced by the West through "modernization," "development," "industrialization," and "secular humanism."

In the first category, the study of ethical principles in the religious tradition dates back to the eighth and ninth centuries, during which two lines of argument were developed: the rationalists, those who subscribed to rational opinion, *ra'y*, argued that where there is no clear guidance from the Qur'an or tradition, the Islamic judges and lawyers might make their own rational judgments on moral and ethical questions. The traditionalists insisted that ethical and moral judgments can be based only on the Qur'an and tradition. This led to major debates among the various groups, which are well known in the study of the Mu'tazilites, the Asharis, the Shafi'is, and the Hanbalis, who took different positions on the questions of ethics in classical Islam.

In addition to these varied schools of thought, there is also a strong tradition in mainstream Islamic philosophy. This is seen primarily as the contribution of Islamic philosophers on *akhlag* (character) in the works of philosophers such as Farabi (870–950), Ibn Sina or Avicenna (980–1037), and Ibn Rushd or Averroes (1126–1198), all of whom have contributed significantly to our knowledge about the sources of mystical and Sufi and Hellenic traditions in the classical Islamic system of ethics.

However, it was Ibn Khaldun, the father of sociology, who theorized about communication as a social institution that grew according to the need of the community. Social communication in terms of *tabligh* provided a vast number of people from diverse races, languages, and histories with a common forum for participation in a shared culture that was Islam. According to Ibn Khaldun, the states, governments, and political systems of wide power and large authority have their origin in religious principles based either on prophethood and propagation or on a truthful *tabligh* carried out by *khatibis* (orators/communicators) (Khaldun, 1955, pp. 310–316; Khaldun, 1967, pp. 125–127). Ibn Khaldun was one of the first thinkers to point out that communication based on ethics is the web of human society and that the flow of such communication determines the direction and pace of dynamic social development. To him, combinations of the *assabieh* feelings and social communication approach provided a more dynamic view of organizational behavior than can be readily derived from the more conventional concepts of states, hierarchical position, and role, which usually had been used in the discussion of politics, government, and large social organizations. He thus concluded that propagation cannot materialize without group feeling. The relationship of social communication and Islam therefore emerges from the very nature of these two institutions. One is the source of society's values; the other propagates, disseminates, and maintains the value system of society, the *ummah* or community.

In the Islamic tradition of epistemology, the sustained discussion on ethics in Islam has been discussed in the *kalam* literature, the theologian's discussion and debate on the sources of right. What follows is an outline of a number of fundamental Islamic concepts that have been the basis of Islam's communication ethics and sense of community. This outline should be at the heart of any journalistic ethics and duties of Muslim journalists. These concepts are the sources of many of the contemporary social, political, and economic debates in the Muslim world, especially in regard to normative secular ethics and in relation to the influences and values coming from the West and the non-Islamic traditions.

THE THEORY OF *TAWHID*

The first and most fundamental outlook regarding man and the universe in Islam is the theory of *tawhid*, which implies the unity, coherence, and harmony between all parts of the universe. Thus one of the most basic ethical pillars of the Islamic world is born: the existence of purpose in the creation and the liberation and freedom of humankind from bondage and servitude to multiple varieties of non-gods. It stands for the need for exclusive servitude to God, and it negates any communication and messages—intellectual, cultural, economic, or political—that subjugate humankind to creatures. The principle of *tawhid* also negates any right of sovereignty and guardianship of anyone except God over human society. Society can be expected to be free from all deviations and excesses only when its affairs are delegated by a Power Transcendental to an individual or a council of rulers, with a power commensurate with responsibilities within the Islamic legal framework.

Thus all man-made laws and ethical codes that arrogate judgment to themselves, or to any authority or institution other than in obedience or enforcement of "Allah's Own Judgment," are void. Therefore, all man-made laws, communication contents, mass media, and public fora that attempt to put restraints upon Allah's sovereignty must be void as well. The concept of *tawhid*, if exercised, provides the principal guide in drawing the boundaries of political, social, and cultural legitimization by a given communication system. The content of *tabligh* must not be in the direction to create and perpetuate political, social, economic, and cultural idols; nor is it allowed under this principle to promote the cult of personality.

Under the principle of *tawhid*, another fundamental ethical consideration in *tabligh* becomes clear: the destruction of thought structures based on dualism, racialism, tribalism, and familial superiority. The function of communication order in Islamic society, according to the principle, is to break idols, to break the dependence on outsiders, and to set the *ummah* or community in motion toward the future. Thus, one of the important functions of *tabligh* is to destroy myths. In the contemporary world, these myths may include "power," "progress," and "modernization." Personalities that represent these must not be superhumanized and superdefined. One of the dualisms, according to this principle, is the secular notion of the separation of religion and politics.

The principle of *tawhid* also requires the absence of any economic, political, intellectual, or other center, including the media, in which power can be amassed. The freedom of expression, assembly, and the communication media do not have meaning when there is no social accountability on the part of the individual and institutions. The fight against the cult of personality and that of any social institutions associated with it is the fight against the communication system that attempts to propagate it.

An additional consideration under the ethical framework of *tawhid* is to campaign against the material foundations of dualism. Since among the characteristics of dualism is a desire for superiority through wealth, the content of journalism and social communication must not stress the value of wealth over spiritual growth and the elimination of dividing lines and forms.

THE DOCTRINE OF RESPONSIBILITY, GUIDANCE, AND ACTION

A second principle guiding the ethical boundaries of *tabligh* in Islam is the doctrine of *amr bi al-ma'ruf wa nahy'an al munkar*, or "commanding to the right and prohibiting from the wrong." Implicit in this principle is the notion of individual and group responsibility for preparing the succeeding generation to accept the Islamic precepts and make use of them. Muslims have the responsibility of guiding one another, and each generation has the responsibility of guiding the next. The Qur'anic verse explains this: "Call people to the path of your Lord with wisdom and mild exhortation. Reason with them in the most courteous manner. Your Lord best knows those who stray from His path and best knows those who are rightly guided" (16:125). This points out the responsibilities of Muslims in guiding each other, especially those individuals and institutions charged with the responsibilities of leadership and the propagation of Islamic ideals. This includes all of the institutions of social communication such as the press, radio, television, and cinema, as well as the individual citizens of each community.

Thus a special concept of social responsibility theory is designed around the ethical doctrine of "commanding to the right and prohibiting from the wrong." This concept has taken on an extra dimension of its own in the Islamic communities and societies throughout history since Islam as an all-inclusive systematic religion. It is an interrelated set of ideas and realities covering the entire area of human notion and action, beliefs and practices, thought, word, and deed. This is particularly important in light of the fact that Islam is not only a set of theological propositions, as are many other religions, but also is a set of comprehensive legal frameworks that govern every action of the individual in society and in the world at large.

For example, on the social and collective levels, the doctrine has been practiced systematically in the mosque in Islamic societies. The mosque, as a major channel of social and public communication, has been pivotal in spiritual and cultural movements since the days of the Prophet. It has fulfilled not only the role of purification of the soul but also the acquisition of knowledge and public affairs information. Mosques and major universities existed side by side or within one another for many years in Egypt, Iran, Spain, many parts of central Asia, and other Islamic areas. In fact, many mosques were the centers of higher education in the Islamic tradition. Today, in a number of Islamic societies, the systems of "mass communication" have been well integrated within the classical and traditional systems of social communication of the mosque, especially the Friday prayers (Mowlana, 1979, 1985, 1986, 1988). The result has been a high level of organization and mobilization, making the process of political, cultural, economic, and military participation extremely effective.

It is here that the concept of martyrdom (*shahadat*) in Islam and the concept of Holy Struggle (*jihad*) may only be understood if the doctrine of enjoying good and forbidding evil outlined here is properly appreciated. The term *Islam* is derived from the Arabic root *salama*, meaning surrender and peace or peaceful submission to the will of Allah. Thus the concept of martyrdom, like all other Islamic concepts, is fully related to the concept of *tawhid*, or the absolute unity of God, humankind, and the universe. In this sense, under the social responsibility theory of "commanding to the right and prohibiting from the wrong," the concept of *jihad* is no exception. So from an Islamic perspective and ethical framework, martyrdom and struggle cannot be explained purely in terms of intercession and mediation; they should be understood within the framework of the principle of causality and not solely as spiritual mediation. In short, according to Islam, there is no martyrdom without struggle and *tabligh* in the course of Allah.

THE CONCEPT OF COMMUNITY

A third fundamental concept in determining the nature and boundaries of *tabligh* and that of social ethics, particularly as it might relate to the political life of the individual and Islamic society, is *ummah*, or community. The concept of *ummah* transcends national borders and political boundaries. The Islamic community transcends the notion of the modern nation-state system: an Islamic community is a religio-economic concept and is only present when it is nourished and governed by Islam. The notion of community in Islam makes no sharp distinction between public and private. Therefore, what is required of the community at large is likewise required of every individual member. Accordingly, the *ummah* must be exemplary, setting the highest standards of performance and the reference point for others. It must avoid excesses and extravagances, be steadfast and consistent, know what to accept and what to reject, and have principles and at the same time remain adaptable to the changing aspect of human life.

Under the concept of *ummah*, race is not accepted as a foundation of the state. Values follow piety, and the social system of Islam is based on equity, justice, and ownership of the people. There is no individual or class of individuals to dominate, exploit, or corrupt the state. Intercultural and international communication (the emphasis here is on nationality and not the nation-state) are the necessary ingredients of Islamic *ummah*. The Qur'an says:

We created you from a single [pair] of a male and a female, and made you into nations and tribes, that you may know each other [not that you may despise each other]. Verily the most honored of you in the sight of God is (he who is) the most righteous of you. (Sura, 49:13)

In the Islamic *ummah* the sovereignty of the "state" belongs to God and not to the ruler or even to the people themselves. The ruler or leaders are only acting executives, chosen by the people to serve them according to the Law of Islam and the concept of *tawhid*. Every citizen in the Islamic "state" is required to offer his or her best advice on common matters and must be entitled to do so. Thus consultative methods in politics are not only recognized but are a moral and an ethical duty of the people and the ruler. Furthermore, man, according to Islam, possesses liberty and free will, so by intervening in the operation of the norms of society and by manipulating them creatively in accordance with the Qur'an and tradition, he may plan and lay foundations for a better future for both the individual and society.

Under the *ummah*, Islam has a new concept of community. One of the most important aspects of *ummah* is that Islam does not differentiate between individual members of its community. Race, ethnicity, tribalism, and nationalism have no place to distinguish one member of the community from the rest. Nationalities, cultural differences, and geographical factors are recognized, but domination based on nationality is rejected. It is the individual and his or her relation to the community that is valued. However, this relationship alone is not the sole purpose in itself; both the individual and society must make their relationship clear to God: are the individuals in society against God or under God? *Ummah*, as a social organization, emphasizes communality and collectivity based on Islamic tenets and not interindividualism. The social contract that becomes the basis of *ummah* is not based on free will of undefined choice but is subject to higher norms: the will of Allah. Communal cohesion is based on divine rights and not on natural rights. The term *theocracy*, often cited in the

West, thus cannot apply to the Islamic community, since the notion of church as an institution is foreign to Islam, which as a religion combines both spiritual and temporal powers. It is an ideology possessing no centralized body, yet its monotheism implies a single global order advocating the universality of moral principles. The *ummah* is beyond the nation-state, in that the notion of community in Islam cannot be compared to the stage series of societal development found in Western community histories—principally that of an independent, incorporated "political community" or "military community."

Modernization movements in Islamic societies over the last 100 years failed in part because they were unable to elaborate a coherent doctrine based on the unity of spiritual and temporal powers, the interconnection of what is known as civil society and the state. Islamic "reformism," despite its idealistic unity, failed to take into account the multidimensional aspects of the society that was the *ummah*. Instead, its political culture, its mode of mobilization, and its administrative framework became ingrained in the concept of the modern nation-state system and its bureaucracy. Attempts were made to shift the models but not the dominant paradigm that stood in contrast to the meaning of the *ummah* (Chay, 1990; Mattelart, 1990; Mowlana & Wilson, 1990; Said, 1978; Schiller, 1990; Shari-ati, 1980; Smythe, 1981; Van Dinh, 1987; Walker, 1984).

It is in this political, spiritual, and ethical framework that journalism must play a pervasive role in the preservation and maintenance of the unity of the Islamic community. Thus communication on both interpersonal and social levels becomes both basic and vital to the functioning of the *ummah*, for it sustains and encourages the integral, harmonious relationship between God, the individual, and society.

THE PRINCIPLE OF *TAQWA*

A fourth principle outlined here to explain the ethical framework of journalism in Islamic societies is the concept of *taqwa*, or, roughly translated, piety. In Islamic societies, *taqwa* is commonly used in reference to individual "fear of God" and the ability to guard oneself against the unethical forces that might control the environment. However, the concept of *taqwa* goes beyond this common notion of piety. It is the individual, spiritual, moral, ethical, and psychological capacity to raise oneself to that higher level that makes a person almost immune from the excessive material desires of the world, elevating the individual to a higher level of prophetic self-consciousness.

The assumption is that human beings possess in their nature a set of divine elements other than the material constituents that exist in animals, plants, and inanimate objects. Human beings are endowed with innate greatness and dignity. Recognizing that freedom of choice is a condition for the fulfillment of obligation, the person is held responsible for performing his or her obligations within the Islamic framework of ethics. In short, it is recognized that human beings perform some of their actions only under the influence of a series of ethical emotions rather than with the intention of gaining a benefit or repelling a harm. Thus as a virtue and as an important element in the ethical framework of Islamic communication, both on the individual and community levels, *taqwa* should be the underpinning ingredient in almost every action of a Muslim.

For example, fasting is an institution that has been practiced by different peoples in different times and places. In modern times, fasting has taken the two extreme forms of either ritualism and hunger strikes or dieting. Islamic fasting, however, is different in the sense that if it does not emanate from and lead to *taqwa*, it cannot be regarded as fasting. The Qur'an says: "O, you believers and faithful, fasting is prescribed for you as it was prescribed for those before you in order that you may develop *taqwa* [piety]" (2:183). On the leadership level of the *ummah* and community, it is the high level of *taqwa* that must be valued and counted most. Technical knowledge, managerial ability, scientific know-how, communication skills, and so on, if not associated with *taqwa*, cannot and should not be the sole criteria for promotion in an Islamic context. In the Islamic tradition, the conduct of politics and journalism is associated with *taqwa*, and those who do not possess a degree of *taqwa* face a crisis of legitimacy.

THE MEANING OF *AMANAT*

The fifth and final principle outlined in this chapter is the concept of *amanat*. The term *amanat* signifies the great responsibility that the Almighty God has imposed on the human being for his or her deeds in this world. The most relevant view of this concept as it may apply to the conduct of the press and the media is that *amanat* refers to Divine Vicegerency, for which human beings alone are fit, and no one else can share this honor with them. The Qur'an says: "Surely, we offered the 'Amanat' into the heavens and the earth and the hills, but they refused to hear it and were afraid of it, and man took it up. Verily, he (man) was unjust, and ignorant" (xxxiii:72).

Thus human beings' fitness for Divine Vicegerency is lower, conditioned by the fact that they must practice the lofty code of morality that brings them to the supreme being. Of all the created beings, human beings are certainly the best and noblest (*Ashraf-ul-makhlughat*). Here it may be noted that rights and obligations are interdependent. Serving the public interest, therefore, becomes one of the principal ethical duties of the media.

Amanat means obligatory duties (*fara'iz*). One aspect of *amanat* is that it can only be given to one who has the capability and power to shoulder the burden of its responsibilities and to fulfill the commandments of Allah. Thus, in Islam, real progress is moral and not just material, for the latter refers to the transitory things of life. Liberty in Islam has quite a different meaning from that understood in the West. It is neither a prerogative nor an absolute right of the individual.

CONCLUSION

An attempt has been made here to evaluate the Islamic implications of our knowledge of the dynamics of communication ecology. A number of concepts have been introduced and examined in order to understand the phenomenon of communication and ethics in an Islamic context. It was shown that Muslim thinkers and philosophers throughout history not only recognized the importance of communication and ethics in determining the cultural profile of the Islamic civilization but also regarded the propitious equilibrium of spatial and temporal biases in Islam as an established fact. Over the last century, however, and especially during the last four decades, a dualism and contradiction have been created within the Islamic countries as a result of the introduction of the secular nationalist framework and the accompanying new concepts and methods of communication and ethics. A crisis of legitimacy has been created as a result of a conflict between the "official culture" of the ruling elites, which in many cases now represents and promotes Western influence, and the "traditional Islamic culture" of the masses, rooted in centuries of religio-political and socioethical experience.

Nowhere is this communication and ethical conflict better illustrated than in the structure and use of the means of communication at the disposal of both cultures. The overwhelming evidence suggests that Muslim societies have, by and large, not responded positively to modern communication ethics coming from outside their own culture, nor in the post-colonial Muslim world has the political and communication system acquired from the West gained a broad popular base. On the contrary, such political and communication systems have become increasingly authoritarian, dictatorial, and military. Thus, as stated earlier, in Muslim societies today, two competing and mutually exclusive ethical methods and frameworks exist: the imported political culture of the ruling classes and the indigenous political culture of the Muslim masses.

A look at the premodernist reform movements of the eighteenth and nineteenth centuries that swept over a large part of the Muslim world might offer some lessons. These movements were generated from the heart of the Islamic world itself and were directed toward correcting social evils and raising the moral standards of the community. Such movements appealed to the Muslims to awaken and liberate themselves from Western economic, political, military, and cultural domination and to carry out the necessary internal reforms that would create ethical and moral regeneration and strength. It would be a mistake to consider these movements as being primarily the result of Western influence on the Muslim world. All of these movements, without exception, emphasized a return to the tradition and ethics of Islam (Christians, Ferre, & Fackler, 1993; Cooper, Christians, Plude, & White, 1989; Merrill, 1997; Mowlana, 1994, 1996; *Sahifeh Noor*, n.d., 1361–1365; Schlesinger & Mowlana, 1993). The current movements in the Islamic world are simply a continuation of the premodernist movements that tried to resolve contradictions created by exogenous forces.

Here the central question is not one of economics but of culture, ethics, and *tabligh*. It is in this context that contemporary movements in the Islamic lands must be studied and understood. The question that Muslims have to answer, therefore, is how best to devise structural changes and institutional setups that would help maintain the precious communication and ethical balance that traditionally has been part of the Islamic civilization.

As outlined elsewhere, the crucial question for Islamic societies is whether the emerging global information communication community is a moral and an ethical community or is just another stage in the unfolding pictures of the transformation in which the West is the center and the Islamic world is the periphery. Throughout Islamic history, especially in the early centuries, information was not a commodity but a moral and an ethical imperative. Thus through an Islamic perspective, it seems that linguistic and political vocabularies and concepts, now at the center of global politics, both celebrate the arrival of a new communication age and hold the key to ultimate information control.

REFERENCES

Balagha, N. (1971). *Sermons, letters and sayings of Hazrat Ali* (S.M.A. Jafery, Trans.). Elmhurst, NY: Tahrike Tarsile Quran.

Chay, C. (Ed.). (1990). *Culture and international relations*. New York: Praeger.

Cherry, C. (1961). *On human communication*. Cambridge, MA: MIT Press.

Christians, C., Ferre, J., & Fackler, M. (1993). *Good news: Social ethics and the press*. New York: Oxford University Press.

Cooper, T. W., Christians, C. G., Plude, F. F., & White, R. A. (1989). *Communication ethics and global change*. White Plains, NY: Longman.

Ellul, J. (1965). *Propaganda: The formation of men's attitudes*. New York: Vintage Books.

Khaldun, I. (1955). *The mugaddimah* (M. P. Gonabadi, Trans.). Tehran, Iran: Bongahe Tarjumeh va Nashreh Ketab.

Khaldun, I. (1967). *The introduction to history: The mugaddimah* (N. J. Dogwood, Ed.; F. Rosenthal, Trans.). London: Routledge and Kegan Paul.

Kirschenmann, P. P. (1970). *Information and reflection: On some problems of cybernetics and how contemporary dialectical materialism copes with them*. Dordrecht, the Netherlands: D. Reidel.

Kroeber, A. L. & Parsons, T. (1958). The concepts of culture and of social systems. *American Sociological Review, 23*: 582–583.

Lasswell, H. D. (1942). Communication research and politics. In D. Waples (Ed.), *Print, radio, and film in a democracy* (pp. 105–106). Chicago: University of Chicago Press.

Lasswell, H. D., Lerner, D., & Speier, H. (Eds.). (1980). *Propaganda and communication in world history* (Vols. 1–3). Honolulu, HI: University of Hawaii Press.

Lenin, V. I. (1935–1939). *Selected works II* (J. Fineberg, Ed.). New York: Macmillan.

Mattelart, A. (1990). *Communication and class struggle, 3: New historical subjects*. New York: International General.

Merrill, J. C. (1997). *Philosophical foundations for news media.* New York: St. Martin's Press.

Mowlana, H. (1979, Summer). Technology versus tradition: Communication in the Iranian revolution. *Journal of Communication, 29*(3): 107–112.

Mowlana, H. (1985). Communication for political change: The Iranian revolution. In G. Gerbner & M. Siefert (Eds.), *World Communication, A handbook* (pp. 294–301). New York: Longman.

Mowlana, H. (1986). *Global information and world communication: New frontiers in international relations.* White Plains, NY: Longman.

Mowlana, H. (1988). Mass media systems and communication. In M. Adams (Ed.), *The Middle East: A handbook* (pp. 825–839). London: Muller, Blond and White.

Mowlana, H. (1994). Civil society, information society, and Islamic society. In S. Splichal, A. Calabrese, & C. Sparks (Eds.), *Information society and civil society: Contemporary perspectives on the changing world order* (pp. 208–232). West Lafayette, IN: Purdue University Press.

Mowlana, H. (1996). *Global communication in transition: The end of diversity.* Thousand Oaks, CA: Sage.

Mowlana, H. & Wilson, L. (1990). *The passing of modernity: Communication and the transformation of society.* White Plains, NY: Longman.

Mutahhari, M. (1982). *Majmoe ghoftarha* [Collection of Speeches]. Tehran, Iran: Sadra Publications.

Mutahhari, M. (1985). *Fundamentals of Islamic thought: God, man, and the universe* (R. Campbell, Trans.). Berkeley, CA: Mizau Press.

Sahifeh Noor: Majmoe rahnemood ha'i Imam Khomeini (Vols. 1–18). (n.d.). Tehran, Iran: Vezarate Ershad Islami.

Said, E. (1978). *Orientalism.* White Plains, NY: Vintage Press.

Schiller, H. I. (1990). *Culture, Inc.* New York: Oxford.

Schlesinger, P. & Mowlana, H. (Eds.). (1993, January). Islam and Communication [Special Issue]. *Media, Culture and Society, 15*(1).

Shannon, C. E. & Weaver, W. (1961). *The mathematical theory of communication.* Urbana, IL: University of Illinois Press.

Shari-ati, A. (1980). *Marxism and other Western fallacies* (R. Campbell, Trans.). Berkeley, CA: Mizan Press.

Smythe, D. W. (1981). *Dependency road: Communications, capitalism, consciousness, and Canada.* Norwood, NJ: Ablex.

Van Dinh, T. (1987). *Independence, liberation, revolution: An approach to the understanding of the Third World.* Norwood, NJ: Ablex.

Walker, R.B.J. (Ed.). (1984). *Culture, ideology, and world order.* Boulder, CO: Westview.

Wiener, N. (1961). *Cybernetics, or control and communication in animal and the machine* (new ed.). Cambridge, MA: MIT Press.

Wiener, N. (1967). *The human use of human beings: Cybernetics and society.* New York: Avon Press.

Chapter 10

Confucian Conflicts in Singaporean Advertising: A Case Study of the "Wonder Bra" Campaign

Linda K. Fuller

Singapore's advertising can best be described as a progressive and controversial element in the Republic's mass media mix. Indeed, advertising stands as one of the many paradoxes that help characterize Singapore's diverse culture. The reason for this paradox may be that some of the values communicated through advertising pull it in opposite directions. The result is a unique Singapore institution that is caught between two competing value systems. On the one hand are a predominantly Chinese population and government steeped in centuries of Confucian tradition. On the other hand, however, are the values imposed by British colonial masters, the English language itself, industrialization, urbanization, Western popular culture, and advertising agencies with names such as Leo Burnett and Ogilvy and Mather (Martin & Sengupta, 1996, p. 6).

Confucianism serves simultaneously, if at times awkwardly, as both a critical strength and a source of concern in the Singaporean business scene. Potential conflicts occur most noticeably in the field of advertising. This chapter describes and discusses the Republic of Singapore in terms of its historical background, particularly with regard to Asian values, the role of Confucianism in Singapore, and Singaporean advertising—focusing on a recent "Wonder Bra" campaign.

SINGAPORE AND ASIAN VALUES

It seems instructive to begin this discussion by briefly reviewing Singapore's history. Singapore was a colonial power dominated by the British for some 150 years. It was conquered by the Japanese during World War II. Singapore has been independent only since 1965. Since 1965, Singapore has been under the leadership of Lee Kuan Yew and his People's Action Party (PAP). It is currently led by his designated successor, Prime Minister Goh Chok Tong. The "Singapore Success Story'' under the Lee Kuan Yew regime is well documented (Bellows, 1989; Chua & Kuo, 1995; Fuller, in press; Quah, 1990).

While Singapore's political legacy has helped its people understand Western cultural ideals, in terms of the country's own nation-building it has drawn on its mostly Chinese traditions. In developing its own unique culture, however, it has mostly depended on the economics of the workplace. Priding itself on being the most corruption-free state in Asia, with strict laws against bribery, the government operates with unspoken adherence to Confucian principles.

Yet with the creeping materialism and consumption that accompanied economic successes beginning in the late 1970s, fear began surfacing that a check on individualism might be needed. Singapore's poet laureate, Edwin Thumboo, writes:

Given the achievement that has been attained and the far-flung benefits that have been accrued, the Singaporean has gained self-esteem, is confident—at times overly so among some—ambitious, on the make. He travels widely, carrying his lap-top computer and his confidence with him. (1989, p. 766)

That national characteristic even has a name for itself: Kiasuism.

Translated literally as "fear of losing," a term borrowed from the dialect of Hokkien Chinese, Kiasuism is described as aggressive behavior exemplified by gluttonous waste at buffet tables, taking more than one seat in a bus, lining up days in advance before new properties were booked, enrolling children in a popular school, stampeding for freebies, reserving tables at several restaurants, and/or pushing to be first in line. (Fuller, in press)

Bremer (1988), who performed the first serious study of the Kiasu phenomenon, offered this explanation:

Kiasuism may be defined as an attitude by which a person undergoes, on the one hand, extreme disquiet if he discovers that he has not got full value for his expenditure of money, time and effort, and on the other, a distinct sense of exhilaration if he discovers that he has got much more than full value for that expenditure. The ultimate distress is when he has got nothing for something, and the ultimate joy when he has got something for nothing. (p. 44)

Bremer suggests several theories for the Kiasuer's behavior: a "hoarding instinct" theory that comes from peasant ancestors; a "second echelon eaters" theory that comes from waiting for the gods, or elders, or even hungry ghosts to go first; and a "raiding instinct" theory that comes from historical exploits of looting and plundering. As such an uncomplimentary adjective, albeit oftentimes used alternatively for humorous self-derision (e.g., Dhaliwal, 1994) or as a signal for a need for civil graciousness (Kestral, 1996), perhaps the most intriguing aspect of Kiasuism is the Singaporean reaction to it and the fact that this national trait has become incorporated into its own form of popular culture (Fuller, 1996e).

Local advertisers, quick to pick up on emerging trends, have incorporated some national symbols of Kiasuism into some of their promotions. McDonald's, for example, which operates 66 restaraunts across the island, incorporated the concept into a recent campaign by offering bigger-than-average Kiasuburgers in buns with, of course, extra sesame seeds. And the Comix Factory, a comic book publisher operated by a group calling itself The Kuppies (Kiasu Urban Professionals), has been extremely successful, reporting revenues of $344,235 in 1994.

In 1990, in response to concerns about pro-Western sentiments and the "deculturation" on the part of some citizens, the government formally proposed a White Paper describing Singapore's five shared values:

1. Nation before community and society before self;
2. Family as the basic unit of society;
3. Consensus instead of community;
4. Racial and religious harmony; and
5. Regard and community support for the individual.

At a deeper level, it becomes increasingly clear that the "values" discussion is applicable to a number of issues. Felix Stravens (1996), executive director of the Institute of Advertising for the Republic of Singapore, points out that although the government recognizes that the country will become even more international in scope, it nevertheless wants to maintain its own culture. Toward that end, the following list cites what those in power consider good and bad Asian and Western values:

- Bad Asian values: caste system of Hindu culture; inferior status of women; practice of nepotism; tradition of authoritarian rulers; parental shame toward children with disabilities and general lack of sympathy for the disabled; attitude of subservience to those in authority; and the deep-rooted Chinese belief that "good boys" should never be soldiers.

- Good Asian values: work ethic; thrift; strong family ties and support; modesty and humility; respect for education; respect for one's elders, teachers, and righteous rulers; and communitarian values.

- Bad Western values: too much emphasis on the rights and interests of the individual and too little emphasis on the rights and interests of the community and state; lack of respect for one's elders, teachers, and upright rulers; mistaken belief that competition in education is bad; inability to make sacrifices in the short term for long-term benefits; excessive materialism and hedonism; and living beyond one's means.

- Good Western values: political system based on democracy; independent judiciary; rule of law; civil service based on merit and free of corruption; equal rights for women; pursuit of science and technology; management based on merit, teamwork, and delegation of power; punctuality and public hygiene; empathy with and support for the disabled; and the egalitarian belief of affording equality with opportunity to all (Stravens, 1996, pp. 277–278).

In terms of consumer segmentation, both demographic and psychographic variables have been identified. Singapore has a fairly young population; the median age in 1993 was 31 years. According to the Department of Statistics, for that same year, the monthly personal income median was nearly $1,000. Stravens has identified 10 groups, based on their characteristics and motivations:

1. "Traditional Chinese," which includes most businesspeople;
2. "Modern Malays," a young, family-centered group;
3. "Comfortable Careerists";
4. "Hard-pressed Providers";
5. "Possession Paraders," which mostly includes the administrative class;
6. "The Dependent Matriarchs," older housewives;
7. The "Bo Chaps," an apathetic, underachieving group;
8. The "Disaffected," who hold lower-status jobs;
9. The *"Jing Di Wa"* (Frogs in the Well), a mixed ethnic population that, like the captured frogs, lives insular lives; and
10. The "Brat Pack," an upwardly mobile group somewhat anti-establishment in its orientation, but it is expected that these members will return to their roots and become model affluent citizens (1996, pp. 279–281).

Claiming that Singaporean political culture as officially proclaimed is artificial, with a cornerstone of its Asian values really meaning Confucianism, Asuncion-Lande and Lande (1995) point out how the country's leaders draw mainly from the aspects of ancient Chinese tradition that best serve their ethnic pride and political needs, simply assuming that Singapore's minorities (i.e., the Muslim Maylays and Hindu Tamils) will comply. According to the Singaporean polity, in contrast to the decadent West, Asian values stress a number of hierarchical aspects integral to Confucianism—specifically filial piety and obedience and deference to governmental authority.

SINGAPOREAN CONFUCIANISM

In addition to being multiethnic, multiracial (75 percent Chinese, 15 percent Malay, 10 percent Indian), and multilinguistic, the nearly 3 million residents of Singapore are also multireligious. Well over half are Taoists and/or Buddhists, two faiths that typically are intertwined with Confucianism and are by no means mutually exclusive. Some 15 percent of the population is Muslim, 10 percent is Christian, and 7 percent is Hindu. Although for the most part Singaporeans enjoy freedom of worship and are encouraged to be tolerant of others' religious choices, in 1990, the Singapore Parliament passed a "Maintenance of Religious

Harmony'' law permitting the government to silence or imprison without trial any members of religious groups with whom it disagreed (Ross, 1990). A classic example of this is the Jehovah's Witnesses, whose members and literature have been banned there for the last quarter century (Solomon, 1997).

While it would be presumptuous to attempt a thorough examination of Confucianism, a basic understanding is important to the current discussion. Confucianism is based on the life of self-educated Confucius (551–479 B.C.), and it represents a way of life followed, mostly by Chinese people, for more than 2,000 years. A philosophical approach to life, an ethical code of personal conduct, and an inspirational form of religion with its own rituals, deities, and temples, Confucianism has been considered one of the greatest forces for social stability in world history. The idea, based in classical Confucian thought on the Chinese character ''jen,'' is that wisdom, or sagedom, is achieved through self-cultivation and inner enlightenment, which then translates to loving others. After steps have been taken for individual growth, concern for society comes next— first the family, then the state, and eventually the whole world. Rights are subsumed under obligations, and expectations for social responsibilities are an expected part of the humanistic creed. By extension, moral qualities such as virtue and righteousness are expected in a ruler.

Writing of *Confucianism and the Chinese Family in Singapore*, Kuo (1987) says that Confucian ethics and Confucian social order are based on the institution of family—consisting of filial piety, ancestral worship, family continuity, and an extended kinship network. The Overseas Chinese feel isolated in Singapore, which they see as being influenced by a number of modernizing social trends:

1. urbanization and urban renewal

2. public housing policies

3. industrialization and economic development

4. family planning and population policies

5. mass education and the promotion of English

Kuo notes a number of incompatibilities, such as achievement is valued more than ascription and birth; the family loses its role as status-conferer; nepotism is frowned upon in modern bureaucracy; geographical and social mobility can weaken kinship ties; women make up more of the workforce; daughters are valued and treated more equitably; and patriarchal power is challenged as family relationships become more symmetrical and reciprocal rather than authoritarian and obligatory. ''Culture is seen here as a dynamic organism,'' he concludes, ''and tradition and modernity should eventually find a balance to reach a synthesis'' (Kuo, 1987, p. 24).

Confucian education has remained a top priority of the Republic since its founding, some three decades ago. Early in 1982, a curriculum stressing moral education, or Confucian Ethics, was introduced (Tay, 1982) as an option for secondary school students' required Religious Knowledge course. Prime Minister Lee Kuan Yew was quoted as declaring,

Confucianism was part of the Chinese school environment, the fables and parables recounted over and over again in books and through the teachers and encapsulated in sparkling sayings and succinct epigrams.... The doctrines and philosophy of Confucianism in the Chinese school syllabus are spread in textbooks on Chinese language, Chinese literature and Chinese history. (*Straits Times*, 1982)

Understandably, there was backlash from some minority Singaporeans who resisted the campaign. Some citizens wondered if it was not part of a government threat, or even a conspiracy, to boost Chinese culture and reinforce its dominance. "With the support and cooperation of government offices, the mass media, and Chinese voluntary organizations, Confucianism was extended from the school level to the societal level and was promoted as a form of a revitalization movement," wrote Kuo (1992, p. 10). Following some entanglements, particularly regarding national identity, Confucian ethics per se were eventually replaced in 1990 by the government-initiated "White Paper for Shared Values," cited earlier. Sensitive to accusations of imposing Chinese Confucian values on the non-Chinese community, it nevertheless stressed that Confucian precepts and practices that had evolved from a rural, agricultural society needed revision for the current urban, industrial society.

Kuo (1992) asks some probing questions. Can Confucianism, or some of its selected elements, be packaged in a changing context and environment and remain relevant to the evolving, new economic, political, and cultural order? In other words, can such selected and reinterpreted Confucian values be made compatible with an urban-industrial social structure and fit in the larger social system of Singapore society? If they can, they will eventually be incorporated into the evolving value system in contemporary Singapore. As and when that happens, of course, it becomes inconsequential to argue whether such values are Confucian, Singaporean, Asian, or universal (Kuo, 1992, p. 22).

SINGAPOREAN ADVERTISING

Singapore, the world's ninth richest country, is ranked second to the United States in world competitiveness by the International Institute for Management Development (IMD). Its robust economy often has been referred to as "The Singapore, Inc." model. "Competitiveness has resulted in dramatic improvements in the standard of living," according to the government-run newspaper *Straits Times* (Latif, 1996). In 1997, the editors of the *Wall Street Journal* and the Heritage Foundation saw fit to single out Singapore as scoring highest in "economic liberty," based on qualities such as its efficient, strike-free labor force, no minimum wage, and no antitrust regulations.

Continually rising, Asian advertising revenues were recently valued at approximately $254.5 million (Asian ad revenue, 1996, p. 11). Even more impressive is the fact that in 1993, expenditures for advertising reached $14 billion in nine East Asian countries, including China. That number increases to $47 billion if Japan is included (Naisbett, 1996, p. 106).

Advertising, one of Singapore's fastest-growing industries, is fueled by highly positive economic growth rates due to the country's growing affluence. Its advertising stands as a $740-plus billion industry (Tan & Soh, 1994, p. 166). Most agencies, joining public relations firms and design studios, are located in the restored shophouses of Singapore's Chinatown (Saini, 1996) and are positioned to target specific market niches (Wee, 1994). The Yellow Pages of the 1996 Singapore telephone book contained some 400 advertising agencies, many of which also double as public relations businesses.

Operating in the same open-door/free marketplace that allows foreign investment companies, advertising agencies are still under the governance of the Singapore Code of Advertising Practice and the Singapore Broadcasting Corporation Programme Code and, as such, they must prescribe to the following rules:

1. ordinary good taste and common sense;
2. respect for the law, religious beliefs, and social institutions;
3. respect for the individual opinions of the public; and
4. proper regard for the special needs of children.

"Through legal control, political maneuvering and structural arrangements, the Singapore government exerts considerable influence over the operation of the mass media" (Hao, 1995, p. 5). "Over the years, a stable hegemonic state-media relationship has evolved whereby the role of the media is prescribed as pro-development and hence pro-government, in the name of national security and public interest" (p. 5).

While for the most part Singaporean advertisers, advertising agencies, and major media owners[1] are said to practice self-endorsed voluntary controls, in actuality, higher governmental laws and regulations dictate advertising practices. Monitoring and enforcement is mainly under the auspices of the Department of Customs and Excise, the Ministry of the Environment, and the Ministry of Health. Since 1976, when it was formed by the Consumers' Association of Singapore (CASE), the Advertising Standards Authority of Singapore (ASAS) has operated to protect consumers from misleading, misrepresentative, and/or offensive advertisements. An advisory council to CASE, its members represent the following media-controlling organizations:

• Advertising Media Owners' Association of Singapore
• Association of Accredited Advertising Agents, Singapore
• Consumers' Association of Singapore

- Ministry of the Environment
- Ministry of Health
- Pharmaceutical Society of Singapore
- Singapore Advertiser's Association
- Singapore Association of Pharmaceutical Industries
- Singapore Broadcasting Corporation
- Singapore Manufacturers' Association
- Singapore Medical Association

Although not a government body, and thereby lacking any legal jurisdiction, the ASAS nevertheless is capable of preventing or stopping offensive advertising from appearing in Singapore. In response to criticisms about how it could be objective when it was set up by the very industry it is meant to monitor, the ASAS was constructed so that not more than half of its council would be advertiser connected. Guided by the Singapore Code of Advertising Practice, whose prescriptions are listed above, the ASAS also prides itself on responding to consumer and competitor complaints. Ultimately, control resides in the government-run media itself—which decides what space is available for particular advertisements. As an example, see the appendix at the end of this chapter for a listing of rules governing the Singapore Broadcasting Corporation.

Wee (1994) notes Singapore's young community and its consumer-led popular culture are influenced by advertising. He finds trendy teens everywhere sporting high-fashion couturier names. He wonders, "Is fashion consumption (along with cinema-going) one of the chief ways youths have of finding fantasy or meaning in Singapore, a place still said to be 'dull' even by many residents of the country?" Young people joke, tongue in cheek, about their quest for the "3 Cs:" luxury car, luxury condo, and gold credit card.

Confucianism often is considered in the development of an advertising campaign. One famous campaign deals with the children's supplement drink known as Sustagen. In the advertisement, a young Chinese boy argues for Sustagen from his father. The boy says, "Come on, Dad. If you can play golf five times a week, I can have Sustagen once a day." After a media outcry, and after the campaign was singled out by the prime minister as part of his 1994 National Day Rally Speech, the ad was pulled. Quantas terminated a radio commercial dealing with its discounted airfares that ended with a husband calling his wife "the last of the big spenders" when it was deemed to portray waste. When McDonald's put together a promo for the Chinese New Year, it included the whole Singaporean family, including grandparents and other extended kin, rather than be accused of being insensitive to the country's value system. Also, a number of billboards in the country deal with Confucianism itself—typically featuring Chinese characters and their translations along with some kind of abstract design. A particularly telling example is the Mass Rapid Transit (MRT) billboard, in which a Confucian statement is juxtaposed with a stylized ad for jeans and the MaXimizer push-up bra. This advertisement is the focus of the case study that follows.

While advertising clearly has become a major industry and, therefore, also a major means of influence in Singapore, Birch (1993) points out that foreign investment brings with it threats to "both Singapore's economic success and its own sense of being an Asian society" (p. 63). Western models are featured in ads, bans on cigarettes and tobacco advertising are difficult to enforce in foreign magazines, and joint ventures muddle the works. Consider, however, the biggest issue of all. Through its very purpose, advertising appeals to the individual—a confusing conundrum for persons primed to consider nation before self.

SINGAPOREAN ADVERTISEMENTS AIMED AT WOMEN

Wong and Leong (1993) point out that Singaporean women are increasingly taking their place alongside their male counterparts as an important advertising target. Along with women in Japan and in other affluent Asian countries, Singaporean women remain quite vulnerable to advertising appeals. Until recently, those messages were mainly aimed at housewives. The editor of Singapore's popular women's magazine *Her World* blames advertising for perpetuating the homemaker stereotypes (Lin, 1993, p. 109). Advertising also is blamed for women wanting cosmetic enhancements such as breast enlargements, eye and nose jobs, and hair transplants (More Thais, 1996).

As key consumers, women worldwide are often the target of advertising, and Singapore women are no exception (Fuller, 1996a, 1996b, 1996d, 1996e). While some people consider those appeals part of conspiracies by media industries as bastions of male privilege to keep women and minorities down (e.g., Faludi, 1992; Kissling, 1995; Wolf, 1991), economics clearly plays a key role. Increasingly, the commodification of women is becoming standard practice. The idea is not only to sell women products but also to sell women themselves as products. Macdonald (1995) phrases the argument this way:

The body has historically been much more integral to the formation of identity for women than for men. If women had defined for themselves the ideals of their bodily shape or decoration, this would not be problematic. It is the denial of this in the history of western cultural representation, in medical practice, and in the multi-billion dollar pornography, fashion, and cosmetic industries, that has granted women only squatters' rights to their own bodies. (Macdonald, 1995, p. 193)

Buslig et al. (1996) analyzed portrayals of women, predominantly shown in submissive and exploited roles, in 18 magazine advertisements and found a dangerous link between those images and harmful eating disorders. Comparing models of 1994 to those of 1954, they found a progressive pattern toward thinness. Ninety-three percent of recent models were ectomorphs, the thinnest somatotype body category. Six percent of that number fell into the thinnest subcategory of ectomorphic body shape. In 1954, only 39 percent was ectomorphic.

Monitoring of Singaporean media for the first six months of 1996 revealed that advertising appeals covered every part of a woman's body, literally from head to toe—"Total Beauty, Under One Roof," a local health center claimed. A slimming center offered an herbal weight loss plan to help get rid of inches, while another featured a "Fat Displacement System" that was paid for by the kilo. A Singaporean pharmacy offered a "Your Body, Your Image" workshop, appealing to women who might hate how they look, who were depressed about having to get into shape and concerned over giving off the wrong signals in social situations.

In a full-page color ad in the only Singapore newspaper, Vidal Sassoon hints, with a sense of disgust, "Do you have Asian hair?" The ad then goes on to read,

Asian hair differs from Western hair in many ways and it is essential to use a product that suits you—giving the salon look even at home! Asian hair differs from Western hair and tends to be:

• Straighter

• Longer, and therefore more susceptible to damage

• On average approximately one third thicker

• Less full and less structured

Many advertisements appeal to women's lack of self-esteem. One company offers an eight-week collagen treatment specifically designed for Asian women. It declares, "Without sufficient collagen tissue, the skin loses its elasticity and pre-mature wrinkle formation will appear . . . from age 23!" A local television personality confesses to using a whitening toothpaste as the secret behind her "winning smile." However, the most frightening of all was the plethora of messages for face whiteners, Carita's Whitening Cleansing Cream ($53 for 125 ml), Kose's Medicated Sekkisei ($90 for 200 ml), Shiseido's Whiteness Essence ($149 for 30 g), and Institute Esthemderm's Whitening Buffing Mask ($45 for 75 ml), Whitening Day Cream ($56 for 50 ml), and Whitening Night Cream ($83 for 50 ml). From a number of feminist perspectives (e.g., Bordo, 1990; Butler, 1990; Fuller, 1996c; Goffman, 1979; Marshall, 1996), advertising aimed at Singaporean women presents classic cases for analysis.

CASE STUDY: THE WONDER BRA

In its review of 1994's most remarkable accomplishments, *U.S. News and World Report* cited the Middle East peace accord, the Republican majority in the U.S. Congress, the end of the white-minority rule in South Africa, and the

Wonder Bra (Breakthroughs: The feats, 1994). Furthermore, as of 1997, there were some 607 Websites devoted to the Wonder Bra.

"History does not record whether Confucius ever considered the Wonder Bra," *Newsweek* reports:

But today there's bad news from the world of lingerie for Asian leaders who hope that Confucianism's stress on propriety will ward off the West's obsession with sex. Asia's growing class of affluent urban women is eager to flaunt their sexuality. And that has created a boom market for the raciest of G-strings and skimpy push-up bras. The hottest market of all: stuffy Singapore, where graffiti artists are caned and the country's government has outlawed chewing gum. (Elliot, 1996)

Recognizing the role of Western popular culture in transforming still-shy Asian women's notions of beauty, research has suggested a direct relationship between the number of racy ads and women's dissatisfaction with their bodies. While one might have thought that the high-fashion padded bra boom that took off in the United States a few years ago would be irrelevant halfway around the world, sales are booming in Singapore.

Most of the citizenry, following both religious and personal dictates, tend to dress very conservatively. Women, for example, rarely expose their arms, and cleavage is simply unheard of. Despite Singapore's location, just one degree north of the equator, scanty clothing is considered extremely improper. In Singapore's train stations, where many people (oftentimes whole families) jostle together, walking by full-sized billboards of women in Wonder Bras is embarrassing. With all the other strictures of Singapore, these advertising freedoms simply do not make sense.

Triumph International, the first company to create a "made-for-Asia" cleavage-enhancing brassiere, maintains a loyal following, holding some 70 percent of the Singapore market (Ong, 1996). Its "ultimate push-up bra," the MaXimizer Glamour, offers "the ultimate in versatility!" by offering four different removable pads for "discreet support," "natural cleavage," "greater Oomph!" or "the ultimate uplift." It is available at Tangs, one of Singapore's starship department stores, in Silk White, Jet Black, Silver Blue, and Fresh Peach. Another padded push-up bra by Triumph International is its Pour Moi version. The company reported that of the 2.5 million bras it sold in 1995, some 90 percent were padded, and more than half were "bust-boosting styles." In 1994, Ms. Doy Teo, marketing manager for Triumph International, predicted "to further pad the bra business" by at least another 30 percent, or 750,000 bras, in the near future.

Singapore's famous Orchard Road, which has been likened to Fifth Avenue, Regent Street, and the Champs Elysees, offers a shopping mecca for tourists and townspeople alike. Reports reveal that from Robinsons at one end to Isetan Scotts at the other end, "gravity-defying" bra sales continue to do a brisk business.

Seeing the success of Triumph International in Singapore, Britain's Gossard entered the market in 1994. The most recent entry is Playtex's One and Only Wonder Bra. "Because the Asian woman has a different skin tone, is less buxom, has narrower shoulders and a smaller chest, Sara Lee has created a Wonderbra model specifically for the Asian cleavage" (Ong, 1996, p. 2). Shameless appeal to a plunging uplift, however, still features a Caucasian model.

Ranging from $20 to $60+ (noticeably higher in Asia than in the United States), push-up bras are quite intricately constructed, boasting some 50 component parts and various removable and tuck-in features. The idea, the manufacturers say, is a "cup-runneth-over" effect. Singaporean women, whether teenagers or grandmothers, are buying into it. Fradric Teo, division manager of Siber-Hegner, the local Wonder Bra distributor who set a 1997 budget of $200,000 for promotion said, "There are still more women who fear going under the scalpel for a good figure than faking what nature has given them with a good old-fashioned bra" (Ong, 1996, p. 2).

Advertising Age (Koranteng & Bruner, 1996) has reported protests to revealing push-up bra advertisements in Mexico and the United Kingdom. As a result of these protests, Playtex changed Wonder Bra billboard advertisements in Monterey, Mexico, which featured a sexy blonde. Similar advertisements in Mexico City were not changed. In the United Kingdom, the large number of complaints about billboard advertisements for Gossard Holding's Glossies bras prompted the United Kingdom's Advertising Standards Authority to undertake an investigation. The investigation determined that the billboards did not violate advertising standards.

The surprising thing about the padded push-up bra campaign in Singapore is the absence of negative coverage. So where do the principles of Confucianism fit in?

IMPLICATIONS

In a country where Buddhism currently claims the largest numbers, where certain religious groups have been banned, and where Christianity (especially Roman Catholicism) is the fastest-growing religion, the underlying pervasive role of Confucianism is still not to be discounted. At the same time, while some worry about the incursion of advertising in Asia as a catalyst toward the acceptance of Western values (Jewell, 1993; Fuller, 1996a; Martin & Sengupta, 1996), several related issues emerge: how to maintain equilibrium among multireligious Singaporeans, how to teach youngsters to critically evaluate the messages that they are being fed by the media for ever-slimmer figures and trendier outfits, how to encourage the use of local, native models for advertising and public relations campaigns, and how to balance governmental imperatives with the basic Confucian emphasis on simple lifestyles.

Women in Singapore, as elsewhere, seem susceptible to glitzy advertising. Marcia Ann Gillespie, editor of *Ms.* magazine, stated:

In a world where women bear the brunt of the beauty hype and hundreds of millions of dollars are spent in pursuit of this ideal . . . I can't forget the high price we've paid. Women have had ribs removed, their feet bound, their thighs suctioned, their breasts siliconed. Women get lifted and tucked and snipped and tightened, and have their faces totally recast. Girls and women binge and purge and starve themselves until their bodies fail. (Springen, 1996, p. 69)

One is reminded of Marshall McLuhan's prediction of a global world tied together by common media perceptions, a concept that seems plausible as multinational conglomerates become the norm. Lazier-Smith's (1989, p. 258) prophetic words strike with resonance: "Status quo ad messages come from another basic source—work routines and traditions in advertising agencies."

Yet Singapore's wholehearted appreciation of Western popular culture should not be mistaken for an acceptance of the value system from whence it comes. Its embrace of Western music and hamburgers hardly means that it agrees with Western philosophies. To think otherwise about notions of "cultural imperialism" in Singapore is to completely miss the point. What remains intriguing, still, is that decision making might, in fact, have some effect on political ideologies.

In the case of Confucianism vis-à-vis the demands of the socially created institution of advertising, the Singapore situation stands as a classic example of conflicting loyalties.

The Confucian emphasis on community is diametrically opposite to individualism as we often understand the term. . . . Confucianism conceives of the self neither as an isolated atom nor as a single, separate individuality, but as being in a relationship. . . . Each relationship contributes to the development and overall constitution of self. (Tu, 1984, p. 5)

If that is truly the case, how does one allow for the sterling success of the "Wonder Bra" campaign?

Looked at in microcosm, the examples here of hedonistic appeals to women in the midst of evolving self-esteem levels bring together the themes of this book in terms of religious and regulative constraints. Kuo (1992, p. 13) has commented on how top-down implementation of Confucianism is "compatible with the dominant political culture in Singapore, specifically in terms of paternalism, communitarianism, pragmatism, and secularism. (To these a critic would add authoritarianism)." From the data presented here, one might imagine any number of forthcoming conflicts between Singapore's versions of Confucianism within the marketplace of opportunities.

APPENDIX: RULES OF THE SINGAPORE BROADCASTING CORPORATION

According to Birch (1993, pp. 58–59), The Singapore Broadcasting Corporation will not accept any recorded programme, script or advertising copy which includes the following:

- Matter that constitutes a breach or incitement to a breach of any law of the Republic of Singapore.
- Any statement that might give offence to the people of any friendly foreign country.
- Matter which is critical of democratic institutions or systems of government in general.
- Obscene or offensive jokes, songs, oaths or expressions and any remark of doubtful propriety.
- Matter of such a nature as would tend to destroy public confidence or create any feeling of insecurity in the community.
- The name of any individual in association with advertising without his [sic] prior permission in writing.
- The use of the Deity's name except in reverence.
- Matter unsuitable for children intended for transmission at times when large numbers of children are likely to be listening.
- Matter that may encourage crime or public disorder or which could be injurious to the well-being of any community or the devotees of any religion.
- Statements that could be regarded as libelous or subversive.

Specifically:

- Dramatic programmes should not simulate the presentation of news or events in such a way as to mislead or cause alarm to listeners.
- Respect should be maintained for the sanctity of marriage and the importance of the home. Divorce should not be treated casually or as a convenient solution to marital problems.
- Reference to mental or physical afflictions should be handled with caution to avoid offence or anxiety to sufferers of similar ailments.
- While certain forms of gambling are acceptable in society, it is undesirable to introduce anything which unduly emphasises betting or which might promote an interest in gambling.
- All aspects of fortune telling or the forecasting of events should be treated with circumspection, even when these form part of the development of the dramatic plot.
- Accuracy of religious rites should be maintained.
- Reference to alcohol and drugs should be limited to the needs of plot and characterisation—never presented as desirable.
- Sex should be treated with discretion—illicit sex may have limited reference but should never be presented as commendable.

- Vices like greed, bribery, cruelty, intolerance, selfishness, unfair exploitation of others should never be presented in a favorable light.
- Crime should not be condoned.
- Deliberate use of horror for its own sake should not be permitted.
- No programmes should contain matter which, if imitated, might be harmful to the well-being of individuals or the community, such as the explanation of the techniques of crime, or anti-social behaviour or the description in detail of any form of violence or brutality.
- Any matter which derides or otherwise discredits the law and its enforcement or which discredits social institutions should not be permitted.

NOTE

1. Singapore's major media owners, all governmental entities, include the Television Corporation of Singapore (TCS), the Radio Corporation of Singapore, (RCS), and the Singapore Press Holdings (SPH). Since 1964, they all have had their own in-house guidelines for advertisers and advertising agencies.

REFERENCES

Asian ad revenue rises 21 percent. (1996, March–April). *AMCB, 26*(2): 11.

Asuncion-Lande, N. C. & Lande, C. H. (1995). *Culture, politics and communication policy—Singapore and the Philippines collide.* Paper presented at the World Communication Association biannual conference, Vancouver, Canada.

Bellows, T. J. (1989). Bridging tradition and modernization: The Singapore bureaucracy. In C. T. Hung (Ed.), *Confucianism and economic development: An Oriental alternative?* (pp. 195–223). Washington, DC: The Washington Institute for Values in Public Policy.

Birch, D. (1993). *Singapore media: Communication strategies and practices.* Melbourne, Australia: Longman Cheshire.

Bordo, S. (1990). Reading the slender body. In M. Jacobus, E. Keller, & A. Shuttleworth (Eds.), *Body/politic: Women and the discourses of science* (pp. 83–112). London: Routledge.

Breakthroughs: The feats of 1994 that have changed our lives. (December 26, 1994). *U.S. News and World Report, 117*(25): 7.

Bremer, A. A. (1988, December). Kiasuism: A socio-historico-cultural perspective. *World Anthropological Studies, 6*(1): 21–36.

Buslig, A.L.S. et al. (1996). *A picture is worth a thousand words: Exploitation of women in magazine advertisements.* San Diego, CA: Speech Communication Association.

Butler, J. (1990). *Gender trouble: Feminism and the subversion of identity.* New York: Routledge.

Chua, B. H. & Kuo, E.C.Y. (1995). The making of a new nation: Cultural construction and national identity in Singapore. In B. H. Chua (Ed.), *Communitarian ideology and democracy in Singapore* (pp. 101–123). New York: Routledge.

Dhaliwal, R. (1994). *The Kiasu traveller: True stories of the ugly Singaporean overseas.* Singapore: Brit Aspen.

Elliot, D. (1996, February 12). Objects of desire. What do women want? Sexy underwear. *Newsweek, 127*(1): 41.

Faludi, S. (1992). *Backlash: The undeclared war against women.* London: Vintage.

Fuller, L. K. (1996a). *Advertising appeals to Asian women: A "head-to-toe" analysis of media aimed at Singaporean and Japanese consumers.* Paper presented at the 61st annual convention of the Association for Business Communication, Chicago.

Fuller, L. K. (1996b). Beauty/body media messages aimed at Singapore women. *Awareness: A Journal of the Association of Women for Action and Research, 3*(2): 27–37.

Fuller, L. K. (1996c). Cultural communication similarities and differences in relationship-seeking: A report on the United States and Japan. Paper presented at the 26th annual convention of the Communication Association of Japan, Tokyo.

Fuller, L. K. (1996d). *Our bodies, our (Singapore) selves: Messages to women in the Singapore media.* Singapore: Association of Women for Action and Research.

Fuller, L. K. (1996e). *When a national characteristic becomes popular culture: The case of Singapore's "Kiasuism."* Paper presented at the Northeast Popular Culture Association Conference, Hamden, CT.

Fuller, L. K. (in press). Reading Singapore's national day: A case study in the rhetoric of nationalism. In L. K. Fuller (Ed.), *National days/national ways.*

Goffman, E. (1979). *Gender advertisements.* New York: Colophon.

Hao, X. (1995). *The Singapore press and public trust.* Paper presented at the Association for Education in Journalism and Mass Communication Convention, Washington, DC.

Jewell, K. S. (1993). *From mammy to Miss America and beyond: Cultural images and the shaping of U.S. society policy.* London: Routledge.

Kestral, L.R.Q. (1996, February 23). Is there a place for a gracious society in a pragmatic economy? *Straits Times,* p. 5.

Kissling, E. A. (1995, November 2). I don't have a great body, but I play one on TV: The celebrity guide to fitness and weight loss in the United States. *Women's Studies in Communication, 18*(2): 109–216.

Koranteng, J. & Bruner, R. (1996, July 15). Sexy bras drawing protests; one marketer alters its ad; another stands firm. *Advertising Age, 67*(29): 16.

Kuo, E.C.Y. (1987). *Confucianism and the Chinese family in Singapore: Continuities and changes.* Revised version of a paper prepared for the International Conference on "The Psycho-Cultural Dynamics of the Confucian Family: Past and Present," Yongpyong, Korea.

Kuo, E.C.Y. (1992). *Confucianism as political discourse in Singapore: The case of an incomplete revitalization movement* (Department of Sociology working papers). National University of Singapore.

Latif, A. (1996, March 16). The Singapore Inc. model: Nothing succeeds like success. *Straits Times,* p. 34.

Lazier-Smith, L. (1989). A new "genderation" of images to women. In P. J. Creedon (Ed.), *Women in mass communication: Challenging gender values* (pp. 247–260). Newbury Park, CA: Sage.

Lin, J. L. (1993). *Voices and choices: The women's movement in Singapore.* Singapore: Council of Women's Organizations and Singapore Baha'i Women's Committee.

Macdonald, M. (1995). *Representing women: Myths of femininity in the popular media.* London: Edward Arnold.

Marshall, H. (1996, May–June). Our bodies ourselves: Why we should add old-fashioned empirical phenomenology to the new theories of the body. *Women's Studies International Forum, 19*(3): 253–265.

Martin, D. G. & Sengupta, S. (1996, June 11). *Exploratory paper: Influence of Chinese culture on Singapore advertising.* Paper presented to the American Academy of Advertising, Vancouver, Canada.

More Thais going to surgery to look Caucasian. (1996, June 11). *Straits Times.*

Naisbitt, J. (1996). *Megatrends Asia: Eight Asian megatrends that are reshaping our world.* New York: Simon & Schuster.

Ong, C. (1996, May 10). Singapore's new bra-vado. *Straits Times*, pp. 1–2.

Quah, J.S.T. (1990). *In search of Singapore's national values.* Singapore: Times Academic Press.

Ross, J. D. (1990, July 31). Suppression in Singapore. *Christian Science Monitor*, p. 19.

Saini, R. (1996, January 10). No suits, but you see people in T-shirts and jeans. *Straits Times*, p. 2.

Solomon, N. (1997, January 10). When "economic freedom" bars chewing gum. *Media Beat*, p. 2.

Springen, K. (1996, June 3). Eyes of the beholders: A sharp exchange of the meaning of beauty. *Newsweek*, pp. 68–69.

Stravens, F. (1996). Advertising in Singapore. In K. T. Frith (Ed.), *Advertising in Asia: Communication, culture and consumption* (pp. 273–292). Ames, IA: Iowa State University Press.

Tan, Y. S. & Soh, Y. P. (1994). *The development of Singapore's modern media industry.* Singapore: Times Academic Press.

Tay, E. S. (1982). *Some issues on education: Issues facing Singapore in the eighties: Talks by ministers at the National University of Singapore.* Singapore: Information Division, Ministry of Culture.

Thumboo, E. (1989). Self-images: Contexts for transformations. In K. S. Sandhu & P. Wheatley (Eds.), *Management of success: The moulding of modern Singapore* (pp. 749–768). Singapore: Institute of Southeast Asian Studies.

Tu, W. M. (1984). *Confucian ethics today: The Singapore challenge.* Singapore: Federal Publications for the Curriculum Development Institute of Singapore.

Wee, C.J.W.L. (1994, January 30). Indulging teenage "techno-consumption." *Business Times*, p. 29.

Wolf, N. (1991). *The beauty myth.* London: Vintage.

Wong, A. K. & Leong, W. K. (Eds.). (1993). *Singapore women.* Singapore: Times Academic Press.

Part IV

Religion, Politics, Media, and Human Rights

Chapter 11

When Size Does Matter: How Church Size Determines Media Coverage of Religion

Michael J. Breen

INTRODUCTION

News provides consumers with a means of surveying the state of society, including its level of social deviance. From the content of news, one can ascertain which groups are perceived as legitimate within a society. In a world where communications are instantaneous and where the pace of life is dramatically faster than it was even 25 years ago, consumers of news are forced to rely on the mass media for their understanding of the world in which they live. Information obtained from the mass media differs in quality and type from that obtained by direct experience (Wilkins, 1973, p. 23). This leaves significant power in the hands of the media. As Dahlgren (1981, p. 101) put it, ''Television news has become the major source of information for a majority of the population, and the only news source for many.'' The possibilities that exist in the mass media for the manipulation of public opinion are well-documented (Iyengar & Kinder, 1987). This is as true of issues of social deviance as it is of issues of political interest.

Press reports, being unable to avail themselves of visuals in the way that television does, vary in their manner of identifying social deviance. In the past, race has most often been used as an identifier in cases involving non-Caucasians involved in crime or other anti-social behavior, whereas in cases of white crime, race is not mentioned. Deviance in media reports commonly reflects the values of the power elite in a society and tends to indicate which groups are regarded as legitimate or otherwise (Thio, 1973). Different elements of media reports serve as surrogates for deviance. Among these are measures of legitimacy, such as social evaluation. The majority are presented in a positive fashion as being law abiding (normative) and the minority in a negative fashion as being law breaking (deviant).

In latter years, particularly with the rise of religious fundamentalism, the growth of terrorism associated with foreign nations, and the social and religious divide regarding abortion, religious affiliation has become a commonly used tag in various news reports. The focus of this chapter is to analyze the factors associated with such reports. Of particular interest is the portrayal of religious groups as being legitimate or not. What manner of reporting is used for religious groups, and how are they or individuals associated with them presented in terms of the overall society to which they belong?

Hoover and Lundby (1997) define religion as the "blind spot" of media studies. While the reason for this may originally have been the lack of dialogue between the empirical base of media studies and the metaphysical/faith stance of religion, current trends in media reporting of religion seem to focus primarily on religion as a sociological phenomenon. The role of the media audience is highly significant in terms of coverage of religion. The media serve as conduit and director of the public debate. In Habermas' terms, it is the media who construct the religious reality for the audience, or at the very least, construct the backdrop against which religious experience is to be gauged. Such construction can be strongly affirming of religious practice, neutral, or strongly opposed. This chapter shows that the relevant size of a religious grouping in a media market affects media coverage. The presumption on which this chapter is based is that minority religions in any given market will be represented as deviant.

BACKGROUND

Scott (1972, p. 12) defined deviance as "a property conferred upon an individual by other people. Seen in this light, it is a natural phenomenon; that is, a property that has meaning to the 'the natives' who employ it in the course of everyday life."

Deviance labels are applied for many reasons, sometimes for behavior, sometimes for appearance, or at other times for a wide variety of reasons. Such labeling, Scott argues, can lead to exclusion from full participation in the community. These labels also are applied unevenly. The definition of exactly who is to be regarded as deviant varies from individual to individual in any given society. Drawing on Erikson's work, Scott says:

There are at least two features of a deviant label that make it distinctive; one is that it carries an imputation of moral inferiority and culpability, and the other, that is an essentializing label. The person to whom a deviant label has been applied is usually viewed as being morally inferior, and his condition, his behavior, or whatever basis is used for applying this label to him is interpreted as evidence of his moral culpability. . . . Thus when a person has been labeled a deviant, he becomes a second-rate citizen, who is in a symbolic sense "in" but not "of" the social community in which he resides. (1972, p. 15)

The use of labels in media reports is not exclusively an American phenomenon. Journal articles can be readily found in the coverage of Iranian Muslims in British media (Asari, 1989), the treatment of minorities in crime reports in the French and Swiss press (Soubiran-Paillet, 1987), the ethnic references in crime reports in Holland (Winkel, 1990), the cultural portrayals of native Canadians (Ungerleider, 1991), and the emphasis on immigrants in conflict issues in France (Hargreaves & Perotti, 1991), as well as a host of similar issues.

In the United States, the use of minority labels in reports of deviance has been a contentious issue for some time. The specifics of the issue include the use of the phrase "black on black violence" in reports on apartheid in South Africa (Fair & Astroff, 1991), the media emphasis on a connection between race and crime (Gomes & Williams, 1991), the ongoing problem of racism in social institutions (Solomon, 1993), the difficulties between different ethnic groups (Singer, 1978), and the opposition experienced by sexual minorities (Clark, 1989).

Wilson and Gutierrez (1985) have carefully researched the treatment of ethnic minorities in the media.

Movies, radio programs, newspapers and newsmagazines generally ignored the issues confronting people of color in the United States, as well as their culture and traditions. When they were treated, it was often in stereotyped roles. These characterizations of minorities were largely based on the perceptions and preconceptions of those outside the groups. (p. 15)

But the media treatment of minorities has not just been a lack of coverage of culture and tradition. The darker side to the lack of coverage of minority culture has been the identification of minorities in reports of socially deviant acts. Schaffert (1992), writing in the context of media coverage of terrorism, states that, "Through semantic labeling, the casual employment of terms . . . the media can create public perceptions . . . that vary in both objectivity and veracity" (p. 64).

Media fascination with deviance has been a well-documented feature of news for many years (Shoemaker, 1987). Boorstin (Cromer, 1978, p. 229) speaks of the media creating "the thicket of unreality which stands between us and the facts of life." Given that the full definition of newsworthiness involves some role for deviance, a news focus on minorities is even more significant when linked to deviance. When deviance becomes the driving force, news is subordinated to it. The lack of general coverage about a minority group becomes the dominant kind of report available to the general (majority) public. It is the very rules to which majorities consent that make deviance possible (Cohen, 1963, p. 4).

But deviance is more than an element of newsworthiness. It serves to prime the audience. Iyengar and Kinder (1987) state that by calling attention to some matters while ignoring others, television news influences the standards that people use for judgment. Because consumers cannot pay attention to everything, they are necessarily selective. Wilkins (1973) indicates that consumers have direct experience of few news items. They take shortcuts by relying on the most accessible information sources. Frequent priming of a given story in the media means people's choice will tend to focus more on that issue. Wilkins adds that it is the more powerful sources in a society that define "deviance." The framing of stories is of key relevance in the issue of priming. Iyengar and Kinder (1987, p. 90) suggest that when more media coverage interprets events within a given frame or context, the more influential that context will be in priming the public's assessment of the events. The routines of news can combine with various interest groups to frame stories in the context of a particular ideology (Reese & Buckalew, 1995).

The connection between agenda setting and deviance is increasingly important. There is a consequence of deviance reporting that affects those who share an identity with those reported as deviant—they appear guilty by association as further deviance stories are reported. This is a consequence of media treatment; as the group is associated only with deviance stories, the deviance reports become new referents for a whole group (Breen, 1997).

Deviance reporting can become a social tool for maintaining power and for the marginalization of minorities. This has important consequences for groups targeted in the media. Shoemaker (1984) found that groups perceived as being deviant by editors were portrayed as being less legal and less viable. She concluded that there was support for the theory that the media acted as agents of social control. As Seymour-Ure (1984, p. 7) puts it, "The churches and religion are subject to quite inappropriate criteria . . . and these are applied by reference to a false stereotype without much basis in popular experience."

In the context of religious groups, legitimacy functions as a surrogate or an encoded term for deviancy. The Waco episode was cast in the media as a highly deviant event; murder, child abuse, tyranny, and separatism were the order of the day in media reports. A religious group, the Branch-Davidians, was presented as being highly deviant by focusing particularly and negatively on the legal aspects of the case. Because the principals were not law abiding, the religious component of their faith was immediately dismissed as being "wacko."

Religious labels, allied to legitimacy reports, have become a common feature in news reports (e.g., pedophile priest, fundamentalist cleric, right-wing Christian, Moslem fanatic, Jewish extremist). What has been true in the past of minorities in terms of media labels in legitimacy reports is true today of the reporting on many religious groups.

This chapter focuses principally on the phenomenon of religious labeling in legitimacy stories by examining the coverage of various religious groups. It shows how the nature of the coverage of such groups is primarily associated with legitimacy reports. Because this chapter focuses on five religious groups—Catholics, Lutherans, Baptists, Jews, and Mormons—there is an opportunity to evaluate the performance of the news media with reference to the publication of legitimacy and its application by the media to different religious groups.

This chapter advances three hypotheses:

H1: That the greater the percentage of the population from a religious denomination, the more prominent mass media stories will be about that religious denomination.

Newspapers appeal to their markets, and news content is most likely to reflect the characteristics of the market. Thus the preponderance of religious stories that do appear should reflect the religious composition of the community. Coverage of religious groups should normally be in proportion to group numbers in the community, so the greatest number of stories should be about the largest group (Shoemaker & Reese, 1996, p. 42).

H2: That the fewer the number of people from a religious denomination in a population, the less legitimate stories there will be about that religious denomination.

Shoemaker (1984) measured article character by evaluation and legality. Those measures will be used in this content analysis as components of legitimacy. Legitimate stories are those whose content is primarily about some event or behavior, the legality of which may be called into question. Such stories about individuals are used to cast whole groups in negative light by association. Religious identification is more likely to be used in stories involving legality, especially given the expectation that mainstream religions are expected to be law abiding, but a failure to act within legal boundaries by a religious group or member identified as belonging to such a group is likely to be highlighted given its relative novelty. Amplification occurs when formerly religious individuals become less so and are then more prone to deviant or illegal behavior (Peek, Curry, & Chalfant, 1985; Ross, 1994). This is further accentuated when the report about behavior is negatively characterized by the author (Shoemaker, 1984).

The practice of labeling in the media is most often associated with socially disadvantaged groups or groups regarded as deviant by the media. The minority religions in a community do not have the same social influence and power that come with being a majority. Stories about majority religious groups will have a natural audience in the community, whereas minority group stories only become newsworthy (i.e., capable of attracting significant readership) if they appeal to a wider readership than the minority, hence the appeal to deviance and the association with illegitimacy.

> H3: That group size and legitimacy interact so that for stories about small groups, the more legitimacy, the less the prominence; for stories about large groups, group size is not a factor in determining prominence.

H3 suggests that smaller groups, lacking social influence and power, will be covered negatively, with a disproportionate emphasis on illegitimacy. Smaller groups are generally more likely to be tolerated than assimilated. Labeling as illegitimate is a protective measure by the stronger over the weaker to ensure the continuation of the *status quo* and the clarification of the lines of demarcation.

CASE STUDY

This study looks at media coverage of religious groups in 10 newspapers throughout 1994. The method used in this research is content analysis of newspaper coverage. Coverage is measured by looking at:

- the prominence of stories about a religious group or an individual affiliated with a religious group; and
- the legitimacy of such stories.

The concepts being investigated are the legitimacy and prominence of media coverage of religious groups. The prominence of media coverage is measured as placement and length of each story (Breen, 1997; Shoemaker, 1984). A value for prominence is given by multiplying the number of words in a story by 3 for front-page stories, by 2 for section front-page stories, and by 1 for all other stories. The legitimacy of the stories is defined along two dimensions, legal and evaluative. Legal is coded as the legality of the event being reported; evaluation is coded as the attitude of the writer toward the group.

The Nexis database was searched with a series of general search terms.[1] The search was limited to 10 newspapers representing 10 states where one of the five religious groups in the study had its largest state population (Bradley, 1992). These were the *Boston Globe* and the *Providence Journal*,[2] the *Atlanta Journal & Constitution* and the *Commercial Appeal*,[3] the *Milwaukee Journal* and the *Minneapolis Star Tribune*,[4] the *Salt Lake Tribune* and the *Idaho Falls Post Register*,[5] and the *New York Times* and the *Miami Herald*.[6]

One caveat is in order at this stage—there may be a ''threshold effect,'' whereby high populations of particular religious groups may not fit the hypotheses because they do not constitute the majority religious group in a given area.

Table 11.1
Percentage of the State's Population Who Are Identified with Each Religious Group*

State	Newspaper	Cath.	Morm.	Bapt.	Jewish	Luth.
Rhode Island	*Providence Journal*	82.30%	0.20%	4.20%	2.10%	0.90%
Mass.	*Boston Globe*	75.10%	0.30%	2.10%	7.20%	0.20%
Utah	*Salt Lake Tribune*	4.80%	90.00%	1.40%	0.20%	0.70%
Idaho	*Falls Post Register*	14.60%	52.80%	3.20%	0.10%	5.10%
Georgia	*Atlanta Journal*	5.60%	0.90%	60.00%	4.90%	1.10%
Tennessee	*Commercial Appeal*	4.60%	0.50%	54.70%	0.60%	1.00%
New York	*New York Times*	61.60%	0.30%	6.10%	15.60%	2.40%
Florida	*Miami Herald*	28.00%	1.10%	30.00%	10.00%	2.80%
Minnesota	*Star Tribune*	39.10%	0.50%	2.20%	1.20%	36.60%
Wisconsin	*Milwaukee Journal*	49.20%	0.40%	3.70%	1.10%	22.70%

*Percentages across religious groups within each state do not add up to 100 percent, either because some people identified with other religious groups, or because they did not identify with any formal religion.
Source: Bradley, 1992, p. 12.

This is most obvious in the case of Jewish populations, which do not constitute the majority in any state, but this may apply to other groups as well. Table 11.1 shows the percentage breakdown of each group for the relevant states.

SAMPLING

The sample was generated as follows. Each pair of newspapers corresponding to one religious group was searched together. There were five searches in all. For each search, all stories resulting from the search were counted, and every nth story was selected to yield approximately 100 stories. The resulting sample of 500 stories was subsequently coded for pertinence to ensure that each story was primarily about a religious group. For example, references on a society page to a wedding performed by a religious minister would not be regarded as pertinent. Non-pertinent stories were not included in the final analysis. All stories also were coded to determine legality, evaluation, prominence, and religious identification.

CODING

Legitimacy was coded on two levels, legality and evaluation. Legality was coded on a five-point scale, with 1 as extremely illegal (homicide, suicide, rape, sexual abuse), 2 as highly illegal (felony, grand larceny, solicitation, conspiracy, perjury), 3 as somewhat illegal (major misdemeanors, assault, adultery), 4 as not too illegal (minor legal infringements, minor misdemeanors), and 5 as entirely legal (not at all illegal oddities, quirks).

Evaluation was coded as the perceived attitude of the writer to the religious group in question, using a five-point scale from 1 (very negative) to 5 (very positive). Legitimacy was to be computed as the sum of legality and evaluation, the lowest possible result being 2 (extremely illegal and very negative), the highest being 10 (not at all illegal and very positive).

Before the formal coding of stories was done, a random sample of 45 stories was made, and a set of these was distributed to two independent coders who were asked to assess the stories according to the coding sheet and instructions listed in the Appendix. Coding guidelines were to be further clarified if this initial coding experience yielded a low level of intercoder reliability. The results for intercoder reliability, using Scott's pi for pertinence, legality, evaluation, prominence, and religious identification, are shown below; the high scores suggest that there was no need for adaptation of the original coding guidelines.

Pertinence	=	1.00
Prominence	=	1.00
Religious	=	1.00
Religious Identification	=	1.00
Evaluation	=	0.91
Legality	=	0.88

OUTCOME

The initial sample yielded a total of 500 stories, but only 293 stories were pertinent to the subject of the study. These break down as seen in Table 11.2 and Table 11.3. The highest percentages were in the 80–90 percent range (Mormons in Utah, Catholics in Rhode Island) and the lowest were less than 1 % (Mormons in most states outside of Utah and Idaho, Jews in Utah and Idaho, and Lutherans in Massachusetts and Utah). Some denominations were not represented in some of the sampled newspapers, and in other cases, the number of articles from a given newspaper turned out to be very small. Table 11.3 lists the variables of interest. Indicating wide variation in prominence and group size, both evaluation and legality are more normally distributed.

The correlation between the measured variables is seen in Table 11.4 and indicates that group size is correlated to evaluation, legality, and prominence.

Table 11.2
Number of Articles about the Religious Groups in Each Newspaper

	Cath.	**Morm.**	**Jew.**	**Luth.**	**Bapt.**	**Total**
Boston Globe	14	2	11	0	3	30
Providence Journal	10	0	7	1	1	19
Salt Lake Tribune	18	50	3	1	11	83
Falls Post Register	2	0	1	0	1	4
New York Times	17	0	21	0	1	39
Miami Herald	0	1	6	0	0	7
Milwaukee Journal	13	0	3	4	1	21
Star Tribune	17	0	10	8	8	43
Atlanta Journal	5	3	5	0	15	28
Commercial Appeal	8	2	2	0	7	19
Total	104	58	69	14	48	293

Table 11.3
Mean, Standard Deviation, and Variance for Group Size, Evaluation, Legality, and Prominence

	Mean	**Standard Deviation**	**N**
Group Size	34.17	35.45	293
Evaluation	3.08	.95	293
Legality	4.20	1.24	293
Prominence	918.97	952.87	293

Hypothesis 1 predicted that prominence and group size are related. Hypothesis 2 predicted that legitimacy and group size are related. Legitimacy was coded on two dimensions, legality and evaluation. A reliability index was created for these, but Cronbach's alpha was low. This hypothesis is therefore tested against the two measures of legitimacy in separate tests. While the correlations shown in Table 11.4 are modest, they are statistically significant and indicate that hy-

Table 11.4
Pearson's Correlation Coefficients for Group Size, Prominence, Legality, and Evaluation (n = 293 for each)

	Group Size	Prominence	Legality	Evaluation
Group Size	1.00			
Prominence	.18***	1.00		
Legality	.12 *	−.003	1.00	
Evaluation	.25***	.08	.12*	1.00

*** p < .005; ** p < .01; * p < .05.

Table 11.5
Partial Correlation Coefficients for Prominence, Legality, and Evaluation with Control for Group Size (n = 293 for each)

	Prominence	Legality	Evaluation
Prominence	1.00		
Legality	−.02	1.00	
Evaluation	.08	.10	1.00

*** p < .005; ** p < .01; * p < .05.

potheses 1 and 2 are supported. The partial correlations with control for group size are shown in Table 11.5, with none of the associations being statistically significant. The primary factor in determining the nature and extent of coverage in relation to religion is group size.

Hypothesis 3 predicts an interaction between prominence and the measures of legitimacy. These relationships are presented graphically in Figure 11.1 and Figure 11.2. Analysis of Variance (ANOVA) was run to test these interactions of legality, group size, and evaluation with prominence. The summary results are shown in Figures 11.1 and 11.2. In Figure 11.1, it is clear that large groups receive more prominent coverage than do small groups for positive stories, while the opposite is true for negative stories. In Figure 11.2, large groups receive more prominent coverage for legal stories than do small groups, while the opposite is true for illegal stories. In both of these figures, evaluation and legality were collapsed from five categories to three for clarity.

The main effect is from group size, closely followed by evaluation; legality is not statistically relevant in regard to prominence. In the two-way interactions,

Figure 11.1
Prominence and Evaluation Interaction by Group Size*

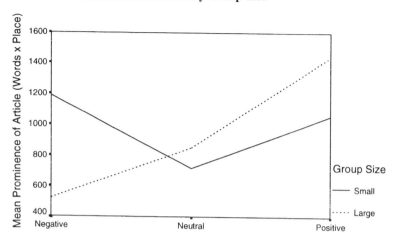

Evaluation of group	
Main effect of group size	$F(1,287) = 4.26$, $p < .05$
Main effect of evaluation	$F(2,287) = 6.87$, $p < .001$
Interaction of group size and evaluation	$F(2,287) = 4.89$, $p < .01$

*Group size was dichotomized for the purposes of this figure.

group size with evaluation is statistically significant, while group size with legitimacy is not. Hypothesis 3 is supported, but clearly the interaction of group size with evaluation is significant in terms of prominence, while the interaction with legitimacy is not statistically so.

COMMENT

These results show clearly that reporting of religious groups is determined principally by group size. Although the religious denomination that makes up the largest or smallest group varies from region to region and from newspaper to newspaper, it is quite clear that group size is the most important factor in determining the kind of reporting that occurs.

It is interesting to note that the media in the United States are devoting more coverage to religious concerns (Shepard, 1995, p. 19), but the quality of coverage leaves something to be desired. As media analyst Ellen Hume puts it,

Figure 11.2
Prominence and Legality Interaction by Group Size*

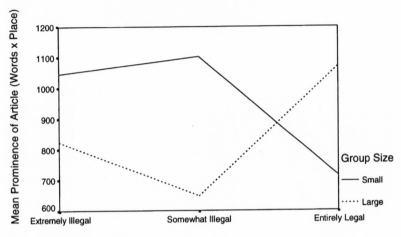

Levels of legality	
Main effect of group size	F (1,287) = 6.40, p < .01
Main effect of legality	F (2,287) = 2.35, p < .10
Interaction of group size and legality	F (2,287) = 1.09, ns

*Group size was dichotomized for the purposes of this figure.

"We cover religion as politics, as a scandal, as a freak show" (Shepard, 1995, p. 22). An increase in coverage is to little avail if there is no quality to that coverage or if coverage is predicted by group size.

The thrust of this chapter is that religion has become the deviancy of the 1990s. In a liberal age, to be associated with a minority religion is to be statistically deviant. Small religious groups and individuals associated with them are reported less prominently, are more prominently reported as being less law abiding, and are evaluated more negatively than their peers in larger religious groupings. In a country already divided into minorities, the media are creating a new regional divide in which religion serves to mark minorities as different and in a very negative fashion.

This study is limited in that it examines only five of the many religious groups in the United States. Other significant questions remain about other religious groups, especially those not in the religious mainstream (e.g., the Branch Davidians or those underrepresented in the national population, although very large in the world population, such as Muslims, Buddhists, and Hindus). There has been no attempt to make a distinction between subgroups in any given religious denomination (e.g., between Hasidic and Reformed Jews or between Catholic clergy and laity). A study of subgroups may provide interesting distinctions in which the smaller subgroup may be treated as a minority, even though its larger parent group is a majority.

Further research is definitely indicated. Would the same results occur with a larger sample representing many more religious groups? Does dividing religious groups into smaller units generate the same effects? What effects, if any, do these realistically have on the general population? Is there a decline in religious faith that can be linked to media representations? How do media reports of religious groups, as outlined in this study, affect social attitudes and values? What other media presentations of religion (e.g., Islam) are associated with terrorism?

The possible research agenda indicated clearly extends beyond religion. All of the various ways in which minorities can be created in a society are possible sources for media bias. These include gender, age, wealth, sexual orientation, and race. In the international context, the question of nationality also becomes an issue. At the heart of this chapter lies a question about the "why" of news content. Unless consumers become aware of the reasons behind the shape and form of existing content, there is little reason to change. This chapter suggests that examination of news content should be thorough and ongoing, as the focus of content changes over time.

Whose interests are being served by a focus on deviance? Is there any role for good news or reports of normative events, or is one to conclude that it is only size and power that matter in the long run, even in the mass media? Hoover and Lundby (1997) suggest that "Interest in religion news is widespread, but readership and satisfaction are lower because they are more closely related to the way people perceive religion news *is* [emphasis added] being covered and the way they believe it *should* [emphasis added] be covered." Religion is an important topic for media attention, but its coverage should not be dependant on power and influence as currently appears to be the case, nor on deviance or eccentricity.

Appendix: Coding Sheet

No.	Pertinent	Source	Place	Count	Cath.		Morm.		Jew.		Luth.		Bapt.	
1	Yes	BG	1	124	5	3			1	5				
2	Yes	MH	2	140									2	3
3	Yes	NYT	3	100							2	2		
4	Yes	MJ	2	80			2	3						
5	Yes	SLT	1	240									5	2

NOTES

1. The Nexis search term was "headline (catholic! or lutheran! or jew! or mormon! or baptist! or fundamentalist!) and date aft 12/31/93 and date bef 1/1/1995."

2. Massachusetts and Rhode Island have the largest populations of Catholics relative to the overall state populations.

3. Mississippi, Alabama, and Tennessee have the largest populations of Baptists relative to the overall state populations. Tennessee was chosen because it has the largest circulation of newspapers in the region.

4. Minnesota has the largest population of Lutherans relative to the overall state population.

5. Utah and Idaho have the largest populations of Mormons relative to the overall state populations.

6. Judaism is the only one of the five faiths that does not enjoy majority status in any of the 50 states. For that reason, the newspapers chosen were from those areas that are listed as having the highest number of resident Jews.

REFERENCES

Asari, F. (1989). Iran in the British media. *Index on Censorship, 18*(5): 9–13.

Bradley, M. B. (1992). *Churches and church membership in the United States, 1990: An enumeration by region, state and country based on data reported for 133 church groupings.* Atlanta, GA: Glenmay Research Center.

Breen, M. J. (1997, Summer). A cook, a cardinal, his priests and the press: Deviance as a trigger for intermedia agenda setting. *Journalism and Mass Communication Quarterly, 74*(2); 348–356.

Clark, M. J. (1989). Institutional religion and gay/lesbian oppression. *Marriage and Family Review, 14*(3): 265–282.

Cohen, Bernard Cecil. (1963) *The press and foreign policy.* Princeton, NJ: Princton University Press.

Cromer, G. (1978). Character assassination in the press. In C. Winick (Ed.), *Deviance and mass media* (pp. 225–241). Beverly Hills, CA: Sage.

Dahlgren, P. (1981). TV news and the suppression of reflexivity. In E. Katz & T. Szecsko (Eds.), *Mass media and social change* (pp. 101–113). London: Sage.

Ericson, R. V., Baranek, P. M., & Chan, J. B. (1987). *Visualizing deviance: A study of news organization.* Toronto, Canada: University of Toronto Press.

Fair, J. E. & Astroff, R. J. (1991). Constructing race and violence: US news coverage and the signifying practices of Apartheid. *Journal of Communication, 41*(4): 58–74.

Gomes, R. C. & Williams, L. F. (1991). Race and crime: The role of the media in perpetuating racism and classism in America. *Urban League Review, 14*(1): 57–69.

Hargreaves, A. G. & Perotti, A. (1991). The representation on French television of immigrants and ethnic minorities of Third World origin. *New Community, 19*(2): 251–261.

Hoover, S. M. & Lundby, K. (1997). *Rethinking media, religion, and culture.* Thousand Oaks, CA: Sage.

Iyengar, S. & Kinder, D. R. (1987). *News that matters: Television and American opinion.* Chicago: University of Chicago Press.

Peek, C. W., Curry, E. W., & Chalfant, H. P. (1985). Religiosity and delinquency over time: Deviance deterrence and deviance amplification. *Social Science Quarterly, 66*: 120–131.

Reese, S. D. & Buckalew, B. (1995). The militarism of local television: The routine framing of the Persian Gulf War. *Critical Studies in Mass Communication, 12*: 40–59.

Ross, L. E. (1994). Religion and deviance: Exploring the impact of social control elements. *Sociological Spectrum, 14*: 65–86.

Schaffert, R. W. (1992). *Media coverage and political terrorists: A quantitative analysis.* New York: Praeger.

Scott, R. A. (1972). A proposed framework for analyzing deviance as a property of social order. In R. A. Scott & J. D. Douglas (Eds.), *Theoretical perspectives on deviance* (pp. 9–35). New York: Basic Books.

Seymour-Ure, C. (1984). *Must the media be bad news for religion?* Birmingham, England: Centre for the Study of Religion and Society.

Shepard, A. C. (1995, December). The media get religion. *American Journalism Review,* 19–25.

Shoemaker, P. J. (1984). Media treatment of deviant political groups. *Journalism Quarterly, 61*(1): 66–75.

Shoemaker, P. J. (1987). The communication of deviance. In B. Dervin & M. J. Voight (Eds.), *Progress in communication sciences* (Vol. 8) (pp. 151–175). Norwood, NJ: Ablex.

Shoemaker, P. J. & Reese, S. D. (1996). *Mediating the message: Theories of influences on mass media content.* White Plains, NY: Longman.

Singer, D. G. (1978). An uneasy alliance: Jews and blacks in the US 1945–1953. *Contemporary Jewry, 4*(2): 35–50.

Solomon, W. S. (1993). Framing violence: Press coverage of the L.A.P.D./Rodney King beating and first trial. *New Political Science, 27*: 85ff.

Soubiran-Paillet, F. (1987). Presse et delinquance ou comment lire entre les lignes. *Criminologie, 20*(1): 59–77.

Thio, A. (1973). Class bias in the sociology of deviance. *The American Sociologist, 8*: 21–22.

Ungerleider, C. S. (1991). Media, minorities and misconceptions: The portrayal by and representation of minorities in Canadian news media. *Canadian Ethic Studies, 23*(3): 158ff.

Wilkins, L. (1973). Information and the definition of deviance. In S. Cohen & J. Young (Eds.), *The manufacture of news* (pp. 22–27). Beverly Hills, CA: Sage.

Wilson, C. C. & Gutierrez, F. (1985). *Minorites and media: Diversity and the end of mass communication.* Beverly Hills, CA: Sage.

Winkel, F. W. (1990). Crime reporting in newspapers: An exploratory study of the effects of ethnic references in crime news. *Social Behavior, 5*(2): 87–101.

Chapter 12

Transcultural Communication and the Antinomy between Freedom and Religion: A Comparison of Media Responses to the Rushdie Affair in Germany and the Middle East

Kai Hafez

The history of Western communication freedom is to a large extent a history of emancipation from religious dogmatism. Until the Reformation, the Catholic Church controlled and censored large parts of what was published about religion, philosophy, and science. In European history, one of the most important relations between "a country's dominant religion" and "communication freedom," which is analyzed in this anthology, consisted of an antinomy between religion (or religious dogmatism) and communication freedom whereby the dominance of religion led to restrictions on the freedom of expression whereas a ban of religious dogmatism from public discourse enhanced open communication.

The case of British-Indian author Salman Rushdie, who was doomed to death by Ajatollah Khomeini of Iran in 1989 for allegedly blasphemous remarks about the Prophet Mohammed and the Qur'an in *The Satanic Verses* (Rushdie, 1988), seemed like a chapter from a European history book with all of the necessary ingredients of religious dogmatism, individuals fighting for the freedom of expression, and clerics threatening the lives of those individuals.

However, the idea that the communication culture in the Islamic world of today, especially of the Middle East, is comparable to that in the European Middle Ages is at least partly mistaken. Even if Khomeini's *fatwa* is clear evidence for such judgment, a comparison of mass media responses to the Rushdie affair both in the Middle East and in the West reveals that the state of communication freedom in the two regions cannot be adequately described in terms of a clear-cut dichotomy of "traditional" versus "modern." Public opinion in many Islamic countries amalgamates religious traditionalism and secular modernity. It combines dogmatic and liberal elements into a somewhat unstable communication culture. Western foreign reporting—like all international communication—is often shaped by distorted, ideological, and sometimes even semireligious presumptions about the world (Sreberny-Mohammadi, et al., 1980). As a result, communication freedom is still limited. Furthermore, the antinomy between religious dogmatism and communication freedom is complicated by a third dimension of intercultural or transcultural communication.

The following contribution is a comparison of the responses of the German prestige press to the Rushdie affair (1989–) with those of English-speaking newspapers in Pakistan, Saudi Arabia, Jordan, Kuwait, and Egypt. The approach is based on the premise that Germany and the Middle Eastern countries are usually considered part of either the "West" or "Islam," respectively. However, since they are not political protagonists of the Rushdie affair like Great Britain and Iran, public debates have not been focusing on matters of *Realpolitik*—British and European efforts to contain Iran's flagrant violation of international law and human rights—but have emphasized the issues of human rights, freedom of expression, and religious "blasphemy," which are of primary concern for the analysis of communication freedom.

This chapter is based on the critical-hermeneutical and qualitative content analyses of a sample of several hundred press reports since 1989 (Hafez, 1996a, p. 139ff.). The results are not necessarily representative, especially since the vernacular press is not evaluated. However, the advantage of qualitative over quantitative methods of content analysis is an in-depth discussion of a selection of significant topics (Merten, 1983). The reports, features, and commentaries are subjected to critical examination with the aid of specialist literature about the Rushdie affair, politics, society, and the mass media in the Middle East, as well as theoretical approaches to transcultural communication and the functioning of media systems.

MEDIA COVERAGE IN THE MIDDLE EAST: BLURRING THE BORDERLINE BETWEEN STATE AND RELIGION

When Ayatollah Khomeini issued his *fatwa*, the Iranian mass media were obliged to follow his line. The media and public opinion had experienced a short period of freedom in the early days of the Iranian revolution of 1978–1979 (Bakhash, 1984). However, in the course of 1979, Ayatollah Khomeini installed the new constitution of the "Islamic republic," which allowed the supreme religious jurist—the *vilayat e-faqih*—to bypass the elected president and parliament in any political decision and to gain theocratic supremacy over the state and civil society. Given the Ayatollah's tight control of the media (Guardians of Thought, 1993), it is not surprising that reports about the Rushdie affair were mere repetitions of Khomeini's dogmatism.

Even a very limited sample leaves doubts about whether extensive quantitative analysis of the Iranian media would provide results beyond these observations. In the reports of Radio Tehran and the Iranian News Association (IRNA), Rushdie was often not only considered blasphemous and destined for death by execution, but his work was seen as part of a "conspiracy against Islam and the Muslims,'' orchestrated by Great Britain to destroy the ''most holy values of Islam,'' which had until then survived other conspiracies such as the ''establishment of the Zionist regime'' in Israel (Mit gottes, 1989). The topic of a pretended cultural ''conspiracy'' was reinforced by semi-Fascist biologist metaphor speaking, for example, of the ''life-spending breath of the Islamic revolution blowing through the universe'' (Radio Tehran, 1990).

However, if the analysis of Islamic media responses to the Rushdie affair is extended beyond the Iranian media system, the picture changes tremendously. It seems as if public opinion in the Middle East evolved in ''concentric circles'' around Iran. Iran was the center of anti-Rushdie criticism and propaganda. Pakistan, being part of the wider Indian subcontinent culture in which Rushdie was born, was divided among supporters and opponents of Iran. Arab media responses in Jordan, Saudi Arabia, Kuwait, and Egypt were by and large reserved and compromising, neither supporting Iran nor Salman Rushdie.

The Pakistani newspaper *Dawn* is an important source of information for the English-reading public, mainly in Karachi. The founder of Pakistan, Mohammed Ali Jinnah, helped launch the paper in the 1930s to advance Muslim viewpoints (Napoli, 1991, pp. 59, 61). *Dawn*'s reports and editorials about the Rushdie affair were shaped by two diverging lines of argument.

The first argument was that while *The Satanic Verses* were considered ''blasphemous'' and should be banned inside of Pakistan, Iran should not be supported in its threat against the author or in its political confrontation with the British government to ban the book. This view corresponded to the reaction of the Organization of the Islamic Conference (OIC), a confederation of 45 Muslim states whose eighteenth conference of foreign ministers in Riyad in March 1989 had confirmed that Rushdie's book insulted Islam, which demanded that the British publisher of *The Satanic Verses* stop printing or circulating the book and that Islamic countries boycott the publisher in case he would not agree. At the same time, the OIC did not confirm Khomeini's *fatwa* demanding the assassination of Rushdie. In *Dawn*, the author was called a ''deviant character'' and ''perverse mind,'' but neither was Rushdie sentenced to death nor was the British government condemned for not interfering with his freedom of expression (Indian Muslims, 1989; OIC verdict on blasphemy, 1989). On the contrary, it was proposed that Rushdie ''deserves to be consigned to the dark pit of oblivion and ostracism rather than to be exposed to the blaze of global publicity'' (OIC verdict, 1989). Beyond that, *Dawn* expressed an understanding that the British government could not interfere without violating its own democratic principles. Even Muslim self-criticism was included when the paper asked

whether certain aspects of our reaction to the Rushdie book served the cause that was meant to be advanced. With so much deep-rooted prejudice and misconception about Islam being part of the West's cultural heritage, any fresh demonstration of frenzy and violence only serves to cast Islam and Muslims in an unflattering light in the non-Muslim world. (OIC verdict, 1989)

A second line of interpretation criticized such a relatively moderate approach to the Rushdie affair, supported Iran, and mainly was based on a position of Islamic anti-imperialism. Iran's policy was considered a reaction to the Eurocentric materialistic world system. As a result of the perceived threat to Islam by the West's solidarity, cooperation and strategic consensus with Iran were demanded (Hossein, 1989). A less anti-Western article emphasized that British society and culture were not the driving force behind *The Satanic Verses*. Instead, the Rushdie affair was a political conflict necessitating close cooperation with Iran as well as a dialogue with the European Community.

The enraged reactions of *Dawn* against Rushdie's alleged "blasphemy" as well as the violent demonstrations in Islamabad, Pakistan, and Srinagar, India, must be explained in terms of the special cultural conditions in Pakistan and India. First, since Salman Rushdie is of Indian descent, his works cause more attention on the Indian subcontinent than in other parts of the world. Second, *Dawn's* coverage of the affair echoed feelings of disintegration and cultural alienation experienced by some members of the Pakistani immigrant community in Great Britain. Third, in the non-Arabic speaking world, where the writings of Islam (Qur'an, Hadith, etc.) can only be approached by certain elites and scholars, the person and life of the Prophet Mohammed have become a "correct model" for life. Mohammed's status is established only "gradually below deity" (Ruthven, 1990, p. 31; Schimmel, 1985, p. 152). Confirming the need for an official ban of *The Satanic Verses*, *Dawn's* coverage revealed a cultural disposition to blur the borderline between state and religion.

The division between hard-line, moderate discourses indicates that support for Khomeini's death verdict against Rushdie was not unanimous in Pakistan. However, by allowing such comments to be published, *Dawn* demonstrated that it, like the whole Pakistani political system that reinstitutionalized the traditional Islamic law (Shari'a) in the 1970s, is susceptible to religious neoconservatism or even radical fundamentalist discourses.

The sample of Arab newspaper reports exemplifies that Arab coverage of the Rushdie affair largely coincided with the "moderate" line of *Dawn's* editorials or other special comments. Content analysis exemplifies that Arab mass media discourses were at least partly rooted in the concept of religious legitimacy. Even if this way of thinking blurred the line between state and religion and limited the freedom of expression in religious matters, it would hardly, however, spill over into Iran-like fundamentalism.

Newspapers such as the *Egyptian Gazette*, *Kuwait Times*, *Arab News*, *Jordan Times*, and *Middle East Times* referred to the blasphemic nature of *The Satanic Verses* by phrases holding that this was a "belief, shared by many Muslims" (Tehran to distance, 1995), even though occasionally more distanced passages could be found saying that the book was "allegedly defaming the Prophet Mohammad" (Rushdie out, 1991). The sample of articles indicates that Arab coverage of the Rushdie affair was in accordance with the OIC declaration. Viewpoints were published similar to those of Saudi Arabia's, that Rushdie must be given a chance to do penance, that he could not possibly be sentenced without a fair trial, and that diverging interpretations of traditional Islamic law existed depending on different schools of Islamic jurisprudence. Egypt Foreign Minister Amr Moussa was quoted saying that the whole affair concerns "just a book and an individual," and that both cannot be "reason enough for conflict between East and West or Islam and Christianity" (Tehran intensifies, 1989).

The West's viewpoint was adequately represented in Arab media coverage; most reports were even based on sources of the Western news agencies Associated Press and Reuters. Personal statements by Rushdie were reported. For example, he was quoted as saying: "I refuse to be an unperson. . . . I have lost my freedom, my home, my family, my daily life and I want them back" (Rushdie refuses, 1992), and "Free speech is life itself" (Rushdie out, 1991). British Prime Minister Margaret Thatcher's apology toward the Muslims and her statement that freedom of expression still was a supreme human and civil right (Tehran signals, 1989) as well as Prime Minister John Major's statement after meeting Rushdie on May 11, 1993 (Major pledges, 1993) and his call for Iran to lift the *fatwa* (Major urges, 1994) were covered at length.

While the sample has not verified any support of Khomeini's *fatwa* in the Arab newspapers, active criticism of Iran was low key. The *Middle East Times* echoed Reuters' comparison between the burning of Rushdie's books in Bradford, Great Britain, in January 1989 and the Nazi book burnings (One year later, 1990). In the *Jordan Times* and *Kuwait Times*, conservative *mullahs* in Iran who supported the Rushdie verdict were called "radicals" or "fundamentalists," and pragmatic forces inside the Iranian government, most notably President Rafsandjani, who were carefully trying to distance themselves from Khomeini's decision, were encouraged (Azmeh, 1993; Khomeini's foreign policy, 1990; London, Tehran, 1990). The Saudi-based *Arab News* asked whether the Iranian leadership would "remain for ever prisoner of the decisions made by Khomeini" (Taheri, 1992).

Only one statement defending Rushdie against persecution could be found in the sample. It appeared as part of an editorial in the *Egyptian Gazette*:

There is, however, the fundamental point that Mr. Rushdie should have used his undeniable talents to defend his religion, not to make fun of it and play havoc with the lives of sincere believers. The order of the Ayatollah Khomeini that Salman Rushdie and the publishers of his book . . . should be murdered is quite another matter. Islam has a long history of religious tolerance; the Ayatollah's command will do more to damage the image of Islam in the West than any words of Mr. Rushdie. (Apologise or face death, 1989)

Arab media responses confirmed the observation that most Islamic countries distanced themselves from the Rushdie affair, which was mainly considered a conflict between the West and Iran (Schulze, 1986–1993, p. 601). However, they also supported the Nigerian winner of the Nobel Peace Prize, Wole Soyinka, who in 1989 complained that, even though religious feelings might have been hurt, the Islamic world should support Rushdie more actively (Soyinka, 1989).

In the final analysis, mass media coverage in Pakistan and in Arab countries about the Rushdie affair represented a proto-democratic communication culture with a high degree of competition between religious and secularist legitimacy and a tendency to tolerate or even advocate restricted freedom of expression where religious issues are concerned but a rather low-key influence of radical fundamentalist views supporting violations of international law or human life as protected by human rights declarations.

THE PRESS IN GERMANY: COVERING HUMAN RIGHTS AND RELIGIOUS BLASPHEMY

The German prestige press consists of newspapers and political magazines covering a wide range of ideologies and political directions. The following analysis is based on a sample for the years 1989 to 1993 from the ultraconservative *Die Welt*, the conservative *Frankfurter Allgemeine Zeitung*, the mainstream liberal *Süddeutsche Zeitung* and *Die Zeit*, the left-liberal *Frankfurter Rundschau*, and the left-alternative *Die Tageszeitung*. All these papers are among the most important opinion leaders inside the German media system. Other mass media, including TV and radio, are strongly influenced by the prestige press (Weischenberg, Löffelholz, & Scholl, 1994).

The Rushdie affair brought about enormous repercussions in the German elite press. Although reports, editorials, and comments concentrated on the first months after Khomeini's *fatwa*, media reporting would remain on a fairly high level for years, especially around the anniversaries of the *fatwa*. The press touched upon a variety of topics, for example, the personal fate of Rushdie and his publishers and translators, demonstrations against Rushdie in several countries, the controversy between Rushdie and Turkish poet Aziz Nesin, and the ban of the Pakistani film International Guerillas in Great Britain (Hafez, 1996a, p. 139 ff.).

The formation of media coverage was reinforced by the Cologne-based International Rushdie Defense Committee, a group of human rights activists, poets, artists, and other known personalities, which demanded solidarity with Salman Rushdie and served as a lobby group in politics and public opinion. Also, the Berlin-based left-alternative *Die Tageszeitung* launched several campaigns on behalf of Rushide and established itself as an important opinion leader for the German mass media.

In the German press, an interpretation of the Rushdie affair through a human rights perspective prevailed. Khomeini's *fatwa* was considered an offense against art. 19 of the Human Rights Declaration of the United Nations (1948), claiming that, ''Every person has the right to express his opinion.'' *Die Tageszeitung* prepublished a German translation of certain controversial passages of *The Satanic Verses* (*Satanische Verse*, 1989) as well as a declaration by the

International Committee for the Defense of Salman Rushdie (ICDSR) and his publishers, a London-based twin committee of the one in Cologne that highlighted the importance of the Rushdie affair for freedom of expression as formulated in art. 19. The ICDSR declaration was signed by a large number of mostly Western intellectuals (Weltweite erklärung, 1989; Widman, 1989). Media coverage in Germany was exemplary for journalistic advocatism on behalf of human rights, the freedom of expression, and the life and basic rights of Salman Rushdie.

However, a significant part of the German media responses in the elite press also was based on the perception of an inherent contradiction between Islam and human rights. While Salman Rushdie himself distinguished between "Islam" and "Islamic orthodoxy" and argued that his life and book were endangered by orthodoxy's "holy war against modernity" (Paasch, 1989), the German press did not apply any clear distinctions. The mainstream-liberal *Süddeutsche Zeitung* observed "indignation of the Western world" about Islam representing a "sinister reality" and "absolutist ideology" (Blau, 1989; Trotz entschuldigung, 1989). Ultra-conservative *Die Welt* wrote about "fanatic Islamic countries" and the contempt of all Muslims for the West (Helm, 1989b). Conservative *Frankfurter Allgemeine Zeitung* perceived an "immense intellectual gap . . . between Christianity and Islam" (Ross, 1989). Mainstream-liberal *Die Zeit* held that "the murderous Muslim" was a character that existed millions of times worldwide and that German society was endangered by values infiltrated through foreign cultures (Krönig et al., 1989). These reactions were similar to those of the poet Hans Magnus Enzensberger, who had become famous for, among other things, his thought-provoking contributions about the democratization of German public opinion and his "media-theory" in the emancipatory tradition of Bert Brecht. Enzensberger announced that, "If Rushdie is harmed, Islam [sic] will have to bear the consequences" (Ich bin, 1989).

While Khomeini excluded Rushdie from the Muslim community, a significant part of the German prestige press, a very rare coalition from ultra-conservative to liberal segments of the media excluded Islam and the Muslims from the world of civilization and virtually equated Islam to barbarism. This reaction was in turn criticized by several intellectuals of Iranian and Arab origin, such as Bahman Nirumand and Khalid Duran, who are known in Germany for their liberal political views. They argued that Western public opinion, instead of pragmatically advocating Rushdie's rights, had started an ideological campaign that reinforced deep-rooted prejudices against Islam, Muslims, and the Middle East in Germany and erroneously upheld allegedly profound differences in the value structures of Islam and the West (Duran, 1989; Nirumand, 1989).

Bahman Nirumand, specialist on Iran, wrote,

It is frightening to see that even those intellectuals, who are usually not susceptible to racism, are adopting a Eurocentric worldview drawing artificial borderlines between Western civilization and Islamic barbarism. . . . Khomeini's death verdict stems from a world of barbarism. But at the same time the racism and ethnic prejudice advocated by many groups and parties in Europe and the numerous attacks on refugees can hardly be called civilized. (Nirumand, 1989)

While the German press looked at the Rushdie affair through the well-established human rights perspective, it hardly considered the issues of religious integrity, taboos and blasphemy, which are important in Muslim countries. Those aspects of the Rushdie affair were only occasionally on the German media agenda (Gegen die, 1989; Helm, 1989a; Hieber, 1990; Steppat, 1989). The perception prevailed that any debate about Muslim resentment of *The Satanic Verses* would be necessarily linked to the concept of "cultural relativism," the idea that cultures should be allowed immanent value definition without reference to human rights and would thus challenge the supremacy of human rights demands toward Iran and the Islamic world (Greiner, 1992). As a result, religious argumentation was almost banned from the German media discourse.

The content analysis of mass media in the Middle East has confirmed that this view was not completely mistaken (Hampsher-Monk, 1991), although it was outweighed. On the one hand, the widespread support for a ban of Rushdie's work in the Middle East media was, in fact, evidence for the prevalence of cultural relativism where religious matters were concerned. On the other hand, the lack of agreement with Khomeini's *fatwa* was in harmony with human rights. This means that an intercultural dialogue on human rights, such as the one currently conveyed by the United Nations, could help reconcile Islam and human rights and root the idea of human rights in a cultural context. However, German media coverage of the Rushdie affair leaves the impression that Western journalism, in its present form, is an obstacle to an intercultural dialogue about human rights.

TRANSCULTURAL COMMUNICATION AND THE ANTINOMY BETWEEN FREEDOM AND RELIGION

The qualitative content analysis of German, Pakistani, and Arab press coverage about the Rushdie affair allows different and somehow contradictory conclusions. On the one hand, the results seem to confirm the conventional wisdom that communication freedom, the freedom of expression, is negatively affected when dogmatic religious interpretations relating to traditional Islamic laws (of blasphemy or apostasy) are dominant elements of political culture. On the other hand, the case study of Germany reveals that the secular-democratic discourse is in itself no sufficient guarantee for communication freedom, since in the transcultural context, misperceptions can severely limit the public discourse. Anti-religious sentiments, banning all religious argumentation from the public discourse and insisting on a monopoly of *secular* human rights interpretations, tend to spill over into new ideologies or even semireligious attitudes that in turn limit the freedom of expression.

Religious Legitimacy, State Control, and Communication Freedom

Islamic media responses to the Rushdie case were influenced by various factors. The newspapers are part of authoritarian political systems that are either neopatriarchal, like on the Arab peninsula, or patrimonial, like in Pakistan, Egypt, and Jordan (Pawelka, 1985; Sharabi, 1988). Newspapers are owned or controlled by governments exerting influence through direct censorship, control of media resources, and intimidation or even imprisonment of journalists (Freund, 1992; Napoli, 1991; Qudsi-Ghabra, 1995). Even though Muslim governments allow various degrees of press freedom, depending on the changing state of political systems and the concrete circumstances of events reported, "benevolent censorship" is a state of structural repression of the freedom of expression.

In the Rushdie affair, the media echoes of the pragmatic policies of the governments in Pakistan, Kuwait, Saudi Arabia, Jordan, and Egypt helped prevent the Islamic world from expressing solidarity with Iran's violation of human rights. However, at the same time, governmental influence or control of the media prevented clear statements on behalf of Rushdie, human rights, and the freedom of expression, since official policies were coordinated within the OIC. Even the monarchies of the Arab peninsula, usually political competitors of Iran on matters concerning the Persian Gulf, felt the need to show a minimum of pro-Iranian solidarity by not openly criticizing and instead ignoring the *fatwa* of Ayatollah Khomeini.

This observation, however, leads to the much more complicated interrelation between state control of the media, communication freedom, and religious legitimacy. Political power in many Muslim countries is at least partly based on religious legitimacy. In Saudi Arabia, the monarchy is considered guardian of the holy places of Mecca and Medina. In Jordan, Hashemite King Hussein is supposed to be a direct descendant of Mohammed, and even in Egypt, the president has nominal control over Muslim scholars (*ulama*), and the Islamic law (Shari'a) is a potential source of the Egyptian legal system. "Legitimacy" in these cases is not perceived in a wider sense as a cultural-religious heritage, such as, for example, the German Christian Democratic Parties, but refers in a strict sense to state monopolies of religious interpretation.

For example, in Saudi Arabia, this policy legacy is handed down to the media system through a "media charter" installed by King Fahd in 1982, stating that media coverage in Saudi Arabia must be based on the ideas of Arab unity and solidarity as well as a rejection of atheist tendencies and materialistic philosophies (Hafez, 1996b; Media charter declared, 1982).

Therefore, communication freedom is severely limited in its ability to transcend the boundaries of the puritan traditions of Wahhabi-Islamic discourses where matters of religion and philosophy are concerned. In the final analysis, the inability of Saudi journalism to separate state and religion in the Rushdie affair is by no means accidental but is an integral part of Saudi media policy.

However, this does not mean that Arab media policies such as those in Saudi Arabia are in general incompatible with human rights, but rather that questions like those touched by *The Satanic Verses*—faith, the Prophet, divine origin of the Qur'an, and so on—are handled dogmatically. For example, the treatment of other human rights seems less problematic as the charter demands journalists to fight against racial injustice for a "humane" and "just" society.

It seems that all of the mass media in the Middle East suffer from similar dogmatic challenges to the freedom of expression as shown in the Rushdie case. They were, therefore, hardly capable of advocating the author's rights, just as they so far have been unable to protect their own rights. However, religious legitimacy as an element of Arab or Pakistani media discourses cannot be considered a one-way street, orders and restrictions handed down solely from the governments to media organizations and journalists. The definition of "legitimacy" as a consensus over values underlying political power holds that these values are shared by society as a whole or at least a significant majority of the population.

All media systems, in authoritarian as well as in democratic societies, are part of the wider social system and, from the perspective of systems theory, media are embedded in so-called "environment systems" or disperse "environments" such as the political and economic systems, public institutions, and various kinds of audiences. Media systems are striving to interact with their environment in such a way as to uphold a certain, sometimes shifting equilibrium. The media might be able to influence public opinion just as they themselves might be influenced by public moods or political, commercial, and ideological factors (Kunczik, 1984; Rühl, 1980).

Even in authoritarian political systems, where the autonomy of the mass media and other forces and institutions of civil society are usually weak and the state seems to define the norms of public discourse, a certain degree of bottom-to-top feedback must be supposed. If this is true, the oscillation in Muslim mass media between pro-Rushdie advocacy, Muslim self-criticism, and the willingness to subscribe to the ban of *The Satanic Verses* might be explained as being at least partially motivated by the journalists and the media themselves reacting to what they considered a social demarcation line for public debates about religion. A definite answer, however, about who caused the blurring of secular and religious arguments in the Rushdie coverage, the state or the media, could only be given if the results of the content analysis were compared to extra-media data such as independent polls on how Muslim public opinion was structured.

Transcultural Communication and Communication Freedom

The most remarkable aspect of the German newspaper coverage of the Rushdie affair was the advocative way in which the author's life and freedom of expression were defended. The quantity and quality of editorials and other comments went far beyond neutral reporting. In theory, advocative journalism is controversial, since the main task of the democratic mass media is to generate information relevant to the public and to represent the different viewpoints held by institutions, organizations, and individuals of society, whereas advocacy tends to harm neutrality. German mass media reacted, perhaps more than other media in Europe, in defense of Rushdie. After the long German history of communication control from monarchic censorship to the Nazi book burnings, contemporary public opinion is sensitive to any restrictions on the freedom of expression.

However, the quantitative content analysis shows that German advocacy—in spite of the credit it deserves for defending Rushdie—often coincided with quite narrow, distorted "frames" of argumentation. Even the very limited empirical basis is ample evidence for the fact that Islamic public opinion, as reflected in the mass media, was anything but monolithic, and that it represented a climate hostile to human rights only in the narrow sense of an almost consensual agreement to the ban of *The Satanic Verses*. The image of the cultural gap between Islam and the West, based on the perception that public opinion in Islamic countries was identical to pro-Iranian, hard-line policy, seems distorted, yet it has had a considerable influence on the most important German national newspapers.

Islamic responses to the Rushdie affair must be analyzed on different levels:

First level—Qur'an. It is controversial whether Khomeini reproached Rushdie out of apostasy (*irtidad*) or blasphemy (*sabb*) (Busse, 1990). In both cases, however, the *Qur'an* recommends punishments only for "the beyond" but not for life on earth (*Qur'an* III, 80; II, 214; IV, 136; V, 59; IX, 67). At the same time, the *Qur'an* lays down several freedom rights, including the freedom of expression (Faath & Mattes, 1992, p. 38).

Second level—Islamic jurisprudence (fiqh). Traditional Islamic law does, in fact, contain the death penalty for apostasy. However, since the Rushdie case is open to different traditional judicial interpretations concerning *irtidad* or *sabb*, the center of Islamic scholarship for the Sunni majority of Muslims, Al-Azhar University in Kairo, did not confirm Khomeini's death verdict. It was confirmed only by extreme radicals such as Egyptian fundamentalist Umar Abd al-Rahman, who was imprisoned in the United States. Azhar instead declared that, "Rushdie's book should receive an answer through another book" (Hottinger, 1989, p. 171).

Third level—Islamic Public Opinion/Media. As already laid out, Muslim public responses to Rushdie varied from advocatism for Rushdie (*For Rushdie*, 1994) to support for a ban of *The Satanic Verses* and confirmation of Khomeini's *fatwa* (Piscatori, 1990).

The comparison of the actual responses to the Rushdie affair in the Middle East to the German media coverage reveals the fact that the German media discourse was characterized by significant shortcomings of transcultural communication. While a coherent theory has not yet been developed, transcultural communication research deals with the construction, deconstruction, and transport of cultural symbols from one cultural sphere to another (Asante & Gudykunst, 1989; Reimann, 1992). Since "cultures" are primordial, antagonistic systems only when "essentialized" to dichotomies, for example, Western "rationality" versus Islamic "irrationality," culturally expressed meaning can be transferred interculturally. In international communication research, "transcultural communication" distinguishes public-to-public from direct person-to-person communication between individual members of different cultures. Journalists bear the special responsibility to "translate" cultural meaning for their domestic audiences who have to overcome the natural distance separating individuals from international affairs. Inadequate transcultural communication, especially wrong interpretations of cultural differences, reinforces definitions of cultural conflict such as those of Huntington's *The Clash of Civilizations* (1996).

German media coverage of the Rushdie case was characterized by a series of distorted transcultural transfers. The heterogenity of responses by the Islamic traditional sector, public opinion, and mass media, and the fact that a majority of Muslim countries would not subscribe to an interpretation of Muslim culture sentencing apostates to death, were only occasionally appreciated. Instead, German media decoded the Islamic context in such a way that the idea of primordial and overall antagonism between Islamic faith and Western human rights was reinforced.

A second shortcoming of transcultural transfers was that the issues of religious insult or blasphemy and of the need to protect the integrity of religion were almost banned from the German media discourse. While the insistence on looking at Khomeini's *fatwa* solely from the perspective of human rights was surely consistent with international law and therefore reasonable, the disregard of Muslim outrage and the lack of understanding for the important role still played by religion in Asia and Africa were something else. Webster has argued that the banning of religious argumentation in the case of Rushdie mirrored anti-religious attitudes of Western liberalism stemming from its own complicated emancipation from the Christian faith and churches (Webster, 1990). In an outstanding editorial announcing the publication of Webster's book in one of the national "papers of record," the *Süddeutsche Zeitung* argued: "In our allegedly liberal society the defamation of other religions—anti-Semitism or, as a new phenomenon, anti-Islamism—has a long tradition" (Nachdenken mit, 1992).

It is paradoxical that the equation of Islam to "barbarism" and the banning of any kind of religious discourse was itself ideological or even semireligious in nature. Part of the German media responses was in accordance with the writings of American poet Norman Mailer, who welcomed the fact that "Khomeini has given us the chance to win back our fragile religion . . . the belief in the power of words" (Ungeheuer, 1989). The liberal, anti-imperialist segment of German public opinion seemed particularly susceptible to anti-religious forms of secularism where the question of human rights was concerned. The reaction was in line with what German political scientist Claus Leggewie called the "fundamentalism of enlightenment" (Mutig und notwendig, 1993).

CONCLUSION

The comparison of media coverage about the Rushdie affair in Germany, Pakistan, Jordan, Saudi Arabia, Egypt, and Kuwait can be summarized in two parts.

First, German public opinion reasonably and advocatively opposed Khomeini's *fatwa* on the basis of human rights and international law, while Muslim media had no clear vision of a separation of state and religious legitimacy. Muslim public discourses were unstable in their ability to defend human rights and the freedom of expression where religious issues were concerned. Communication freedom was curtailed by traditional religious dogmatism.

Second, beyond the necessary defense of Salman Rushdie, German media coverage was to a large degree a case of failed transcultural communication based on distorted images of Islam and anti-religious ideological legacies of public opinion. The Islamic and Western countries apply quite different methods in restricting communication where their "religion" (meaning, Islam or human rights) is concerned. Islamic countries are mostly authoritarian. Western societies restrict discourses through subtle means of stereotyping, agenda setting, or the so-called "framing" of topics. Yet reciprocal effects between "a country's dominant religion" and "communication freedom," which are analyzed in this anthology, can be observed on both sides.

In the final analysis, the concept of an antinomy between religion (or religious dogmatism) and communication freedom, whereby the dominance of religion leads to restrictions of the freedom of expression, and whereas a ban of religious dogmatism from the public discourse enhances open communication, is simplistic. Transculturality is an additional component influencing communication freedom, independent of whether a media system is shaped by secular discourses or religious legitimacy.

While Western societies may be emancipated from religious restrictions, they face new challenges in the age of "globalization" to favor transcultural communication and minimize erroneous definitions of cultural conflicts.

REFERENCES

Apologise or face death, Rushdie told. (1989, February 19). *Egyptian Gazette.*

Asante, M. K. & Gudykunst, W. B. (Eds.). (1989). *Handbook of international and intercultural communication.* Newbury Park, CA: Sage.

Azmeh, Y. (1993, February 6). Iranians puzzled by Western "misunderstanding." *Jordan Times.*

Bakhash, S. (1984). *The reign of the Ayatollahs: Iran and the Islamic revolution.* New York: Basic Books.

Blau, F. (1989, February 25, 26). Blasphemie oder krise des glaubens. *Süddeutsche Zeitung*.

Busse, H. (1990). Salman Rushdie und der Islam. *Geschichte in wissenschaft und unterricht, 4*: 193–215.

Duran, K. (1989, February 27). Woher kommen die Verse denn nun wirklich? *Frankfurter Allgemeine Zeitung*.

Faath, S. & Mattes, H. (1992). Demokratie und menschenrechte im Islamischen politischen Denken. In S. Faath & H. Mattes (Eds.), *Demokratie und menschrechte in Nordafrika* (pp. 19–48). Hamburg, Germany: Edition Wuquf.

For Rushdie. (1994). New York: Braziller [Original publication in French, 1993].

Freund, W. S. (1992). Nicht gerade vielfältig—von gelenkt bis eben frei: Die arabische presse. In U. Steinbach (Ed.), *Arabien: Mehr als erdöl und konflikte* (pp. 321–325). Opladen, Germany: Leske und Budrich.

Gegen die verhöhnung des Islam. (1989, February 25). *Frankfurter Rundschau*.

Greiner, U. (1992, June 5). Wider den kulturrelativismus. *Die Zeit*.

Guardians of Thought. (1993). *Limits on freedom of expression in Iran, Human Rights Watch*. New York: Human Rights Watch.

Hafez, K. (1996a). Salman Rushdie im kulturkonflikt: Zum problem der transkulturellen kommunikation in der Deutschen presseberichterstattung. *Orient, 37*(1): 137–161.

Hafez, K. (1996b). Hörfunk und fernsehen in Saudi-Arabien. In Hans-Bredow-Institut (Ed.), *Internationales handbuch für hörfunk und fernsehen 1996/97* (pp. 91–95). Baden-Baden, Germany: Nomos.

Hampsher-Monk, I. (1991). Salman Rushdie, the Ayatollah and the limits of toleration. In A. Ehteshami & M. Varasteh (Eds.), *Iran and the international community* (pp. 162–172). London: Routledge.

Helm, S. (1989a, March 1). Schadensbegrenzung. *Die Welt*.

Helm, S. (1989b, February 18). Zwischen Asien und Europa—Die geburt Satanischer Verse. *Die Welt*.

Hieber, J. (1990, February 24). Klage über den abwesenden Gott. *Frankfurter Allgemeine Zeitung*.

Hossein, I. N. (1989, March 13). Mirroring contempt. *Dawn*.

Hottinger, A. (1989). Die Schwierige koexistenz von Orient und Okzident. Die hintergründe der Rushdie-Affäre. *Europa—Archiv, 44*: 165–171.

Human Rights Declaration of the United Nations, art. 19 (1948).

Huntington, S. P. (1996). *The clash of civilizations*. New York: Simon & Schuster.

Ich bin für eine offensive antwort. (1989, February 18). *Die Tageszeitung*.

Indian Muslims warned of dire consequences. (1989, March 20). *Dawn*.

Khomeini's foreign policy legacy. (1990, June 11). *Kuwait Times*.

Krönig, J., Kruse, K. Merkel, R. Robben, B., & Tilgner, U. (1989, February 22). Tod dem dichter des Satans. *Die Zeit*.

Kunczik, M. (1984). *Kommunikation und gesellschaft: Theorien der massenkommunikation*. Köln, Germany: Böhlau.

Major pledges support for Rushdie against Iran. (1993, May 18–24). *Middle East Times*.

Major urges Iran to lift Rushdie death sentence. (1994, February 15). *Jordan Times*.

Media charter declared. (1982, October 19). *Arab News*.

Merten, K. (1983). *Inhaltsanalyse. Eine einführung in die theorie, methode und praxis*. Opladen, Germany: Westdeutscher Verlag.

Mit gottes hilfe ging der schuß nach hinten los. (1989, March 8). *Deutsche Welle Monitor-Dienst*, p. 2.

Mutig und notwendig. (1993, October 9). *Frankfurter Rundschau.*

Nachdenken mit einer pistole an der schläfe. (1992, February 15). *Süddeutsche Zeitung.*

Napoli, J. J. (1991, Spring). Benazir Bhutto and the issues of press freedom in Pakistan. *Journal of South Asian and Middle East Studies, 14* (3): 57–76.

Nirumand, B. (1989, May 6). Die affäre Rushdie und die Europäische zivilisation. *Die Tageszeitung.*

OIC verdict on blasphemy. (1989, March 20). *Dawn.*

One year later, still no mercy for Salman Rushdie. (1990, February 20–26). *Middle East Times.*

Paasch, R. (1989, February 17). Kann denn literatur sünde sein. *Die Tageszeitung.*

Pawelka, P. (1985). *Herrschaft und entwicklung im Nahen Osten: Ägypten.* Heidelberg, Germany: Ullstein.

Piscatori, J. P. (1990, October). The Rushdie affair and the politics of ambiguity. *International Affairs, 66*(4): 767–789.

Qudsi-Ghabra, T. A. (1995). Information control in Kuwait: Dialectic to democracy. *Journal of South Asian and Middle Eastern Studies, 18*(4): 58–74.

Radio Tehran. (1990, March 15). *Deutsche Welle Monitor—Dienst* [untitled], p. 11.

Reimann, H. (Ed.). (1992). *Transkulturelle kommunikation und weltgesellschaft: Zur theorie und pragmatik globaler interaktion.* Opladen, Germany: Westdeutscher Verlag.

Ross, T. (1989, February 22). Der streit um die "Satanischen verse" zeigt die tiefe kluft zwischen Islam und Christentum. *Frankfurter Allgemeine Zeitung.*

Rühl, M. (1980). *Journalismus und gesellschaft: Bestandsaufnahme und theorieentwurf* (Kommunikationswissenschaftliche Bibliothek 9). Mainz, Germany: V. Hase & Koehler.

Rushdie, S. (1988). *The satanic verses.* London: Viking.

Rushdie out of hiding. (1991, December 15). *Egyptian Gazette.*

Rushdie refuses "to be an unperson." (1992, February 16). *Jordan Times.*

Ruthven, M. (1990). *A satanic affair: Salman Rushdie and the wrath of Islam.* London: Hogarth.

Satanische Verse. (1989, February 22). *Die Tageszeitung.*

Schimmel, A. (1985). *And Muhammad his messenger: The veneration of the prophet in the Islamic piety.* Chapel Hill, NC: University of North Carolina Press.

Schulze, R. (1986–1993). Die Arabissche welt in der jüngsten gengewart. In U. Haarmann (Ed.), *Geschichte der Arabischen welt* (3rd ed.) (pp. 592–616). München, Germany: C. H. Beck.

Sharabi, H. (1988). *Neopatriarchy: A theory of distorted change in Arab society.* New York: Oxford Press.

Soyinka, W. (1989, May 26). Heiliger krieg für Satanische Verse. *Die Tageszeitung.*

Sreberny-Mohammadi, A., Nordenstreng, K., Stevenson, R., & Ugboajah, F. (1980). *The world of the news—The news of the world* (final report of the "foreign images" study undertaken by the International Association of Mass Communication Research for UNESCO). London: UNESCO.

Steppat, F. (1989, February 24). Der Islam trug viel zu Europas aufklärung bei. *Die Tageszeitung.*

Taheri, A. (1992, March 2). Is Iran becoming a secular state? *Arab News.*

Tehran intensifies anti-Rushdie drive. (1989, March 16). *Kuwait Times.*

Tehran, London pave way for resuming relations. (1990, June 10). *Kuwait Times.*

Tehran signals mellowing position on Rushdie now. (1989, March 5). *Jordan Times.*

Tehran to distance itself from Rushdie *fatwa.* (1995, June 6). *Jordan Times.*

Trotz entschuldigung Rushdie weiter in gefahr. (1989, February 20). *Süddeutsche Zeitung.*

Ungeheuer, B. (1989, March 17). Im schatten des teufels. *Die Zeit.*

Webster, R. (1990). *A brief history of blasphemy.* Southwold, England: Orwell Press.

Weischenberg, S., Löffelholz, M., & Scholl, A. (1994). Merkmale und einstellungen von journalisten: Journalismus in Deutschland II. *Media Perspektiven 4*: 154–167.

Weltweite erklärung. (1989, March 2). *Die Tageszeitung.*

Widman, A. (1989, February 28). Weltweite kampagne fur Rushdie. *Die Tageszeitung.*

Chapter 13

Japanese Media, Religion, and the Law

Dan Tinianow

INTRODUCTION

A discussion of Japanese communication freedom, religion, or law provides sufficient material for an entire volume, let alone a single chapter. The complex interplay of these three elements cannot be investigated exhaustively in a single chapter. Rather, a basic summary of each topic is presented, followed by illustrations of a variety of convergences of all three.

The first such convergence explored is the Aum Shinrikyo sarin attack and subsequent trial, which is still ongoing as of this writing. The Aum Shinrikyo case illustrates how media cover a cult-like religious group before and after an attack, how the legal system deals with an apparently religiously inspired mass murder, and how the media cover the subsequent trial.

The second example investigated is the Imperial Household Agency (IHA) and its relationship with the media and the state religion of Shinto. At one time, the emperor of Japan was considered divine. Although this has not been true for some time, the emperor is still the high priest of the Shinto religion. The Imperial Household Agency controls the Japanese royal family's contact with the outside world, as well as any media coverage.

The final case study offered is the Komeito Party. This moderately powered political party is openly affiliated with the Nichiren Shoshu Buddhist sect. How the media cover this party and how the religious group affects it are both of interest.

These three examples will provide a diverse view of communications freedom, religion, and the law in Japan.

JAPANESE MEDIA OVERVIEW

Since the author of this chapter is a media specialist, the issue of communication freedom will be addressed primarily as it applies to the mass media. Because of this, it is necessary to provide some basic information about the nature of the mass media in Japan.

Physically, the mass media in Japan are quite similar to those in any developed nation, although perhaps somewhat more advanced. In organizational structure, however, Japanese media are unique. Individual elements of the Japanese media mix may resemble counterparts in other nations, but the combination is purely Japanese.

The primary characteristics of Japanese mass media are the influence of the national daily newspapers and the Japan Broadcasting Corporation (Nippon Hoso Kyokai, or NHK) and the relative lack of localism.

The Importance of Newspapers

The Japanese media are dominated by five national daily newspapers. The *Asahi, Mainichi, Nihon Keizai, Sankei* and *Yomiuri Shimbun* all publish both a morning and an evening edition, with a total circulation of more than 40 million copies a day (Cooper-Chen, 1997, p. 53). Of the world's 10 highest daily circulation newspapers, the top three are Japanese, with the fourth highest having a circulation of just over one-third of the circulation of the *Yomiuri Shimbun* (the United States is not represented in this list) (p. 54). It is not surprising that Japan has the highest ratio of newspapers to people in the world, with 578 copies a day for every 1,000 people (p. 52).

Local newspapers are smaller than the nationals, and many are published only once or twice a week, even in cities with populations above 100,000. However, the national newspapers all have regional sections.

The national daily newspapers also are involved in other media. All of the commercial television networks are either affiliated with or owned by a national newspaper (p. 115). Newspapers also are heavily involved in radio broadcasting, although their presence is less influential.

Japanese book and magazine readership is also quite impressive. In addition, Japan has a thriving comic book, or *manga*, industry. Japanese comic books are for all ages and all types of people. One can see people reading manga in restaurants, coffee shops, trains, buses, and even schools and offices. Sales of manga for 1984 totaled 297 billion yen (US$ 1.2 billion), although this figure does not include any of the income from manga-related products (Schodt, 1986, p. 138).

NATURE OF TELEVISION BROADCASTING

There are five major commercial network and two public television networks in Japan. The public networks, Nippon Hoso Kyokai (NHK) general and education, are funded by annual license fees paid for every television set in the country. Although NHK is an independent entity, it enjoys a close and favored relationship with the government. NHK is modeled after the British Broadcasting Corporation in many ways. It also oversees radio networks, including shortwave broadcasts. In addition, NHK runs a publishing arm that prints workbooks that accompany its educational programs and guidebooks that provide additional insight into its historical dramas.

Generally speaking, Japanese citizens view a great deal of television. They watch an average of over three hours of television a day. The average Japanese television set is turned on for eight hours and eight minutes a day (Cooper-Chen, 1997, p. 105). Of the Japanese citizens surveyed by NHK (1995), 54.9 percent watch, on average, at least three hours of television a day.

Local broadcasting is relatively uncommon in Japan. With a population approaching 200 million, there are barely more than 100 local affiliates of national television networks, with these local affiliates carrying the network schedule for 70 percent to 90 percent of the broadcast day (p. 113). Large cities such as Tokyo and Osaka certainly receive a great amount of local broadcasting, whereas a city of more than 250,000 (Mito in Ibaraki prefecture) has no local television broadcasting but retransmits a signal from Tokyo, 100 kilometers away.

Retransmission is the nature of Japanese television broadcasting. Of the 1,502 VHF and 9,453 UHF television stations operating in 1992, NHK used 1,113 and 5,338 of them, respectively, to retransmit its signals (DeMente, 1992, p. 276). The remaining stations were operated by 46 commercial broadcasting companies, with the majority owned by the "big five" commercial networks—NTV, TBS, Fuji, ABC, and TV Tokyo (Cooper-Chen, 1997, p. 113).

Other Traditional Media

NHK was the only player in broadcasting until 1950. Commercial radio broadcasts began during that year. Growth continued steadily, so by the end of the decade, all of Japan could receive both NHK and commercial radio broadcasts (Cooper-Chen, 1997, p. 108). Localism is more common in radio broadcasting than in television. Most cities of even moderate size have their own radio station. In 1992, there were 1,018 radio stations, in Japan—504 were AM stations, 491 were FM stations and 23 were shortwave stations. NHK owns 315 of the AM stations, 484 of the FM stations, and 21 of the shortwave stations (DeMente, 1992, pp. 239–240).

Starting in 1970, "mini-FM" radio stations began broadcasting in densely populated areas. Although these stations had signals that only carried 1 kilometer, they could reach thousands of people in urban areas. An incident in 1985 in which a mini-FM broadcaster was arrested for signal strength and content violations made mini-FMs much less common (Cooper-Chen, 1997, p. 109).

New Media

It is ironic that Japan, a nation with a high-tech image, until recently had one of the lowest rates of Internet use. A 1996 study found that Japan had only 3 percent of the world's Internet-connected computers (Cooper-Chen, 1997, p. 221). The United States had 70 percent. This is a great disparity but is worded ambiguously. Stated differently (and taking into account the relative proportion of computer ownership), Japan was only one-tenth as "wired" as the United States. Some of the reasons for this disparity include the following:

1. Computer ownership is, by some estimates (Cooper-Chen, 1997 p. 221), more than three times more common in the United States than in Japan; Japan's telephone company (NTT) was extremely slow in meeting customers' needs.
2. Internet expenses were considerably higher in Japan.
3. There was little Japanese content on the Internet. More recently, Internet adoption has picked up its pace in Japan (Cooper-Chen, 1997 pp. 221–222).

In other ways, Japan is a technological trendsetter. It began HDTV (high definition television) broadcasts in 1989 (under the direction of NHK), although only 2.1 percent of households in Japan had a receiver in 1995 (NHK, 1995, p. 17). It had a major Direct Broadcast Satellite system in place that same year (under the direction of NHK) (Cooper-Chen, 1997, pp. 218–219). Satellite receiver penetration was 27.9 percent in 1995 (NHK, 1995, p. 17). Cable television penetration, however, was relatively low, with figures varying between 7 percent (NHK, 1995 p. 17) and 25 percent (Cooper-Chen, 1997 p. 107).

JAPANESE RELIGION OVERVIEW

The native religion of Japan is Shinto, a form of animism that is closely tied to national identity and the royal family. Buddhism also is widespread. There is an expression that says the Japanese are born Shinto and die Buddhist. A second version of this saying adds that atheism or agnosticism comes between the two. The reference to Shinto birth and Buddhist death is justified by the Shinto ceremonies performed when a child is born and the Buddhist funeral rites that most Japanese receive. The addition of the comment on atheism/agnosticism indicates that many Japanese are non-religious.

The Japanese seem to have no difficulty picking and choosing elements that they like from disparate religions, having multiple affiliations with different religions, or switching religions. In fact, it is relatively uncommon to find an individual in Japan who regularly practices a single faith throughout life. This is demonstrated by the fact that if one adds up the number of people professing membership in various faiths in Japan, one gets a total that is greater than the population (DeMente, 1992, p. 242). Christian faiths have many adherents in Japan, as do other major world religions (although these are minor compared to

Buddhism and Shinto). However, the majority of Japanese consider themselves "non-observant."

As the Japanese are fad-driven in other respects, religious beliefs also are influenced by short-lived trends. Cults (or cult-like pseudo-religions) flourish in Japan. By some counts, there are as many as 200,000 religions in Japan (DeMente, 1992, p. 256; Nomura, 1995).

Shinto is set apart because it is institutionalized. The emperor is the leader of the Shinto faith (DeMente, 1992, p. 256) and is called upon to perform certain rites throughout the year (e.g., planting and blessing the first rice seedling of the season). Until this century, the emperor of Japan was considered a direct descendant of the Japanese pantheon. Although the connection between the government and Shinto is tenuous, it is exclusive. Any official religious activity involving the government is Shinto (DeMente, p. 256).

JAPANESE LEGAL SYSTEM OVERVIEW

The primary features of the Japanese legal system are its hierarchical structure, its lack of jury trials, its relative underemphasis on precedent, and its automatic review by the voting public. The hierarchical structure starts at the top with the Supreme Court, which consists of a chief justice and 14 justices. All except the chief justice are directly appointed by the cabinet. The chief justice is appointed by the emperor (based on the advice and consent of the cabinet). At the next level are the eight high courts, which are distributed according to geography and population density. The next level is the district court. At roughly the same level as the district court, but in a separate system, is the family court, which handles domestic matters such as divorce and child custody. Finally, there is the summary court, which is a rough equivalent of a traffic court, where relatively minor infractions are adjudicated. The appeal process goes in the reverse direction, although the highest level to which a summary court may be appealed is a high court (Hayes, 1992, pp. 65–66).

There are numerous other facets to the Japanese legal system. Japan lacks jury trials. Defendants are not absolutely required to enter pleas (Reuters, 1996). Implicit in this is the trust of the Japanese people in the fairness of their judicial system.

Precedent does not have as much power in the Japanese legal system as it does in many other nations. While judges are free to follow precedent, they are not obliged to do so. They are more likely to base their decisions on the current dominant social and political views (Hayes, 1992, p. 64).

Judges are subject to regular review by the public. Such reviews are held as part of standard elections every 10 years (starting with the tenth year of a judge's term). Because of low voter familiarity with a judge's record, as well as low interest, no judge has ever been removed from the bench due to such a vote (p. 65).

The wheels of justice turn more slowly in Japan. It is not unusual for a trial to be in session only once a week, particularly for a high-profile case. With such practices, a major trial can last decades. For example, the trial of former Prime Minister Kakuei Tanaka lasted 19 years. The defendant was dead by the time a final verdict was reached (Ueno, 1997).

Although litigation is becoming more common in Japan, the population is nowhere near as litigious as that of the United States. This is borne out by the fact that the proportion of lawyers in the Japanese population is only about one-twentieth of that proportion in the United States.

CASE STUDY: AUM SHINRIKYO

Aum Shinrikyo (alternately Aum Shinri Kyo), or the Supreme Truth church, is formed on the foundation of Shoko Asahara's apocalyptic visions. Asahara foresaw that the world would end in 1997 (Cooper-Chen, 1997, p. 45). He had a list of signs of this impending doom, and the great Hanshin earthquake of January 1995 was supposedly an early one. This would be followed by wars, disease, and poison gas attacks, among other things (Nomura, 1995). When later signs did not appear, Asahara decided to become proactive. Supposedly, Aum Shinrikyo planned a series of poison gas attacks, either as a means of improving Asahara's credibility forcing his prophecies to occur, or both.

Aum Shinrikyo represents itself as a Buddhist sect. Buddhism has strict codes against causing suffering and killing, yet Asahara's followers could have no doubt that their actions would directly lead to deaths. As previously observed, however, contradictions do not necessarily interfere with the practice of religion in Japan.

Some scholars have suggested that the popularity of manga, particularly those manga featuring post-apocalyptic themes, such as *Akira* and *Fist of the North Star*, has greatly influenced a generation, priming it to follow an apocalyptic visionary like Asahara (Nomura, 1995).

When the sarin gas attacks occurred on March 20, 1995, they were the immediate focus of intense media attention. Within days, Aum Shinrikyo was identified as the primary suspect. Aum facilities were raided, and angry calls were made for the forced disbanding of the group. Understandably, people were terrified by a massive attack on a transit system everyone had assumed was perfectly safe. Over the days that followed, a number of mini-panics occurred, most likely triggered by nothing more than unusual odors.

Prior to the 1995 sarin attack, Aum Shinrikyo received little media attention. What attention it did receive was centered around the 1989 disappearance of a lawyer representing the concerned parents of a group of cult members. The lawyer's child and wife also disappeared (Cooper-Chen, 1997, pp. 44–45). Interestingly, Tokyo Broadcasting Company producers, who had shown cult members raw footage of an interview with this lawyer and had reason to suspect them after the lawyer disappeared, refused to come forward during the subsequent police investigation (pp. 205–206).

The Aum Shinrikyo trial was a popular public event. The courtroom only has space for 48 observers, but over 12,000 people participated in a lottery for those seats (Reuters, 1996).

When the trial opened, Asahara refused to enter a plea on his own behalf. He claimed no concern for his own life and therefore no stake in the outcome of the trial (Reuters, 1996). One part of Asahara's attorneys' strategy was to assert that Asahara was being subjected to religious persecution. The court's refusal to call Asahara by his chosen name (rather than his birth name Chizuo Matsumoto) and its refusal to allow him to wear his religious robes were important parts of this assertion (Reuters 1996).

In December 1997, the trial was put on the fast track, going from one to two sessions a week. This move was intended to cut the expected length of the trial by eight years. Previously the trial had been expected to run 25 years. Prosecutors also made concessions on the classification of "injured" parties in order to speed the wheels of justice. With fewer victims, presentation of evidence would supposedly be shortened. These changes were made at least partly because of concerns about public opinion. "The prolongation of Asahara's trial would sharply amplify public distrust in Japan's criminal justice," explained Deputy Chief Prosecutor Kunihiro Matsuo in a press conference (Ueno, 1997). Nevertheless, in late December 1999, the *Japan Times* reported that Asahara's trail was proceeding "at a snail's pace" and that prosecutors had addressed "only nine out of the 17 counts that he faces." However, since many of the individual trails of other Aum Shinrikyo members were finished or near completion in December 1999, the pace of Asahara's trail would pick up, the *Japan Times* reported (Japan Times Court Reporters, 1999).

CASE STUDY: THE ROYAL FAMILY AND MEDIA COVERAGE

The most direct interplay of media, law, and religion can be seen in examining media coverage of the Japanese Imperial family. The emperor of Japan is not only a living embodiment of the nation, he also is the high priest of Shinto, Japan's national religion, a role of which everyone in Japan is aware. Even Toshiaki Nakayama, a photographer whose career was ruined because he did not follow official protocol, admits the importance of this, saying, "The Imperial family is like a religious treasure" (Tokyo Broadcasting System, 1993).

All access to the Imperial family is through the Kunaicho, or Imperial Household Agency (IHA). In times past, the IHA's duties matched its name more precisely. It provided household services and security to the royal family and little else. Since this would involve handling mail and other communication with the outside, when media emerged as a dominant force, the IHA also took responsibility for media contact.

Media coverage of the Imperial family is restricted in the extreme. While restrictions are usually imposed with a gentle touch, the IHA does not hesitate to be forceful when necessary.

Reporters are assigned to cover the Imperial family by their employers. If the IHA approves them, they become members of the Kunai Press Club. At this point, they are legally employed by the IHA and are subject to discipline and sanctions from it directly. A Kunai reporter who draws the displeasure of the IHA will almost certainly be fired. If his or her transgression is particularly offensive to the IHA, it may pressure the reporter's employer to fire him or her as well. A reporter's career can be destroyed by displeasing the IHA.

What types of actions have provoked disciplinary measures from the IHA? Kunai photographer Toshiaki Nakayama was present to take commemorative photos after the wedding of the emperor's younger son. Nakayama instinctively took a picture when the new princess smiled and neatened the prince's hair. The image was charming and human and was picked up by newspapers and magazines throughout Japan. However, because the photograph was not officially designated as commemorative, Nakayama was fired by the IHA and, subsequently, by his original employer.

Another incident concerned a whimsical magazine article in which Prince Hiro (the older of the emperor's two sons) was depicted with a number of different computer-generated hairstyles. This displeased the IHA, as it was seen as disrespectful. It demanded and received an apology from the publisher of the magazine that had presented the article. If an apology had not been given, most likely the IHA would have expelled from the Kunai Press Club any reporters from that magazine.

If these infringements seem rather minor, it is because the IHA exerts such control that more shocking behavior is nearly impossible. In fact, only one journalist has made a successful career of flouting the IHA. That reporter is Toshiaki Kawahara, who first gained prominence by sneaking onto the grounds of the Imperial Palace, nearly gaining access to the main palace. The article he wrote about the experience created a sensation that included 11 guards being fired. Kawahara undoubtedly earned himself a high ranking on the IHA's "most despised journalists" list!

Since then, Kawahara has employed what he calls "guerrilla journalism" tactics to write numerous articles and best-selling books about the Imperial family. Clearly, what is considered "guerrilla journalism" in Japan must seem mild in comparison to the standards in other countries.

For example, one story that Kawahara cultivated with his tactics was a self-invited personal interview with Prince Hiro, something unheard of in Japan. Kawahara learned that Prince Hiro had been attracted to a Norwegian reporter some time in 1985. Kawahara interviewed this reporter about her experience meeting the prince and also took several pictures of her. He then visited Oxford, where Prince Hiro was then a student. He presented the prince with the pictures of the reporter. This greatly pleased the prince, so Kawahara took the opportunity to ask for a personal interview. The request was granted.

An IHA "press conference" is an unusual event. A small group is invited to meet with the IHA director from the Kunai Press Club. Any note taking is forbidden at this meeting, and attendees are prohibited from reporting anything they hear at the conference until permission is given. The group of reporters elects one of their own to serve as chair, and this individual is permitted to ask a single question. The answer may be given directly, later in writing, or not at all. This ends the conference. The IHA-imposed restrictions on access to the Imperial family, as well as on how journalists may gather and report information about them, are referred to as the *Kiku Kaaten* (Chrysanthemum Curtain). It is a constant source of frustration to those who make a living covering the Imperial family.

The clearest illustration of the interaction of media, law, and religion can be seen in the chronology of events surrounding the coverage of Prince Hiro's marriage in 1993. What follows is a summary of these events.

In June 1992, Iwao Miyoa, assistant director of the IHA, visited the upper management of all major media outlets. His purpose was to request restraint in the coverage of Prince Hiro's search for a wife. The media had shown an interest in this emerging story, focusing primarily on identifying who he would marry. Without fail, everyone who was asked agreed not to cover this story.

Meanwhile, the IHA was obligated to give something to the media in exchange for their agreement to abide by the gag order. It arranged for Prince Hiro to make a statement directly to representatives of the press. This statement was brief, consisting of the fact that "maybe there is someone special, and maybe there is not," along with an apology for not saying more.

By December 1992, Masako Owada had accepted the prince's proposal, but there was not a whisper of this in the Japanese media. The identity of the future princess was actually revealed by the *Washington Post* on January 6, 1993. That publication, of course, had nothing to fear from the IHA. However, since the information could be obtained from a source other than the royal family, Japanese media were able to report on what the *Washington Post* had reported. The IHA did not like it, but it had to accept it. On January 8, 1993, official permission came from the IHA for media contact with Ms. Owada.

Mari Ujiie, a reporter for the Tokyo Broadcasting System (TBS), was selected as the reporter who would be allowed to ask a question. The topic of the question, by order of the IHA, had to be Owada's health. Other reporters staked out the Owada mansion, but they were not allowed to approach her. When Owada emerged from her house, Ujiie asked her if she was over her cold, to which Owada replied that she was. Ujiie added the follow-up question, "So you are completely recovered?" Owada said that she was. Then Ujiie added, "All the people convey their congratulations." This seemed to embarrass Owada, who said thank you but reminded the reporter that nothing was official yet (the required betrothal ceremony had not yet been performed). For this transgression, the IHA threatened to cut off Ujiie's and TBS's access to Imperial family information. The reporter and the network both apologized, and both were forgiven by the IHA.

On January 19, the IHA officially announced the engagement of Prince Hiro and Masako Owada. Media coverage of this story could now switch into high gear, within the limits imposed by the IHA.

These limits, it turns out, were quite severe. Access to all involved parties was impossible, aside from infrequent, tightly controlled events. The major focus of media attention, therefore, turned to the wedding date itself. Aside from speculation about the date, all media coverage was based on the same IHA-supplied information, therefore, it had a certain sameness to it.

Within the restrictions imposed, the media went as far as they could to cover the story. Reporters staked out the Owada mansion and covered the betrothal ceremony and an Owada family observance at a cemetery, all under the watchful eye of the IHA.

Interestingly, the date of the wedding (June 9) was finally revealed by a sports newspaper. Why would a sports paper do this? For the sales boost, no doubt, and because limits on future access to information about the Imperial family held little threat for it.

Now the media could focus on the minutiae of wedding plans, or at least they could try. The IHA gave out information sparingly, and all of it came with restrictions about when it could be revealed in the media. In every case, all media outlets were given the same release time, so no one had an advantage. A further illustration of the type of control the IHA is accustomed to can be found in the story of Ms. Owada's sash clip. The IHA gave out some information about this sash clip, along with a fairly lengthy gag order on it. The media complained, demanding an earlier release time. This request was denied, and the media honored the timetable that was given. Still, the IHA did not like to be questioned, and information released after this incident was more terse and more sparse. Apparently even objecting to the IHA's actions, without actually breaking a rule, can have repercussions.

As the wedding approached, the media had to work out details of how to cover the wedding itself. Each television network planned its own coverage, only to have the Tokyo police department mandate that all television networks must pool coverage, with the exception of national public network NHK, which often receives special treatment. This, like almost everything else, served to lessen the differences between the coverage offered by the different networks. All remote video would be identical.

CASE STUDY: THE KOMEITO PARTY AND SOKA GAKKAI

Soka Gakkai ("Value-Creation Society") is an extreme faction of Nichiren Shoshu Buddhism that ran candidates for office in the late 1950s with considerable success. As a result of this success, Soka Gakkai decided to form a political party, the Komeito (or "Clean Government") Party. The Komeito Party found great success, rapidly rising to become the third most powerful political party in Japan and then, some time later, the second (Hayes, 1992, pp. 104–105). Implicated in scandals and intimidation schemes in the late 1980s and early 1990s, the party officially disbanded in 1994, almost immediately reforming as the Komei Party and the New Komei Party (Komeishinto), while other former Party members joined the coalition New Frontier Party (Shinshinto) (Yomiuri, 1997). Since then, the old Komeito power structure has been accused of influencing a number of other political parties, and Soka Gakkai has caused enough problems that open hostilities exist between these sects, with each accusing the other of straying from the true path. That is the short version.

The central point is that Komeito is the only political party in Japan's history to openly affiliate itself with a single religion. It was successful as a political party, and Soka Gakkai was successful as a religion, therefore it can easily be argued that Soka Gakkai, through Komeito, had more influence on the Japanese government than any other religious group. Soka Gakkai has always vigorously prosecuted attacks against it through the use of strong-arm tactics and in the courts (Desmond, 1995). Naturally, both individuals and media outlets hesitated to criticize Soka Gakkai (but still did). In the end, the tactics the party and the religion used backfired, causing damage to both. In other words, it was the media, not the religion or political party, that emerged from the scandals unscathed.

In 1996, the Japanese government made changes to the 1951 Religious Corporations Law, which granted broad legal and tax protection to religious groups. The curtailment of this protection surely was inspired by the Aum Shinrikyo sarin attack, but it also was motivated by concerns about Soka Gakkai and its political ambitions. With Soka Gakkai's political clout at least temporarily diluted, this was an ideal time to enact such a change (Desmond, 1995).

As a result of these recent changes and continuing changes in the political landscape of Japan, the current political power and influence of Soka Gakkai are unclear.

CONCLUSION

Law is the most powerful of the three forces (law, media, and religion) in Japan when push comes to shove. The media are certainly a more significant presence in the life of the average Japanese citizen than the law or religion. The most powerful media forces are NHK and the national daily newspapers. Although Aum Shinrikyo certainly captured the attention of the media and the law, the only religious group with significant, orchestrated political power is Soka Gakkai. Religion is a less forceful presence in Japanese culture than it is in many other world cultures. Typically, when religion exerts a noticeable force on Japanese society, it is in a context associated with a scandal or a crisis.

It is much more difficult to present a concise sketch of the interrelationship

Religion, Politics, Media, and Human Rights

of media, law, and religion in Japan. The political nature of modern Japan is constantly shifting. Since law is influenced less by precedent and more by the current social climate, it would seem likely that law also is shifting in similar ways.

REFERENCES

Cooper-Chen, A. (1997). *Mass communication in Japan.* Ames, IA: Iowa State University Press.

DeMente, B. (1992). *Everything Japanese.* Chicago: Passport Books.

Desmond, E. (1995, November 20). The power of Soka Gakkai. *Time,* International Edition, pp. 21–23.

Hayes, L. D. (1992). *Introduction to Japanese politics.* New York: Paragon House.

Japan Times Court Reporters. (1999). Aum trials tail off as Asahara's day nears. The Japan Times Online Edition. Available: http://www.japantimes.co.jp/news/news12-99/news12-29.html (December 29, 1999).

Nippon Hoso Kyokai (NHK). (1995). *The Japanese and television.* Tokyo: NHK Public Opinion Research Division.

Nomura, Y. (1995, June–July). Where AUM Shinrikyo is coming from. In Kansai Forum Online Osaka: International Business House. Available: http://home.inet-osaka.or.jp/~forum21 (April 17, 1998).

Reuters. (1996, April 24). Cult leader's trial draws a crowd. *The Seattle Times Online,* Today's Top Stories, World. Available: http://www.seattletimes.com/extra/browse/html/cult_042496.html (April 24, 1996).

Schodt, F. (1986). *Manga! Manga! The world of Japanese comics.* Tokyo: Kodansha.

Tokyo Broadcasting System. (1993). *Houdou media supesharu* [News media special]. Tokyo. (Rebroadcast on KIKU-TV, Hawaii).

Ueno, T. (1997) Reuters. http://204.71.177.75/headlines/971202/international/stories/subway_1.html (December 2, 1997).

Yomiuri Shimbun. (1997). At least 5 new parties beginning to emerge. Available: http://www.gwjapan.com/yomiuri/rpydy.html (December 19, 1997).

Chapter 14

Economic Liberalization and Political Conservatism as Reflected in China's Media Development (1978–Present)

Guo Ke

INTRODUCTION

During the past 20 years, China has been undergoing the greatest changes in its history, earmarked by rapid economic growth. In 1997, the average annual income of Chinese residents reached 5500 yuan ($660 US), about eight times the 1990 annual amount (Xie, 1998). While low compared to the Western standard, the increase is remarkable, considering the fact that China has a population base of more than 1.2 billion.

This rapid economic growth has promoted the development of China's media system. In 1978, China had only 32 television stations and 93 radio stations (Chan, 1994). The number jumped to 2,000 television stations and 1,416 radio stations in 1997. The audience size for radio increased from 36.1 percent in 1980 to 84.2 percent in 1996, and for television, the audience size has increased from 30 percent in 1980 to 86.3 percent in 1996 (Xie, 1998). The number of newspapers in China also rose from 186 in 1978 to 2,163 in 1996, an almost twelvefold increase. Journals also flourished in China. Their numbers jumped from 930 in 1978 to 8,135 in 1997. Advertising, once considered the capitalist taboo, saw fast development during this period. Since its debut in 1979, the total ad income of the above four media has been increasing by a factor of 10 every five years. In 1996, it reached 18.28 billion RMB yuan (Xie, 1998).

This chapter discusses media development in China from 1978 to 1998, characterized by a combination of economic liberalization and political conservatism. The development can be divided into two periods. In the First Period (1978–1990), despite the backward and forward swings, media development in China was consistent. In the Second Period (1991–1998), when the market economy concept gained recognition, the competitive consciousness became dominant in China's media system. This has brought about unprecedented changes. Media development in Shanghai, the dragonhead of China, is used to discuss the trends in media development and the impact of economic momentum and political orientation on the whole process.

BACKGROUND

Politically, the media in China still remain in a Communist Concept, as defined in the traditional Four Theories of Press (Merrill, 1983). The Chinese media, owned and operated by the State, are regarded as organs of the Communist Party of China and the government, not the watchdog of the government, as is the case in the United States (Streitmatter, 1994). Freedom of press legislation is yet to come (Lee, 1990).

However, in terms of their economy, the media no longer fit exclusively into the Communist Concept. They fall more coherently into the Development Concept, a combination of the Authoritarian and Communist theories (Stevenson, 1994). This trend became more obvious in the Second Period (1991–1998), when the media in China were endowed with a kind of dual function: continuing to be the voice of the government (political conservatism) while becoming the voice of the marketplace as well (economic liberalization).

While it is true that the government still exercises control over the media system, a notion to which most Westerners would object, the control itself does not necessarily mean the stagnation of the media system. In fact, reasonable control can encourage the development of the media system (Xie, 1998), as evidenced by the Chinese media system in the past 20 years.

THE THREE PHASES OF THE FIRST PERIOD (1978–1990)

Media development in China in the First Period (1978–1990) can be broken down into three phases that featured political campaigns aimed to rein in media development. These political campaigns signaled the end of each phase but laid the foundation for the media development in the following phase.

The first phase ended in 1984, when the campaign against "Spiritual Pollution" started. The second phase lasted from 1985 to 1986, when the brakes were applied during the campaign against "Bourgeois Liberalization." The third phase reached its climax in 1989, when the government cracked down on the students' movement and fought against "peaceful evolution" by Western countries (Chu, 1994).

These political campaigns stimulated rather than suppressed media development. In fact, media development was accelerated on an escalating scale in each phase and was usually coupled with a renewed emphasis on liberalization.

First Phase (1978–1984)

The year 1978 was a watershed for Chinese politics and media development (Lee, 1994). The nation began to open up, adopting a reform policy aimed at modernizing the country.

One immediate and dramatic media change was the elimination of the pompous reporting style of the "Cultural Revolution (1966–1976)," summed up in the phrase "falsehood, exaggeration, and empty talk" (Polumbaum, 1990). Chinese media such as the *People's Daily*, the party's mouthpiece, called for shorter news reports and a more lively style. The new philosophy also called for timeliness in news reporting and coverage of growing economic activities.

An increased volume of information in the media is another sign of progress in this phase. The *People's Daily* took the lead by increasing its length from four pages to six pages in 1978 and then to eight pages in 1980, while the number of magazines and newspapers rose greatly from 1978 to 1984 (see Table 14.1).

After a long silence in the "Cultural Revolution," advertising began to appear in Chinese media for the first time—although it did not get into full swing until after 1990. China's first TV ad—more of an announcement than an ad—made its debut in Shanghai on January 28, 1979 (Guo, 1993). The ad for a herbal wine lasted one minute and 35 seconds, too long by Western standards, but it represented the start of China's TV ad industry.

Meanwhile, journalism education also expanded rapidly in the early 1980s to meet the increasing demand for media development and to accelerate information flow, badly needed for the economic reforms (Polumbaum, 1990). The number of journalism teachers and undergraduate students increased almost fourfold from 1980 to 1984, while the number of graduate students remained the same (Guo, 1993).

Also, in 1983, China started five international journalism programs that integrated English language training into the curriculum. The six-year programs exposed students to a wide variety of Western journalism concepts under their English-speaking journalism professors. These open-minded students constituted a major reform force, pushing media development in China forward.

Second Phase (1985–1986)

Following the campaign against "spiritual pollution" in 1984, Chinese media were silenced for awhile, especially after then Party General Secretary Hu Yaobang's speech in 1985, which emphasized the media's role as organs of the government (Polumbaum, 1990). However, it seemed that the party leadership only paid lip service, as it still tolerated liberal ideas in media practices, such as independent editorials. Meanwhile, media practitioners asked for "a free hand" in media content. This was supported by the Publicity Department, the Chinese counterpart of the U.S. Information Agency (Polumbaum, 1990).

One major trend toward liberalization during this phase was a formal recog-

Table 14.1
Total Printed Sheets for Magazines and Newspapers, 1978–1994

Year	Magazines Total Printed Sheets (100 million)	Newspapers Total Printed Sheets (100 million)
1978	22.7	113.5
1979	30.1	123.0
1980	36.7	141.7
1981	45.4	133.6
1982	46.0	129.1
1983	52.5	142.7
1984	64.3	162.3

Sources: China Journalism Yearbook, various years; Chu, 1994.

nition of the entertainment function of media in the nation's seventh Five-Year Plan. The focus on entertainment coincided with the rapid development of television, a powerful medium of entertainment. In fact, television development and the focus on entertainment reinforced each other's growth during this phase.

Since 1985, entertainment has become an integral part of most Chinese TV stations. Television entertainment programs include music, opera, literature, variety shows, ballad singing, acrobatics, and TV dramas. For Shanghai Television Station (STV), entertainment programs comprised over 60 percent of all airtime in 1986 (Guo, 1993).

Of the entertainment fare, TV drama is the most popular. After 1983, TV dramas saw growth in popularity. Foreign TV dramas also began to appear on Chinese screens. In 1986, the Chinese dubbed the Walt Disney cartoon series *Mickey Mouse and Donald Duck*, and it became a national favorite as soon as it was broadcast over the Central China Television Station (CCTV).

In fact, foreign TV dramas were generally preferred, since there were few high-quality domestic TV series during this phase. In a national survey by CCTV in 1987, 72 percent of the respondents favored foreign dramas (Yu, 1990).

In 1983, China decided to build a nationwide television system by the end of the twentieth century. State expenditures on television began to increase. In 1985, the expenditure jumped to 1,780 million yuan (over \$210 million) compared to 670 million yuan (\$83 million) in 1980 (Lee, 1994). Increased financial resources led to rapid television development during this phase. The number of TV stations in 1986 was almost six times more than in 1983, while TV set ownership rose from 88 percent in 1983 to 103 percent in 1986, and the TV audience size expanded from 400 million in 1983 to 580 million in 1986 (Yu, 1990).

Third Phase (1987–1990)

This phase, studied meticulously in the Western world, saw the most dramatic social changes in China. These changes resulted from media development. While maintaining the liberalizing trends of the first two phases, China's media became more aggressive and direct. They actually pushed for democracy and press freedom, sponsored seminars on these topics, and organized university students to participate. They also pushed for democracy and a free press to such a degree that the government felt that they were actually instigating the public to overthrow the government. Action for independence and democracy became a reality rather than just lip service.

The World Economic Herald, published in Shanghai, was shut down in 1989. It was considered a pioneering venture by the West in this process of "Peaceful Evolution." Western-minded opinion leaders such as Fang Lizhi and Qin Benli were encouraged by then Premier Zhao Ziyang's work report in 1987, which did not mention the media's role as an official mouthpiece (Polumbaum, 1990). The results reflected in journalistic operations were a more diversified style of news reporting and a greater openness in the handling of information. Bad news and critical reports (negative reports), seldom seen since 1957, began to reappear in the media (Polumbaum, 1990). During this period, the negative reports comprised more than 10 percent of the total number of news stories for some major newspapers such as *People's Daily, Jiefang Daily, Wenhui Daily*, and *China Daily*, China's only national English-language newspaper (Guo, 1993). The increase in negative reports was seen as a sign by the media to push for more reforms in government and to ask for more freedom and independence in their practices. To some degree, these reforms led to the massive student demonstration in 1989.

Media development in this phase also was motivated by an influx of external influences in the form of "cultural imperialism" (Stevenson, 1994). Foreign broadcasts from the Voice of America (VOA) and the British Broadcasting Corporation (BBC) enjoyed much popularity among Chinese audiences and exercised great influence on them. The Chinese government accused the United States and Great Britain of trying to undermine the stability in China through propaganda (Guo, 1993). Major influences also came from the inflow of official imported foreign media culture such as movies, soap operas, foreign news, and even talk shows and sitcoms (Chan, 1994). The foreign programs on STV, the second-largest television station in China, increased almost fourfold from 1985 (11.8%) to 1990 (42.6%) (Chan, 1994).

SECOND PERIOD WITH COMPETITION MODEL (1991–PRESENT)

After the Tiananmen Square event in 1989, many Western media scholars and politicians predicted an end to media development in China. However, a new competition model of media development debuted in Shanghai shortly thereafter. The new model went into operation on October 28, 1992, when an independent 24-hour radio station known as Oriental Radio Station (ORS) was established. An independent TV station, Oriental Television Station (OTV), was set up three months later, on January 18, 1993.

The establishment of ORS and OTV ended the monopolistic media policy of one radio station and one television station per market, which had existed since 1949. These new stations started fierce market competition with the established Shanghai People's Radio Station (SPRS) and STV.

Advertising Competition

Competition, the essence of the new media model, first intensified in advertising revenues, which became the bulk of income for broadcast stations in Shanghai following the end of government subsidies in 1993 (Steitmatter, 1994). This is especially true for ORS and OTV, which started operations with bank loans rather than with government subsidies.

Of course, competition for advertising, different from that in the West, still retains Chinese characteristics—*Guo Qing*.[1] Instead of competing for a greater number of clients and ads, STV and OTV are vying for only the richest customers, as the economically vibrant Shanghai has far more potential advertisers than available airtime. The head of the chief editor's office at OTV said, "The demand for ad time far surpasses the supply. So our real competition is for richer clients—foreign-funded companies such as Johnson & Johnson and Procter & Gamble—that can pay premium rates and guarantee long-term contracts" (Streitmatter, 1994).

Competition has led to a sharp increase in ad revenues for all stations. STV doubled its ad revenue from 1991 to 1994, while OTV jumped from zero in 1991 to 150 million yuan ($20 million) in 1993. The same is true with SPRS and ORS. Though the rate of increase in advertising revenues for these media has become somewhat smaller, the advertising revenues have continued to rise (Xie, 1998).

Albeit somewhat soft, keen competition for higher ratings still exists. Ratings are released on a monthly basis by an independent agency, Shanghai Urban and Rural Sampling Team. These monthly ratings, ignored by media and advertisers before 1990, received great attention when ad competition started. Ad rates now are based primarily on these ratings.

Lively Styles

Competition for a piece of the advertising pie inevitably resulted in reforms in reporting styles and programming. To end the dominance of STV and SPRS, OTV and ORS improved timeliness and focused on lively coverage of news. Reporters were dispatched into the field, sent to the different provinces in China

Table 14.2
Spot News in STV's and OTV's 30-Minute News Programs, 6:00–6:30 P.M.

	STV	OTV
Total News Items	270	268
Spot News	167	171
Percentage of Total	61.2	63.8

Source: X. Xiaowei, personal communication regarding "composite week" randomly selected by Xiaowei from December 1 to December 29, 1997.

and even abroad for international coverage. Western reporting techniques such as radio actualities and TV voice-overs and stand-ups were introduced to Chinese audiences. Instead of just reading news scripts prepared in advance, common before 1990, radio and TV reporters now often provided spot news (including live reports), reporting news stories from the field just as their Western counterparts did (Streitmatter, 1994). In 1997, as shown in Table 14.2, spot news consisted of more than 60 percent of STV's and OTV's news programs.

STV, on the other hand, makes full use of its rich human resources to add variety to its programming. In September 1995, STV premiered an English channel to cater to the needs of the growing foreign population in Shanghai. The channel broadcasts four hours a day and includes news, features, foreign movies, weather reports, and ads.

Phone-in hot-line and magazine shows also are gaining in popularity. SPRS's phone-in program *990 Citizens and Society*, which started in 1993, has become so popular that national and local officials often join the phone talk and discuss policies with ordinary citizens over the phones. During his visit to Shanghai, U.S. President Bill Clinton and Xu Kuangdi, the mayor of Shanghai, became the guest speakers of the program and talked with eight listeners via the hot lines.

OTV's magazine show *Dongfeng 110* covers actual criminal cases. Not only is it produced with the permission of the Shanghai police, it also features a uniformed officer as an anchorwoman. Another of OTV's groundbreaking programs is the 50-minute show *Across the Pacific*, which features interviews with Chinese residents now living overseas. It is a joint venture between OTV and two American companies (Streitmatter, 1994).

TV game shows also are in great demand in Shanghai. The two competing 60-minute game shows for STV and OTV are *Great World (da shijia)* and *Oriental Space (dongfeng shikong)*. The shows air at the same time, weekdays at 8:00 P.M.

Table 14.3
Electronic Media Development in Shanghai

Year	Number of Radio Stations (TV Stations)	Average Daily Broadcasting Hours (For TV Stations, Weekly Hours)
1991	3 (4)	149 (256)
1992	4 (7)	182 (345)
1993	9 (10)	263 (512)
1994	9 (10)	281 (586)
1995	10 (10)	285 (597)
1996	10 (10)	298 (662)
1997	11 (10)	307 (669)

Source: Office of the Shanghai Broadcasting Bureau, personal Communication, June 17, 1998.

Restructuring

Competition calls for a change in the structure of the rapidly developing electronic media. In order to raise efficiency and competitiveness and get rid of unqualified employees, with the approval from the relevant government authorities the electronic media system underwent an organizational restructuring in early 1995. The restructuring introduced a producer-responsibility system and established specialized stations, much like the Western system.

As is clear from Table 14.3, the restructuring of the electronic system in Shanghai has resulted in consistent growth in the daily broadcasting hours for radio and the weekly broadcasting hours for TV. These two figures more than doubled between 1991 and 1997. During the same period, the number of radio and TV stations almost tripled. For radio stations, Shanghai now has specialty stations devoted to music, finance, traffic, opera, sports, storytelling, English audience, and so on.

Pressure on Newspapers

The vitality within the broadcasting system puts great pressure on newspapers in Shanghai. Radio and TV are pulling away their readers, which means fewer subscription fees and, in the long run, fewer advertisers. In order to compete for advertising, the 87 newspapers in Shanghai started to expand their number of pages in an attempt to increase their information volume and advertising space (Xie, 1998). Since 1995, the three major newspapers, *Jiefang Daily*, *Wenhui Daily*, and *Xinmin Evening News*, have consistently expanded their pages. In 1998, *Jiefang Daily*, the party organ, increased its page count to 20. *Xinmin Evening News*, the largest circulating evening newspaper in China, prints 32 pages daily. *Wenhui Daily*, which mainly targets intellectuals, rolls off 20 pages each day.

The establishment of newspaper groups is another way for newspapers to enhance their competitiveness with the electronic media. Following the example of the formation of three newspaper groups in Guangzhou and two newspaper groups in Beijing, *Xinmin Evening News* and *Wenhui Daily* in Shanghai merged in November 1998 to form the largest newspaper group in China. The deputy chief of the central publicity department in charge of all of the media in China, Xu Guangchun, said the purpose of these newspaper groups is to expand the influence and strengthen the economic vigor of the Communist Party's newspapers to keep these newspapers dominant in news reporting (Xie, 1998).

DISCUSSION

From a 1978 perspective, media in China have developed beyond recognition. It is a mixed process earmarked by political conservatism and economic liberalization. In the past, a political campaign in China would normally stifle the intellectual inspiration and prohibit all of the related activities, whatever their nature. However, during the past two decades, political conservatism, as reflected in the three political campaigns against "Spiritual Pollution," "Bourgeois Liberalization," and "Peaceful Evolution," did not slow down the development of the media system in China. Rather, it promoted development through media reforms, restructuring, and the increased amount of media information.

This political conservatism stimulated economic liberalization, resulting in a form of economic independence for the media in China through increased advertising revenue and a complete end of government subsidies in 1993. Enormous advertising revenues have created great wealth in the media system in China. This newfound wealth, in turn, edged off the political conservatism and made it possible for the journalistic reforms of the first three periods.

Therefore, to some degree, political conservatism and economic liberalization, as reflected in the media development in China, have been two interrelated stimulating factors that have contributed to the rapid development of the media system in China.

This may sound contradictory and even unacceptable to most Western scholars and journalists, who are used to a different set of concepts and systems in regard to media development, but it is an accurate reflection of the cultural values and current political system in China. As former U.S. Ambassador Winston Lord concludes, "As so often in China, contradictions reflect reality. China is on the move. But the very speed of its pace and rigors of its course will require it to apply the brakes often" (Duan, 1988).

The competitive Shanghai model in the Second Period of media development has proven to be a kind of special economic zone experiment for media development in China. The experience of the Shanghai model is now radiating across

China. Though journalistic reforms may appear in different forms in other parts of China, the essence of competition still dominates (Xie, 1998).

Despite the aggressive reforms and development of the media system in China, it still remains within the conservative framework of Communist politics in accordance with the indigenous cultural values in China. The media system may be subject to constant external influences, but it maintains its own characteristics.

NOTE

1. *Guo Qing* is a vague term used to describe anything particular to China that cannot be explained by Western notions.

REFERENCES

Chan, J. M. (1994). Media internationalization in China: Processes and tensions. *Journal of Communication, 44*: 70–87.

China Journalism Yearbook (various years). Bejing, China: China Social Sciences Publishing House.

Chu, L. L. (1994). Continuity and change in China's media reform. *Journal of Communication, 44*: 4–21.

Duan, L. C. (1988). *How to help foreigners to know China: Principles and skills of communication.* Beijing, China: China Reconstructs Press.

Guo, K. (1993). External influences: Positive and negative—a Chinese perspective. *The Journal of Development Communication, 4*: 86–93.

Lee, C. C. (Ed.). (1990). *Voice of China: The interplay of politics and journalism.* New York: The Guilford Press.

Lee, P. S. (1994). Mass communication and national development in China: Media roles reconsidered. *Journal of Communication, 44*: 22–37.

Merrill, J. C. (1983). *Global journalism* (2nd ed.). New York: Longman.

Polumbaum, J. (1990). The tribulations of China's journalism after a decade of reform. In C. C. Lee (Ed.), *Voice of China: The interplay of politics and journalism* (pp. 33–68). New York: The Guilford Press.

Stevenson, R. L. (1994). *Global communication in the twenty-first century.* New York: Longman.

Streitmatter, R. (1994). *The Americanization of Chinese journalism.* Unpublished manuscript.

Xie, J. W. (1998). *On China's media market and development.* Unpublished doctoral dissertation, Fudan University.

Yu, J. L. (1990). The structure and function of Chinese television, 1979–1989. In C. C. Lee (Ed.), *Voice of China: The interplay of politics and journalism* (pp. 69–87). New York: The Guilford Press.

Chapter 15

Faith in Human Rights: Human Rights in Faith

Nazila Ghanea-Hercock

EFFECTIVE UNIVERSALISM AND HUMAN RIGHTS

Since the end of the Cold War and the 1993 Vienna World Conference on Human Rights, the call for a deepened commitment to ensuring that human rights standards are effectively implemented worldwide is becoming increasingly vocal. Such a universal respect for human rights requires more than the enhancement of international and national human rights monitoring machinery, critical though that may be. Even with the best will in the world and consistent support across the board, it is impossible for a centralized international human rights machinery and bureaucracy to have oversight over all international, national, and local situations. The cost of policing all such abuses would be phenomenal. It is for this and other reasons that calls have been made for the development of a grassroots commitment to human rights. Should such a commitment indeed be universal, it would itself act as the "guardian" of such standards.

However, such calls for the universalization of human rights assume that the human rights discourse will not face any serious challenges by the masses. One possible hindrance, however, is the questionable relationship between religion and human rights. Without trying to juxtapose these two phenomena, it is clear that this is an area that needs fuller exploration and is ripe for the further development of both internal discourse and crosscultural dialogue (An-Na'im, 1992, p. 37). One writer has argued that, "Religion must be seen as a vital dimension of any legal regime of human rights. . . . Religions will not be easy allies to engage, but the struggle for human rights cannot be won without them" (Witte, 1996, p. 2). Why this claim for the indispensability of religion to human rights? Some scholars in fact have highlighted religion as a complicating factor in the human rights debate.

If religion is so complicated, so difficult, why deal with it? Why not be content with casual recourse or willful reversion to non-religious or anti-religious arguments derived from Enlightenment-era understandings of secular reasoning? If religion brings as much heat as light, why not extinguish it, or at least bracket it in polite discourse? (Marty, 1996, p. 9).

The value of engaging religion in the struggle for human rights becomes clearer when the need for nurturing a culture of human rights is appreciated. The nurturing of such a culture needs the creation of a new mind-set. As human vision can be significantly informed through visions of faith, religion becomes indispensable to the creation of the vision of universal human rights. Also, human action is often profoundly motivated through deeply held belief. "Without committed individuals and groups, human rights will become a dead letter" (Künnemann, 1995). The grounding of human rights in religion will assist in the widening of both the enforcement and the effectiveness of human rights.

COMPLEXITY, MODERNITY, AND HUMAN RIGHTS

The realities of the day further imply the need for human rights. In an increasingly globalized world, varying cultures, races, and beliefs have to adjust to living in much closer proximity. One aspect of this contraction in world affairs has been the need for the emergence of a new ethic that will regulate relations between the multiplicity of groups. International human rights law has been codified as a response to the social need for regulation in increasingly complex societies. Janis has delegated this task of regulation to international law by claiming that, "The greatest task, weighing on modern international lawyers is to craft a universal and legal process capable of ordering relations among diverse people with differing religions, histories, cultures, laws and languages" (1991, ix).

Though skepticism may exist about such high levels of optimism about the role of human rights, increasing support has meant that its norms are emerging as a key means for upholding the dignity of all human beings. "Human rights rest on an account of a life of dignity to which human beings are 'by nature' suited" (Donnelly, 1998b, p. 21). As religions also are involved in the provision of universal ethical norms for the dignity of the individual and the betterment of society, it is not surprising that religious leaders and believers have at times considered human rights a threat to the sanctity and uniqueness of *their* voice in social relations. With both human rights and religion regulating some of the same "turf" insofar as normative loyalties are concerned, competition may dominate collaboration.

In this clash of normative loyalties, proponents of human rights put human rights forward as a unique language of morality, to be contrasted sharply to the self-referential subjectivities of specific belief systems. They emphasize their belief that human rights are a non-ideological moral currency and are, therefore, singularly positioned for the moral dialogues necessary in present times. Within such readings of human rights, one detects a widespread rejection of religion and its overt positioning within an ideology of secularism[1] (Wilson, 1988, 1991, p. 196). The assumption underlying this perspective seems to be that the only way human rights norms and standards can be "universalized" is through such secularism. Some have argued that the modern human rights movement itself was brought into existence as "an attempt to find a world faith to fill a spiritual void" (Witte, 1996, p. 9), thus denying the necessary maneuverability for the involvement of religious values in the early development of human rights (situated as it was on secularism's negative evaluation of religion). Another significant reason for this rejection of religion has been the problematic consequences of religious claims of exclusivity in an increasingly heterogeneous world. As diversity is the law of current times, the more neutral setting of the discourse on human rights is being utilized to channel our response. Human rights has attempted to seek consensus in a complex world of believers, non-believers, cultures, religions, and races by replacing God as the foundation of the law with the inborn dignity of each and every human being. Human rights assets are its severance from particularities attached to individual belief systems. Nevertheless, there is much controversy about this suggestion of neutrality for human rights. A closer focus on the emergence of human rights enables us to more vividly realize its historical and sociopolitical underpinnings. Human rights, like individual religions, are not timeless categories insofar as their social manifestation in this world is concerned. The political voices and power structures lurking behind the emergence of human rights discourses cannot be underestimated. As Luf has argued, "Human rights have not been a feature of all periods and all cultures. They are a phenomenon of the modern world, bearing the marks of its experience of reality and its normative ethical notions" (1986, p. 236). In their societal manifestation, rather than their inner essence, both rights and religion are historical constructs. This bond of historical relativity actually unites rather than distinguishes between the social norms of religion and human rights. Both aspire toward universality in their validity and discourse while actually being partially a reflection of the historical circumstances of their emergence.

Furthermore, while a sketchy look at the bloody conflicts in history seems to justify some skepticism about the viability of basing international human rights standards on the foundations of religious belief, basing international human rights standards on secularism does not necessarily alleviate the problems either. Though such an approach has the potential to unite the atheists, agnostics, and Western-educated elites from the various religious groups to a nominal commitment, it seems to have had the effect of alienating larger sectors of the world population and whole civilizations whose "worldview" is closely intertwined with religion. Even for those who have not been overtly alienated, association with a man-made standard has not inspired the most committed following. International legal norms often inspire little more than tokenism, superficial statements made only to attract attention to limited policy objectives rather than any profound concern for those outside the orbit of their immediate political agendas. By trading in the foundation of "God" for the humanist alternative of "human dignity," it could be argued that "depth" of commitment to human rights has been replaced by an elusive "breadth" of appeal that has not been entirely successful. It is not clear that such problematic foundations will ever lead to genuine and wholehearted participation by the masses, thus putting the entire project of a universal culture of human rights in jeopardy. Many believers have felt alienated by secularization and share Mitra's call to "communicate in sharing our spiritual insights . . . in order to counteract the dangers of secularisation, which leads to dehumanisation" (1986, p. 123). While acknowledging the modern-day desire for a neutral and universal standard of norms, absolute neutrality is not implied or even possible. Rather, "a set of *neutrally formulated* common human rights" (An-Na'im, 1995, p. 229) can be identified. Since human rights represents a specific value system, the purpose of identifying a set of neutrally formulated common human rights is to make it non-discriminatory toward the "other" and to "reconcile commitments to diverse normative regimes with a commitment to a concept and set of universal human rights" (p. 229). Therefore, although many scholars have associated the neutrality of human rights with its separation from religion, such absolute neutrality from religious, cultural, or ideological motivations is altogether illusory and unnecessary. Instead, religions should be encouraged to pour their visions and moral resources into the progression of human rights, while allowing "room for neutral norms and values independent of such traditions" (deSilva, 1995, p. 133).

ON WHAT BASIS TO COOPERATE?

If a need for the involvement of religions in human rights exists, several questions arise. On what basis should such an engagement proceed? What is the framework under which this dialogue is to occur? What is the collaboration to look like? To vaguely picture such cooperation is relatively unproblematic, a fact that many documents outlining the commitment of various religious groups to the cause of human rights bear testament. Indeed, boiling down the essence of both religion and human rights to that of the upkeep of human dignity and the enrichment of human life and society puts them in a similar light. There are, however, occasions on which the two normative systems clash, where there is a contradiction in their mutual concerns. There is no question that there are numerous aspects of international law and of various beliefs that are quite distinct and do not impinge on one another. The determination of international fishing zones or decisions on prayers for the dead does not require a reconciliation between religions and human rights. However, there is much overlap between the two worldviews, where circumstances bring them into contact. The imposition of limits of the right to evangelize or proselytize, the status of religious minorities, and political involvement on the basis of religious symbols or loyalties all demand some kind of negotiation or prioritization between human rights and various belief systems. The question is whether and in which circumstances the two will clash, enrich, inform, or dismiss one another. Although ideally these parallel forces may often act in harmony, inevitably situations of serious dissension also will arise. Resignation to "a process of osmosis" and "eventual absorption" (Arjomand, 1996, p. 346) between the two, leading to the resolution of *all* clashes, may prove idealistic and sidelines questions about how disagreements will be resolved and which system will trump the other. When the two systems clash, which is to act as the standard against which the other is to be judged? How can the essential paradox between such universalist principles and particularist positions be reconciled?

APPROACHES TO RELIGION–HUMAN RIGHTS PARADOXES

A range of options for the resolution of religion–human rights paradoxes exists. Each relies on varying assumptions about the role of both human rights and religion in human life and society. These options are not necessarily mutually exclusive.

A strict demarcation of the public-private divide may sideline religion to the private domain and assign priority to human rights in the public sphere. Such a position may tend to leave religious matters to each individual to decide, while occasionally recognizing the right of religious representatives to mediate on community concerns. On the positive side, such a position has the advantage of clarity. The correlating disadvantage is its simplicity and the fact that it ignores societal complexities and the arbitrary power implications behind its subjective public-private categorizations.

Another position is to make decisions about the role of religion dependent on the will of the majority. Under this approach, decisions regarding the outcomes of religion–human rights clashes are based on the democratic will of the majority within the community concerned. While on the face of it this seems to resolve the dilemma, the preference attached to the majority clearly falls short of the whole spirit of human rights itself. As Donnelly argues, "Human rights are fundamentally nonmajoritarian. Human rights are concerned with each, rather than all. They aim to protect every person, against majorities no less than against minorities" (Donnelly, 1998b, p. 155). In fact, the whole purpose of human rights is the protection of the vulnerable, often minority, position (the only exception is when this contradicts other human rights norms), and the democratic approach to human rights is not able to extend its protection to the vulnerable.

Much of the history of modern human rights has prioritized the legal over the religious. This springs from the popular secularist perspectives of human rights law. The disadvantage of such a stance is the ensuing frustration and alienation of the religious. This position often is disguised behind subjective terms such as *modernity*. Referring to the Rushdie affair, for example, Howard states, "This conflict between religious and secular worldviews is rooted in the social changes consequent on the transition from traditional to modern societies" (1995, p. 98). The implication of a hierarchy of man-made norms over divine revelation predictably leads to much controversy. In contrast, religious norms may be clearly positioned over human rights. Proponents of positioning religious norms over human rights often are condemned with derogatory terms such as *fundamentalist*. Even if a lot less popular, the position is no different than the previous one. Interestingly, Falk *does* use the term *secular fundamentalism*, which he recognizes as potentially being just as repressive as the religious variety (1992, p. 58).

However, distinctions do indeed need to be made between those who have a genuine desire to further human rights and maintain their fundamentals and others who are trying to thwart the very purpose of human rights. Though the line between the two cannot be drawn very easily, the distinction *is* necessary to prevent the meaning of human rights from being lost in the reconciliation of human rights and religion. The problem, however, is that human rights has come to mean all things to all people. Nevertheless, perhaps the distillation of the very basic tenet of human rights to the norm of "non-discrimination" could at least serve as a guiding principle. Howard, for example, strongly condemns fundamentalists and traditionalists who try to engage in the human rights dialogue while attempting to hide that they are actually against human rights; that they disagree with the ideals of equality, autonomy, and respect for all; and that they prefer societies in which certain categories of people are considered unequal and undeserving of respect, in which the assertion of human rights would be punished (1995, p. 98).

Some may argue that conflicts between religion and human rights need to be negotiated on a case-by-case basis. The assumption is that genuine and open negotiation will always be possible between the coexisting, parallel, and equal systems of religion and human rights. With priorities not being determined, this dual system has the strength of maintaining the breadth of universal human rights and the depth of rooting it in individual belief systems. However, the question of whether human rights trumps religion or vice versa, and in which circumstances, remains unanswered. In the deeply held passions that issues such as blasphemy may give rise to, does this position not just make the subjective basis of such negotiations appear objective? Another factor that needs to be kept in mind is that negotiations about the agenda and content of human rights are largely determined by and dependent on States. Are States really in the best position to make such normative decisions between religion and human rights? Can such State-centered processes really lead to the level of engagement that such issues deserve? The systemic realities of human rights negotiations unfortunately perpetuate claims of great power monopolization and continued imperialism. Some writers propose the determining factor in cases such as the question of suffering. "Taking suffering seriously is the Archimedes point for intermediation between the universal claim and the particular practice when it comes to resolving antagonisms between widely endorsed human rights norms and culturally ordained patterns of behavior'' (Falk, 1992, p. 49). The genius of this position, however, is called into doubt when one is faced with circumstances where suffering potentially exists on both sides. Does one then resort to utilitarian interpretations of greater versus lesser suffering?

A variation of the ''essential unity'' thesis claims that free and open dialogue within and between the religious and human rights cultures would lead to ''cultural reconstruction'' (Falk, 1992, p. 57) and the emergence of a unity of understanding. This thesis relies on its emphasis that both religion and human rights ultimately aim for the inherent dignity of human beings, seeing religion and human rights as parallel universes, evolving and being reinterpreted in relation to themselves and to each other. While this dignity may be assigned to the inner spiritual nature or just the potential for a good life, both religion and human rights would agree on the ends (i.e., of dignity) if not the basis of such dignity. Witte accepts this ''essential unity'' thesis and creates a vivid picture of the compatibility between religion and human rights law.

Law and religion stand not in monistic unity, nor in dualistic antimony, but in dialectical harmony. . . . Law and religion are distinct spheres and sciences of human life, but they exist in dialectical interaction, constantly crossing-over and cross-fertilizing each other. (Witte 1996, p. 5)

They are distinct, but Witte suggests that they are related conceptually, methodologically, institutionally, and professionally. The two are seen as seamless universes of meaning, existing in a cross-fertilizing, harmonizing relationship ebbing in and out of each other's realms of existence. This position does not respond directly to the question of how to empirically resolve conflicts giving rise to the question of hierarchy.

CONCLUSION

It seems that no ultimate solution can be found to this question of on what basis to resolve all conflicts that are to ever emerge between human rights and the endless wealth and diversity of religious or other beliefs. The underlying problem in determining a final solution to this question is in the monolithic assumptions it would have to make about both human rights and *all* religions. Furthermore, any solution would have to risk treating the two and the whole variety of traditions and cultures they carry as static entities not capable of change, thus rejecting the natural process of cross-cultural penetration leading to new understandings. The problematic aspect of ''freezing'' worldviews is that it has the tendency of polarizing positions and exaggerating differences. After all, both human rights and religions are clearly subject to evolution and change. Religious truth has been described as an, ''ever-revolving kaleidoscope of meanings composed of a multitude of infinite perceptions'' (Hart, 1995, p. 163), and even a cursory glance at the history of human rights will demonstrate its ever-changing concerns. A further dimension of the debate is the political context. The politicization of the human rights debate by States has further invested strong power connotations to the question of whether religion, tradition, culture, ''Asian''/''African'' values, or universal human rights will win out.

While the ultimate answers to this complex debate cannot be given without indefensible simplification and perhaps should not be attempted in the highly charged political and social contexts of modern times, the empirical strengthening of cooperation between religions and human rights should not be put on hold. The world may have to be satisfied with less conclusive and deterministic conclusions, submitting to Falk's observation that, ''There are no fixed points of normative reference'' (Falk, 1992, p. 60). Nevertheless, two interim understandings may be proposed.

The first is that even believers may appreciate that human rights can act as an interface between the system of ethics imparted to a particular faith at a particular historical period and the more fluid, more immediate, more inclusive political and legal role of minimum standards for human dignity supported through the system of human rights. Though religions play a primary role in highlighting the moral values that their followers attempt to translate into daily living, given the fact of pluralism, these religions also will be judged by what is considered morally acceptable. Within the pluralism of modern times, *all* traditions and practices have to ''pass the test of some sort of universal moral code'' (An-Na'im et al., 1995, p. viii), and religions cannot expect immunity from this process. Within social and political circles, such decisions often are judged through the ''lenses'' of human rights. Willing support for such a process rests on the assumption that religious traditions concede that the pursuit of *their* moral code necessitates prior belief in the validity of the grounds on which that code has been built. Human rights needs to bypass such particularities. However, if the subject matter of human rights is the universal quest for what it means to be human, then *every* human being must have a say in the answer to this question. The discussion about human rights therefore needs to be larger and wider than the choice of religion, belief, or commitment of each individual and yet not totally alien from it.

The question remains, ''Can human rights be interpreted and justified from within religious traditions, such that they are supported, rather than undermined, as the 'common core' of a universal morality among these traditions?'' (An-Na'im et al., 1995, p. xiii). As the U.N. special representative on the human rights situation in Iran has reiterated,

Traditional culture is not a substitute for human rights; it is a cultural context in which human rights must be established, integrated, promoted and protected. Human rights must be approached in a way that is meaningful and relevant in diverse cultural contexts. (Economic and Social Council, 1996, Introduction § A)

Only time will tell how far such projects for the support of human rights, utilizing a variety of cultural symbols and commitments, are able to collaborate toward the realization of a universal code of human rights.

The second interim understanding regards the acceptance of the utility of human rights in relation to statecraft. As human rights is a man-made code, human rights' ultimate claims lie no higher than representing the latest register of agreed upon and negotiated standards for a decent human existence. As social conditions and circumstances change, its nuances can be adjusted to register more appropriate measures for altered circumstances. As Clayton explains, "Testing and being contested—by this means the discourse of rights creates itself afresh and the hierarchy of rights is subjected to public scrutiny" (1995, p. 266). All of this can be achieved on a platform that has the potential of being recognized as being more dispassionate, bypassing particular belief systems that "are perceived . . . as parochial or local in scope and as being grounded in context-specific commitments" (p. 260). The problem does not lie in the notional benefits that members of a particular belief system may feel that they have been divinely graced with, but the fear that with time this may "easily degenerate into hostility and antagonism towards the 'them' and solidarity with the 'us' " (An-Na'im, 1995, p. 231). Many religious groups have put their weight behind the campaign for strengthening human rights (Swidler, 1986), precisely because they have come to realize that the only means of ensuring nondiscrimination on a basis such as belief is through shared standards of human rights. However, this only succeeds when human rights is "justified" through the religious norms of the group concerned, hence highlighting the indispensability of religion to the mass absorption of human rights standards.

The challenge is therefore an intricate one: that of allowing human rights to "transcend all differences in the subjectivities and practices of peoples" (Falk, 1992, p. 44), while also "mediating international human rights through the web of cultural circumstances" (p. 45).

NOTE

1. Wilson distinguishes between the terms *secularisation* and *secularism* by defining the former as "that process by which religious thinking, practice and institutions lose social significance, and become marginal to the operation of the social system," and the latter as, "an ideology . . . it denotes a negative evaluative attitude towards religion, and might even be appropriately seen as a particular 'religious' position, in the sense that secularism adopts certain premises a priori and canvasses a normative (albeit negative) position about supernaturalism" (1988, 1991, p. 196).

REFERENCES

An-Na'im, A. A. (1992). Toward a cross-cultural approach to defining international standards of human rights: The meaning of cruel, inhuman, or degrading treatment or punishment. In A. A. An-Na'im (Ed.), *Human rights in cross-cultural perspective: A quest for consensus* (pp. 19–43). Philadelphia: University of Pennsylvania Press.

An-Na'im, A. A. (1995). Toward an Islamic hermeneutics for human rights. In A. A. An-Na'im, J. D. Gort, H. Jansen, & H. M. Vroom (Eds.), *Human rights and religious values: An uneasy relationship?* (pp. 229–242). Grand Rapids, MI: William B. Eerdmans.

An-Na'im, A. A., Gort, J. D., Jansen, H., & Vroom, H. M. (Eds.). (1995). *Human rights and religious values: An uneasy relationship?* Grand Rapids, MI: William B. Eerdmans.

Arjomand, S. A. (1996). Religious human rights and the principle of legal pluralism in the Middle East. In J. D. van der Vyver & J. Witte, Jr. (Eds.), *Religious human rights in global perspective: Legal perspectives* (pp. 311–347). The Hague, the Netherlands: Martinus Nijhoff.

Clayton, J. (1995). Religions and rights: Local values and universal declarations. In A. A. An-Na'im, J. D. Gort, H. Jansen, & H. M. Vroom (Eds.), *Human rights and religious values: An uneasy relationship?* (pp. 259–266). Grand Rapids, MI: William B. Eerdmans.

de Silva, P. (1995). Human rights in Buddhist perspective. In A. A. An-Na'im, J. D. Gort, H. Jansen, & H. M. Vroom (Eds.), *Human rights and religious values: An uneasy relationship?* (pp. 133–143). Grand Rapids, MI: William B. Eerdmans.

Donnelly, J. (1998). *International human rights* (2nd ed.). Boulder, CO: Westview Press.

Economic and Social Council. (1996, March 21). Commission on Human Rights, Fifty-second session, Item 10 of the provisional agenda, Question of the violation of human rights and fundamental freedoms in any part of the world, With particular reference to colonial and other dependent countries and territories, Report on the situation of human rights in the Islamic Republic of Iran, prepared by the Special Representative of the Commission on Human Rights, Mr. Maurice Copithorne (Canada), pursuant to Commission resolution 1995/68 of 8 March 1995 and Economic and Social Council decision 1995/279 of 25 July 1995. (E/CN.4/1996/59).

Falk, R. (1992). Cultural foundations for the international protection of human rights. In A. A. An-Na'im (Ed.), *Human rights in cross-cultural perspective: A quest for consensus* (pp. 44–64). Philadelphia: University of Pennsylvania Press.

Hart, D. A. (1995). *One faith? Non-realism and the world of faiths.* London: Mowbray.

Howard, R. E. (1995). *Human rights and the search for community.* Boulder, CO: Westview Press.

Janis, M. W. (Ed.). (1991). *The influence of religion on the development of international law.* Dordrecht, the Netherlands: Martinus Nijhoff.

Künnemann, R. (1995, May). A coherent approach to human rights. *Human Rights Quarterly: A Comparative and International Journal of the Social Sciences, Humanities, and Law, 17*(2): 323–342.

Luf, G. (1986). Human rights in Christian and Islamic thought: A report on the Tubingen "human rights project." In L. Swidler (Ed.), *Religious liberty and human rights—In nations and religions* (pp. 235–244). Philadelphia: Ecumemical Press.

Marty, M. E. (1996). Religious dimensions of human rights. In J. Witte, Jr. & J. van der Vyver (Eds.), *Religious human rights in global perspective: Religious perspectives* (pp. 1–16). The Hague, the Netherlands: Martinus Nijhoff.

Mitra, K. (1986). Exploring the possibility of Hindu-Muslim dialogue. In L. Swidler (Ed.), *Religious liberty and human rights—In nations and religions* (pp. 109–123). Philadelphia: Ecumenical Press.

Swidler, L. (Ed.). (1986). *Religious liberty and human rights—In nations and religions.* Philadelphia: Ecumenical Press.

Wilson, B. (1988, 1991). ''Secularisation'': Religion in the modern world. In S. Sutherland & P. Clarke (Eds.), *The world's religions: The study of religion, traditional and new religion* (pp. 195–208). London: Routledge.

Witte, J., Jr. (1996, Fall). Law, religion, and human rights. *Columbia Human Rights Law Review, 28*(1): 1–31.

Selected Bibliography

Akiyama, T. (undated, post-1985). *Trends in research on Japan's educational broadcasts*. Tokyo: NHK Broadcasting Cultural Research Institute.

Baker, E. C. (1989). *Human liberty and freedom of speech*. New York: Oxford University Press.

Bar-Kima, O. (1998, May 5). A new organization offers to pay journalists who give "fair coverage" to the ultra-orthodox community. *Ha'aretz*, p. A3.

Blondheim, M. & Caplan, K. (1993). On communications and audio cassettes in "Haredi" society. *Quesher, 14*: 51–62 [in Hebrew with English abstract].

Chang, W. H. (Ed.). (1989). *Mass media in China: The history and future*. Ames, IA: Iowa State University Press.

Curran, C. (1986). Religious freedom and human rights in the world and the church: A Christian perspective. In L. Swidler (Ed.), *Religious liberty and human rights— In nations and religions* (pp. 143–165). Philadelphia: Ecumenical Press.

Donnelly, J. (1998, January). Human rights: A new standard of civilization? *International Affairs 74*(1): 1–23.

Edwards v. Aguillard, 107 S. Ct. 2605 (1987).

Eichner, A. (1995, January 2). The ultra-orthodox plan to censor advertising broadcasts on buses. *Ma'ariv*, p. A17.

Emerson, T. I. (1970). *The system of freedom of expression*. New York: Random House.

Fairman, C. (1949). Does the Fourteenth Amendment incorporate the Bill of Rights? *Stanford Law Review, 2*: 5–139.

Foreign Press Center Japan. (1996). Opening of the trial of Aum Shinrikyo leader Shoko Asahara. Available: http://www.nttls.co.jp/fpc/e/shiryo/jb/j8.html (May 9, 1996).

Frankfurter, F. (1965). Memorandum on "incorporation" of the Bill of Rights into the Fourteenth Amendment. *Harvard Law Review, 78*, 746–767.

Fuller, L. K. (1999). Singapore's Mr. Kiasu, Kiasu Krossove, Kiasu Max, and Kiasu the Xtraman: Comics reflecting a nation's personality and culture. In J. A. Lent (Ed.),

Cheap, cute, mad, and sexy: Themes and issues in Asian cartooning (pp. 77–90). Bowling Green, OH: Popular Press.

Hoover, S. M. & Lundby, K. (Eds.). (1997). *Rethinking media, religion, and culture.* Thousand Oaks, CA: Sage.

Hu, J. W. (1994). Debates contribute to the development of the journalistic science. *Journal of Communication, 44*: 40–51.

Janis, M. W. (Ed.). (1991). *The influence of religion on the development of international law.* New York: Martinus Nijhoff.

Joya, M. (1985). *Things Japanese.* Tokyo: Japan Times Press.

Kestral, L.R.Q. (1996, February 23). Is there a place for a gracious society in a pragmatic economy? *Straits Times*, p. 5.

Koch, A. (1943). *The philosophy of Thomas Jefferson.* New York: Columbia University Press.

Laycock, D. (1986). Non-preferential aid to religion: A false claim about original intent. *William and Mary Law Review, 27*: 875–924.

Levy, L. W. (1972). *Judgments: Essays on American constitutional history.* Chicago: Quadrangle Books.

Marsh v. Chambers, 463 U.S. 783 (1983).

Note: Towards a constitutional definition of religion. (1978). *Harvard Law Review, 91*: 1056–1089.

Pharr, S. J. (1996a). Media and politics in Japan: Historical and contemporary perspectives. In S. J. Pharr & E. S. Krauss (Eds.), *Media and politics in Japan* (pp. 3–17). Honolulu, HI: University of Hawaii Press.

Pharr, S. J. (1996b). Media as trickster in Japan: A comparative perspective. In S. J. Pharr & E. S. Krauss (Eds.), *Media and Politics in Japan* (pp. 19–43). Honolulu, HI: University of Hawaii Press.

Pongsudhirak, T. (1995, July 31). The unsettling "Asian values" of Singapore's Confucius. *Christian Science Monitor*, p. 19.

Singer, Z. (1993, March 19). The broadcast was cancelled "in order not to annoy the religious." *Yediot Aharonot*, p. A5.

Smith, C. (1988, June 30). Throwing dirt at Mr. Clean: Party rebels denounce covert control by Buddhist sect. *Far Eastern Economic Review*, 32–33.

Stone, G. R. (1986). Constitutionally compelled exemptions and the free exercise clause. *William and Mary Law Review, 27*: 985–986.

Stout, D. A., & Buddenbaum, J. M. (Eds.). (1996). *Religion and mass media: Audiences and adaptations.* Thousand Oaks, CA: Sage.

Tillich, P. (1963). *Christianity and the encounter of the world religions.* New York: Scribner.

Van Cise, J. G., Lifland, W. T., & Sorkin, L. T. (1986). *Understanding the antitrust laws* (9th ed.). New York: Practicing Law Institute.

Welch, H. (1967). *The practice of Chinese Buddhism.* Cambridge, MA: Harvard University Press.

Yamamoto, F. (1995). *Nihon masukomyunikeshon-shi, zouho* [History of Japanese Mass Communication]. Revised ed. Tokyo: Tokai University Press.

Table of Cases and Laws

CASES

LAWS

Index

About the Editors and Contributors

JOEL THIERSTEIN is Professor and Acting Director of Telecommunication in the Department of Communication Studies at Baylor University. He has also taught at Southern Illinois University at Edwardsville and Purdue University Calumet, and served as a visiting professor of Communications Law at Syracuse University. Dr. Thierstein has nearly 10 years of media experience. He has worked in the radio, television, cable television, and newspaper industries, and he has written extensively in telecommunications law. He is the author of several books, including *Birds in Flight: Satellites in the New Millennium.* He has also been quoted extensively by the press as an expert in telecommunications, and he has been an invited panelist and a guest speaker on numerous occasions.

YAHYA R. KAMALIPOUR is Professor of Mass and International Communications and Director of Graduate Studies at the Department of Communication and Creative Arts, Purdue University Calumet, Hammond, Indiana. He has also taught at universities in Ohio, Missouri, Illinois, England (Oxford), and Iran. His published books include *Images of the U.S. Around the World: A Multicultural Perspective* (1999); *Cultural Diversity and the U.S. Media* (1998); *The U.S. Media and the Middle East: Image and Perception* (Greenwood, 1995; Praeger, 1997); and *Mass Media in the Middle East: A Comprehensive Handbook* (with H. Mowlana) (Greenwood, 1994). In addition to numerous speeches and media interviews, Kamalipour's articles on media effects, broadcast education, image and perception, international communication, and the Middle East have appeared in professional and mainstream publications in the United States and abroad. He has received several significant awards, including the *1996 Distinguished Scholarship Award in International and Intercultural Communication* from the National Communication Association and the *1996 Edgar Mills Award for Outstanding Service in Communication* from the Communicators of Northwest Indiana.

NAIIM BADII is an Associate Professor and Director of the Department of Communication Sciences at the Allameh Tabatabai University, Tehran, Iran.

ALAN BAUMLER is Visiting Professor at Stanford University. His specialization is in Modern China, and he is working on a monograph on the role of opium in modern Chinese history.

MICHAEL J. BREEN is Head of the Department of Communication and Media Studies at Mary Immaculate College, University of Limerick, and a priest of the Archdiocese of Dublin. His media interests include public opinion, media treatment of religion, and the causes and effects of media content.

LINDA K. FULLER is Associate Professor in the Communications Department of Worcester State College. She is the author/co-editor of more than a dozen books, including the five-volume series *Beyond the Stars: Studies in American Popular Film* (1990), *Communicating Comfortably: Your Guide to Overcoming Speaking and Writing Anxieties* (1990), *The Cosby Show: Audiences, Impact, Implications* (Greenwood Press, 1992), *Community Television in the United States: A Sourcebook on Public, Educational and Governmental Access* (Greenwood Press, 1994), *Communicating about Communicable Diseases* (1995), *Media-Mediated Relationships* (1996), and *Media-Mediated AIDS* (1996).

NAZILA GHANEA-HERCOCK is a doctoral candidate and part-time lecturer at the Department of International Relations at Keele University (United Kingdom). She has published a number of journal articles and chapters. Her interests lie in the relationship between religion and human rights, international organization (particularly the United Nations and its human rights machinery), and Middle Eastern politics.

KAI HAFEZ is an Associate Research Fellow of the German Institute for Middle East Studies (Deutsches Orient-Institut) in Hamburg, Germany, and a lecturer at the Institute for Political Science of the University of Hamburg. Among his special fields of study and research are mass media in comparative and international perspective and the relationship between the Middle East, Islam, and the West.

CEES J. HAMELINK is Professor of International Communication at the University of Amsterdam. He is the editor-in-chief of the *International Journal for Communication Studies: Gazette*. He has authored 14 books on international communication, culture, human rights, and information technology.

GUO KE is an Associate Professor and Deputy Chair of the College of Journalism & Communications, Shanghai International Studies University. He was the 1995–1996 Fulbright Scholar at Kansas State University. He has been teaching journalism for about 10 years. His focus is on international and intercultural communications, and he has published several papers related to the Chinese media.

YEHIEL LIMOR is Senior Teacher in the Department of Communications of Tel Aviv University, Israel. Before entering academic life, he served for many years as a senior correspondent and editor for the daily newspaper *Ma'ariv*. His publications include five books: *The In/Outsiders: The Media in Israel* (1999, with D. Caspi); *The Mass Media in Israel—A Reader* (1998, with D. Caspi, in Hebrew); *Journalism—Reporting, Writing and Editing*. (1997, with R. Mann, in Hebrew); *The Media Institution* (1996, with D. Caspi, in Hebrew); and *The Mediators: The Media in Israel 1900–1948* (1992, with D. Caspi, in Hebrew).

RON MANUTO is a former faculty member at Oregon State University and the University of Texas, Pan American. His primary research areas are legal argument, propaganda, coercive persuasion, and issues regarding freedom of speech. He has published articles on aspects of First Amendment theory and the law as well as journalistic pieces in such newspapers as the *Philadelphia Inquirer,* the *St. Louis Post-Dispatch*, the *Los Angeles Times*, and the *Chicago Tribune*. Dr. Manuto is currently in private consulting and is completing a book on coercion, cults, and the First Amendment.

RILEY MAYNARD is Professor of Mass Communications at Southern Illinois University at Edwardsville. In addition to his 20 years of academic experience, he has worked in media for 30 years, including television and radio journalism. During 1997, he was a Fulbright Professor of Communication at the University of Latvia in Riga, Latvia.

KAZEM MOTAMED-NEJAD is Professor of Communication Sciences, College of Social Sciences, at Allameh Tabatabai University, Tehran. He has taught as a visiting professor at Universities of Paris, I, II, and Universities Rennes I, II.

HAMID MOWLANA is Professor of International Relations and Director of the International Communication Division at the School of International Service at American University, Washington, D.C. He is president of the International Association for Media and Communication Research (IAMCR).

BALA MUSA is an Assistant Professor at Northwestern College in Iowa. He taught at the University of Maiduguri and the University of Jos in Nigeria from 1987 to 1994. His publications cut across the subjects of media and religious communication, including West African popular culture and freedom of expression; media, diplomacy, and conflict management; development communication; and communication policy in Africa.

HILLEL NOSSEK is a Senior Lecturer and the head of Mass Communications Studies at the New School of Media Studies, the College of Management, Tel-Aviv, Israel. His publications include articles in the *Journal of Narrative and Life History* (1994), *Leipziger jahrbuch zur buchgeschichte* (1995, with Y. Limor) and *International Journal of Public Opinion Research* (1996, with H. Adoni).

MANNY PARASCHOS, Professor of Mass Communication at Boston's Emerson College, has taught at the University of Missouri, has chaired the Journalism Department at the University of Arkansas at Little Rock, and has served as Dean of the European Institute for International Communication in the Netherlands. He has been a U.N. correspondent and an editorial page editor and has lectured widely in universities in Europe. He is co-publisher of *Media Ethics* magazine.

TANYA STORCH is Assistant Professor of Chinese Buddhism and Religion at the University of Florida. She has published several articles discussing various aspects of the early and medieval periods of the history of Buddhism in China and East Asia, and she is now finishing her monograph *Three Baskets of Paradoxes*, which is devoted to the principles and methods of Buddhist historiographical writing.

DAN TINIANOW is an Assistant Professor in the Communication Arts Department at Austin College in Sherman, Texas. He lived and worked in Japan for one year, teaching English in public junior high schools as a JET Programme participant, and he has returned for extended stays in Japan four times since 1995, leading student groups on two occasions.